2nd Edition

Entrepreneur's Guide to Starting a Business

by enodare publishing

Bibliographic data
- International Standard Book Number (ISBN): 978-1906144951
- Printed in the United States of America
- First Edition: March 2014
- Second Edition: April 2017

Published by: Enodare Limited
                                 Athlone
                                 Co. Westmeath
                                 Ireland

Printed and distributed by: International Publishers Marketing
                                 22841 Quicksilver Drive
                                 Dulles, VA 20166
                                 United States of America

For more information, e-mail books@enodare.com.

IMPORTANT NOTE

This book is meant as a general guide to starting a business. While effort has been made to make this book as accurate as possible, every situation and every person's circumstances are different. As such, you are advised to update this information with your own research and/or counsel and to consult with your personal legal, financial, tax and other advisors before acting on any information contained in this book.

The purpose of this book is to educate and entertain. It is not meant to provide legal, financial, taxation or other advice or to create any form of advisory relationship. The authors and publisher shall have neither liability (whether in negligence or otherwise) nor responsibility to any person or entity with respect to any loss or damage caused or alleged to be caused directly or indirectly by the information or documents contained in this book or the use of or reliance on that information or those documents.

ABOUT ENODARE

Enodare, the international self-help publisher, was founded in 2000 by a group which included lawyers, entrepreneurs, business professionals, authors and academics. Our aim was simple - to provide access to quality business and legal products and information at affordable prices.

Enodare's Will Writer software was first published in that year and, following its adaptation to cater for the legal systems of over 30 countries worldwide, quickly drew in excess of 40,000 visitors per month to our website. From this humble start, Enodare has quickly grown to become a leading international self-help publisher with legal and business titles in the United States, Canada, the United Kingdom, Australia and Ireland.

Our publications provide customers with the confidence and knowledge to help them deal with everyday issues such as setting up a company, running a business, preparing a tenancy agreement, making a last will and testament and much more.

By providing customers with much needed information and forms, we enable them to protect both themselves and their families through the use of easy-to-read legal documents and forward planning techniques.

The Future….

We are always seeking to expand and improve the products and services we offer. However, in order to do this, we need to hear from interested authors and to receive feedback from our customers.

If something isn't clear to you in our publications, please let us know and we'll try to make it clearer in the next edition. If you can't find the answer you want and have a suggestion for an addition to our range, we'll happily look at that too.

USING SELF-HELP BOOKS

Before using a self-help book, you need to carefully consider the advantages and disadvantages of doing so – particularly where the subject matter is of a business, legal or tax related nature.

In writing our self-help books, we try to provide readers with an overview of a specific area. While this overview is often general in nature, it provides a good starting point for those wishing to carry out a more detailed review of a topic.

However, we cannot cover every conceivable eventuality that might affect our readers. Within the intended scope of this book, we can only cover the principal areas in a given topic and even where we cover these areas, we can still only do so to a moderate extent. To do otherwise would result in the writing of a text book which would be capable of use by professionals. This is not what we do.

It goes without saying (we hope) that if you are in any doubt as to whether the information in this book is suitable for use in your particular circumstances, you should contact a suitably qualified professional advisor for advice before using it. Remember the decision to use this information is yours! We are not advising you in any respect.

In using this book, you should also take into account the fact that this book has been written with the purpose of providing a general overview of setting up a business in the United States. As such, it does not attempt to cover all of the various procedural nuances and specific requirements that may apply from state to state. It therefore remains possible that your state may have specific requirements which have not been taken into account in this book.

Another thing that you should remember is that the law changes – thousands of new laws are brought into force every day and, by the same token, thousands are repealed or amended every day! As such, it is possible that while you are reading this book, some of the legal references in it might well have been changed. Let's hope they haven't but the chance does exist.

Anyway, assuming that all of the above is acceptable to you, let's move on to exploring the topic at hand...............setting up your own business.......

TABLE OF CONTENTS

CHAPTER 1:
THE START-UP LANDSCAPE

Chapter 1

CHAPTER 1

THE START-UP LANDSCAPE

An Overview

So, you're thinking of starting your first business! Like most new entrepreneurs at the idea stage, you're probably feeling both exhilarated and terrified at the prospect of leaping into the world of self-employment. As with most things in life, your trepidation most likely stems from a fear of the unknown—and that is where this book comes in. By the time you have finished reading the ensuing chapters, the unknown will become the known and you will be acutely aware of the steps you need to take and the issues you need to address in order to lay a solid foundation for a successful new business.

Being new to the world of entrepreneurship, you most likely fall into one of two categories: either you don't have substantial business experience, but feel you have a good idea for a new enterprise and are keen to run with it; or you have worked in a specific area of business, such as marketing or product development, and you are in search of a broader perspective on starting a new business before launching out on your own. In either case, this book will help you by acting as a road map for starting your new business and giving you a sense of what to expect and what needs to be done at each stage of the start-up process.

The first few chapters of *"Entrepreneur's Guide to Starting a Business"* focus on the planning stage of starting a new business. These chapters cover the steps you should take long before beginning to offer a product or service to the market (for ease of communication, throughout this book we will refer to a product or service offered by a business as a "product"). This process commences with the need to evaluate both your own personal qualities and goals and those of the business you propose to launch. Particular emphasis will be placed on the research and planning required in order to give your business the best possible chance for success.

While it is true that anyone can start a business, not everyone is cut out to be an entrepreneur any more than everyone is cut out to be a teacher or a doctor. So before launching into the life-changing event of starting a new business, and possibly leaving your current job, you should take a hard look in the mirror and decide whether your particular strengths and weaknesses are conducive to self-employment, particularly if your business will require you to manage and motivate a team of employees. **Chapter 2** will guide you through that self-evaluation process and prompt you to think about what lies ahead.

If having taken that hard look in the mirror you feel that you have what it takes to start and build your own business, the next step will be to put your business idea under the microscope of market research. This is a process that could reveal many more obstacles than appeared on the surface of your initial brainstorm. But don't be alarmed—this upfront analysis often uncovers additional opportunities as well, and in the end will leave you feeling much more confident about whether your idea has a chance at success if implemented properly. Informed confidence is an ingredient for success; misplaced confidence is not. After reading **Chapter 3**, you will know how to become informed.

Assuming your market research confirms that your concept is a potentially profitable one, it will be time to do the hard—but absolutely necessary—work of writing a business plan. This will require you to think through every aspect of bringing your product to market, as well as analyze the competitive waters that you will be diving into and forecast the financial results that could reasonably be expected to flow from your efforts. If you do nothing else, read **Chapter 4**, because having read it you will understand why you need to read all of the other chapters before starting out on your new venture.

Another step in the planning stage will be to decide on a legal structure for your business. This is not a formality, but a decision that can have profound financial consequences both for your business and you personally. **Chapter 5** will walk you through your options, the pros and cons of each, and make some recommendations depending on the size and nature of your proposed new enterprise. More likely than not, the outcome of your legal structure analysis will be to form some type of corporation. **Chapter 6** will teach you how to incorporate, and suggest where to do so. This chapter will also assist you in the very important process of choosing and clearing a name for your business, which in many cases will be your primary brand as well.

At this point, before launching into an examination of the most important aspects of implementing a business idea from scratch, we will diverge for a chapter and explore the possibility of buying an existing business. This is an important option to consider because, for many reasons, it may be the best way for you to enter the market you desire to compete in. **Chapter 7** will help you understand the circumstances in which buying an existing business might be better than building one, and vice versa, and give you a handle on the process of purchasing a business if that's what you decide is the best course of action.

Assuming you've decided to begin at square one and start a new business, it's time to consider how many dollars you will need and where you should look to find them. The failure to accurately assess the cash required to start and build your new business could doom the venture to failure before it even starts. So the first question you must answer is: How much cash will my business need before it can achieve sufficient cash flow to sustain itself? If the answer to that question is "more than I have," then you will need to raise money. In that case, you will need to answer several other important questions:

- Who should I raise money from?

- How much money should I raise and when?

- Should I give an ownership interest to investors and, if so, how much?

Chapter 8 will lay out the most important factors to consider in determining how much money you need to start your business, and then point you in the right direction if you need to raise external funds.

OK, all of the discussion about preparation is now finished, and it's time to execute the business plan that you painstakingly created. No business can run without talented people to manage its operations, so you need to assemble a top-notch team to launch your business and maximize its potential. **Chapter 9** will help you identify the positions that need to be filled and the qualities you should look for in the people you choose to surround yourself with. Remember, you will be seeing more of them than you will your family, and your family's well-being will be dependent on them. In other words, this is important.

Once your management team is in place, they will need skilled people to perform the tasks they were hired to manage. The question then becomes whether a particular function will be performed by a full-time or part-time employee, or whether an independent contractor or consultant will be retained to do the work. You will also need to know the best and most efficient way to recruit, hire, compensate, and retain good employees and independent contractors, and the legal requirements of doing all of this. **Chapter 10** will provide an overview of this complicated subject.

All of these people, of course, are going to need a place to work. While you may be able to run your business out of your home office during the concept stage, most businesses will inevitably need premises from which to operate. Renting commercial property usually represents a major portion of the operating costs involved in running any business. Therefore, it's very important that you get the right premises for your present and future needs, and that you don't commit yourself to something you can't afford. It is also critical that you understand every aspect of a business lease and your obligations under it. In **Chapter 11**, we'll educate you on the most important things to look for in identifying the right commercial property to run your business, and the best terms to negotiate in the lease.

So now that you have the right people in the right place, together with a well-conceived business plan providing a blueprint for executing on a great product idea, it's time to attract some customers. The best way to make this happen is to develop and implement a comprehensive marketing plan for your business, and the steps involved in putting together and executing such a plan include:

- Conducting Market Research and Analysis

- Setting Marketing Goals

- Developing Strategies and Tactics with respect to the Four Ps—Product, Price, Place, and Promotion

- Budgeting

- Executing Marketing Strategies and Tactics

- Measuring Effectiveness and Return on Investment

The marketing plan must be developed to work in tandem with all aspects of your business and help achieve the overall goals of your organization. We'll show you how to do this in **Chapter 12,** and will devote a large portion of that chapter to the increasingly important topic of Internet marketing.

It follows that creating a website will likely be one of the first items that you and your new team should turn its attention to, because websites have become an integral part of running almost any line of business in today's technology-driven economy. Although it may still be possible to do business the old fashioned way based on print and broadcast advertising, as well as word of mouth, it is almost guaranteed that a properly conceived, established, and managed website will deliver a good return on the time and money invested. For that to be the case, however, the website must be created and operated in the right way, or the beneficial results you anticipated could be reversed. **Chapter 13** will introduce you to the right way to create a website, as well as introduce you to the world or e-commerce.

Despite outward appearances, however, the business world does not run on technology alone. Most companies still find it necessary to send people out in the field to pitch their products to potential customers. Does this mean you need a sales force to start a business? Well, yes and no. You do need someone to meet with potential customers and educate them about your product, the value it has to offer, and the reasons it is better than that of the competition. But if you want to meet your start-up sales force, then take a look in the mirror. For many reasons, you personally should be spearheading the sales effort until your product is launched and gains traction. As your company grows and your product is refined, you can look to form a sales team and hire someone to manage them. In **Chapter 14**, we'll give you some tips on how to be an effective start-up salesperson, and then some advice on how to create a sales force that can springboard off your initial efforts.

Often in business the intangibles are as important as the tangibles, and that begins with your company's intellectual property. Intellectual property rights allow you to legally protect the inventions, brands, logos, written material, software, and the like that you create for your business. The legal protections come in the form of patents, trademarks, and copyrights, all of which allow the owner to prevent another person from using the work created and sue for damages if unauthorized use occurs. These rights can be very valuable. So in operating your business it is important to first understand what intellectual property rights you have or may acquire, and then take the necessary steps to secure, protect, and enforce them. **Chapter 15** will teach you the basics of this complex area of business and law.

In order to support and coordinate all of the business operations just described, you will need financial systems and controls in place to properly record, track, and manage your sales, receipts, and expenses. In addition, you will need to provide your management team with the information it needs to conduct its ongoing strategic and financial planning. This is an area where more attention should be paid than you might think necessary, because the failure to put in place the right financial systems and controls, including the right software, could result in a nightmare that may be very difficult to unwind down the road. Also, the failure to produce the right kinds of reliable financial reports will invariably lead to bad decisions based on bad information. **Chapter 16** will tell you what you need to be aware of with respect to your accounting systems and financial reports.

Unfortunately, you and your management team are not the only ones that will be looking at the financial information your business generates and expecting it to be in proper order. The Internal Revenue Service ("**IRS**") and state tax authorities will also be taking a keen interest. Good tax planning can make the difference between a profit and loss for your business, and the failure to understand the tax law—including all relevant filing, withholding, and payment requirements—could lead to stiff penalties and fines. The first step is to understand the basics of federal and state income tax and employment tax law, as well as state sales tax requirements, which are applicable to your business. We will provide an overview of these topics in **Chapter 17**.

For better or worse, the law touches almost every aspect of running a business. When you incorporate, raise money, hire employees, lease property, market and sell products, etc. etc. etc., you will need to be aware of, understand, and comply with the relevant laws and regulations. While we cannot cover every law that will apply to launching and running your business, in **Chapter 18** we will hit the highlights, and help you understand the importance of not giving short shrift to compliance matters.

Now that you have a broad overview of the main steps involved in getting your business up and running and laying a foundation for success, in the ensuing chapters we will take you through each one of these steps in more detail so you have a basic working knowledge of the issues and action items involved. In order to make our discussions throughout the book more concrete and realistic, we will use the case study in the box below as a reference point throughout the book. By following this case study on a chapter by chapter basis, you will better understand how the subjects we discuss actually play out in a real life start-up scenario.

Exotic Universe, Inc.

Cindy McKay has been teaching art and art history at a high school in Boulder, Colorado for ten years. During that time, she has spent her summers traveling to exotic locations such as Patagonia, South Africa, India, and Southeast Asia. On all of her excursions, she has made an effort to seek out local artists and artisans to research their artwork and handmade crafts, and has kept in contact with many of the people she met in this endeavor. A few years ago, at the end of each trip Cindy began shipping a crate of local products back from the region she was visiting, and then selling those products to retailers in the Rocky Mountain area. Word of mouth has increased the demand for her products, and Cindy now wants to launch an e-commerce business selling the paintings and sculptures, jewelry and handbags, furniture and other home décor items she sources. She believes she could expand well beyond the small informal sales effort she has undertaken over the last few years, and is ready to leave her teaching career behind to give it a go full time. Will this be a good decision? And what should Cindy do to ensure she has the best chance of success from the start-up? At the end of each chapter of this book, we will explore the issues Cindy must be aware of and the actions she must take to give herself the best opportunity to build a sustainable and profitable business.

CHAPTER 2:
A HARD LOOK IN THE MIRROR

Chapter 2

CHAPTER 2

A HARD LOOK IN THE MIRROR

Starting with Self-Assessment

Many people who have a great business idea fail when starting their own enterprise. One of the primary reasons for this is that they go into business for the wrong reasons. Another is that they fail to adequately assess their own strengths and weaknesses to determine if they "have what it takes" to succeed in the business world. In other cases, would-be entrepreneurs are just not prepared for the impact that starting a new business will have on their lives and those of their loved ones.

'Potentially' Good Reasons to Start a Business

Starting a business for the right reasons is critical, because your reasons for going into business will affect the strategic plans you make and the goals and objectives you set when operating that business. Just as importantly, if you start your business for the right reasons the experience can be rewarding regardless of whether it makes you a millionaire or not. On the other hand, going into business for the wrong reasons can be a miserable experience even if you are financially successful.

So what are some valid reasons for launching a new business? The answer is not always so clear cut, and that is the reason this section is entitled *'Potentially' Good Reasons to Start a Business*. Some motivations can be a double-edged sword— productive if pursued with the right expectations and in the proper frame of mind, but counterproductive if not.

Here are a few potentially good reasons to begin a new business:

- Be Your Own Boss

- Obtain Increased Responsibility

- Play by Your Own Rules

- Make Your Passion Your Occupation

- Build a Sustainable Enterprise

- Grow Professionally

- Make More Money

Be Your Own Boss

Many business commentators site "the ability to be your own boss" as a good reason to start your own business. In theory, and often in practice, this is true. As an entrepreneur you will be able to determine what line of business you enter, dictate your company's strategy, hire your own management team, and make the key tactical decisions. No longer will you have to carry out the orders of a boss you directly report to.

However, if you think that owning your own business means you will never have to answer to anyone else, you will find out very quickly that you were mistaken. In order to be a successful business owner, you will have to interact with and respond to the demands of dozens of "bosses" that you may never have had to worry about when working for somebody else. The most important of these will be your customers, followed closely by your suppliers, investors, bankers, board members, and any other person or entity your business is closely engaged with.

Obtain Increased Responsibility

Another good reason for starting a business is a desire to be the person who is ultimately responsible for the success or failure of the enterprise—the one sitting behind the desk where "the buck stops." Once again, this is laudable, and any successful entrepreneur wants to be that person. But remember, this means you actually have to shoulder that responsibility, and the responsibility of running a business is a heavy burden to bear.

Play By Your Own Rules

A third valid reason for starting a business is gaining the ability to play by your own rules—to set the terms on which you will conduct your business. You may have previously worked for someone who you felt "didn't do things the right way," whether strategically, operationally, or ethically. Running your own business will allow you to set the standards for yourself and your organization.

But be aware, there will be many forces that can blow your ship off course. It is very tempting to cut corners on quality or push the envelope on ethics when struggling to kick-start a new business. But if you get into business for the right reasons, then you can keep your eye on the type of enterprise you want to build and resist such temptations.

Make Your Passion Your Occupation

Another good reason to start a business is to "do what you love" or "follow your dream." As we'll discuss in more detail in a moment, passion is a key to entrepreneurial success, because people are never more determined to succeed than when they are working on a project they are passionate about.

You need to be extremely careful, however, because making your passion your occupation is the sharpest double-edged sword of them all. Passion can blind one to the obstacles that must be objectively assessed in starting and running a business, so you must be able to temper that passion when necessary in order to make good business decisions. And you will soon find that the reality of running a business forces you to spend most of your time on business planning and operational details, rather than engaging in the activity you are so passionate about. You have to be ready for the daily grind of doing business, not just the joy of doing what you love.

Build a Sustainable Enterprise

The desire to build a sustainable enterprise that contributes to the lives of your customers, employees, and the community is another good reason to start a business. Keeping your eye on a goal such as this allows you to focus simultaneously on being financially, personally, and socially successful. This will help motivate you to ensure that you are building something not just for yourself, to achieve your own dream, but for others as well. Taking pride in building and being the leader of such an enterprise will not only help you personally, it will rub off on everyone around you and help ensure the success of your business.

Grow Professionally

Many talented business people hit a glass ceiling with the organization they work for. Starting your own business in order to break through that barrier and challenge yourself to grow professionally is also a valid reason for starting your own business. Related motivations include the desire to think strategically, manage an organization's entire operations, and engage in diverse tasks, rather than just being pigeon-holed into a segment of a business.

Make More Money

Very few businesses make their owners rich, and focusing solely on profits can undermine the integrity of your business, so there needs to be other motivations such as those just described. However, the chance to make a lot of money is still a valid reason for starting a business, as long as it is not the sole reason. In fact, if a healthy profit is not one of your primary motives, this may cause planning failures that sink all of your non-financial goals. And running your own business can in fact provide the opportunity to make more money than working for someone else—there is just a lot more risk involved.

Once you have determined that you have valid financial and non-financial motivations for starting a new business, the next step in your entrepreneurial self-evaluation is to ask yourself the following critical question: Am I really cut out for this?

Traits of a Successful Entrepreneur

Many doctors would like to be a brain surgeon, but they don't have the necessary skills and talents. Many musicians would like to play for the New York Philharmonic, but no matter how hard they practice they will never be good enough. Many programmers with great ideas would like to be the next Bill Gates, but are never able to translate their ideas into a successful business.

Fortunately, to start and operate a small business does not require you to be the next Bill Gates. But in order to achieve any level of success, there are some traits that almost all good entrepreneurs possess and deploy on a daily basis. The most successful have most of these qualities to some degree, but few have all. However, they are able to make the most of the talents they have and compensate for the ones they don't.

Take a close and honest look at yourself, and determine to what degree you have or lack these characteristics:

- Passion for Your Business

- Determination and Commitment

- Good Work Ethic and Ability to Work Hard

- Self-Awareness

- Self-Confidence and Optimism

- Vision and Creativity

- Strategic Thinking Capability

- Analytical Skills

- Business Judgment

- Leadership Ability

- Management Skills

- People Skills

- Resilience

- Ability to Manage Risk and Stress

Passion for Your Business

The one characteristic that every successful entrepreneur has in common is passion, because passion is what fuels many of the other traits of a good start-up business person. All successful entrepreneurs care deeply, at a gut level, about every aspect of their business, from their employees to their customers to the quality of products they provide. There is an involuntary nature to this trait: while passion can be nurtured, it cannot be manufactured. So if you're just starting a business as a hobby, or just because you think it would be nice to try something different, then think twice.

Determination and Commitment

Passion breeds the determination and commitment necessary to drive a business to a successful destination. In fact, many businesses succeed due to the sheer force of will of their founders. Those who saw Michael Jordan play basketball know that he came to play hard every night and simply refused to lose. This quality rubbed off on his teammates and resulted in six championships. Steve Jobs was the business equivalent of Michael Jordan, refusing to accept failure and continuously pushing Apple Inc. to greater and greater heights. Successful entrepreneurs know how to make things happen, not just talk about them. They know how to close the deal.

Good Work Ethic and Ability to Work Hard

A disciplined work ethic and the ability to work long hard hours—which are not necessarily the same thing—are qualities related to drive and determination. There is no easy road from A to Z in business; even the best business ideas and plans require an extreme amount of time and effort to execute, and the founder must be the one that summons the necessary focus and energy even on the days and evenings he or she just doesn't feel like it. A business only runs as fast as its owner.

Self-Awareness

Successful entrepreneurs are as aware of themselves as they are of their business. Since they personally represent a key component of the business, they know their own strengths and weaknesses inside and out. And just like any other vital aspect of the business, they take advantage of their strengths and work to improve their weaknesses.

Self-Confidence and Optimism

If an entrepreneur doesn't believe in the value of his idea and his own ability to succeed with that idea, then no one else will either. This does not mean arrogance or blind optimism. It means a strong and steady belief that the business will overcome any obstacles and his or her vision will be realized. Self-confidence and optimism allow an entrepreneur to take the risks necessary to grow a successful business; to seize opportunities that others may let pass by.

Vision and Creativity

All of the best business persons think outside the box. They see possibilities and opportunities where others see brick walls; they find solutions to problems that were not apparent on the surface; and they are flexible and able to adapt to fast changing environments. Most importantly, successful business persons are able to visualize the type of organization they want to create and fashion the means to get there.

Strategic Thinking Capability

The entrepreneur must be able to think strategically and see the big, long-term picture when making every decision, while at the same time focusing intensely on the task at hand in order to ensure that short-term goals are realized. Multi-tasking is a continuous process—there is never a moment in an entrepreneur's existence when he or she doesn't have to keep several balls in the air at once.

Analytical Skills

Successful entrepreneurship also requires disciplined thinking and excellent analytical skills. The first business idea that comes to mind is often not the best, and impulsive owners commonly take their business down the wrong road by simply failing to think through the options and select the best one under the circumstances.

Business Judgment

Doing business is both an art and a science. In most situations, the best course of action is gray rather than black and white. Good entrepreneurs have an aptitude for business judgment and are not afraid of making and implementing tough decisions in the face of that uncertainty. They are confident that more often than not, they will have made a good decision, and with that track record the business will prosper. If you are afraid of going out on a limb and making a decision when the outcome is far from certain, then you may be better off working for someone else.

Leadership Ability

An entrepreneur presiding over a business must have the simultaneous ability to think independently and lead and manage teams of people. On the one hand, an entrepreneur is an island unto himself. He must make virtually all key decisions and accept personal responsibility for the organization's success or failure. But on the other hand, he cannot do it alone, and must be able to lead and inspire a team to be as motivated as he is for the company to succeed.

Management Skills

There is a quantum leap between performing a task yourself and motivating another person to perform it equally as well, if not better. In addition to leadership ability, good managers must have strong organizational abilities, excellent communication skills, the empathetic ability to understand the needs of their team, a willingness to delegate and trust its members to do their job, and the self-confidence to hire the best and the brightest, even if in some circumstances they are better and brighter than their boss.

People Skills

Most good entrepreneurs also have good interpersonal skills. This does not mean they are all the most likeable people on the planet, but they do have the ability and presence to command respect, and the interpersonal skills to work together with others and motivate them to perform at a high standard and provide valuable input to the organization. Good entrepreneurs value good advice and are not afraid to hear differing opinions.

Resilience

Inevitably, your business will hit bumps in the road, sometimes even craters. So resilience in the face of adversity is another necessary quality of a successful entrepreneur. Some of the world's most successful businesses were left for dead at one point or the other. But the founders stuck with their vision, bounced back, learned from their failures, and grew their business stronger than ever.

Ability to Manage Risk and Stress

Risk and stress are the constant companions of an entrepreneur. The pressures and uncertainties of running a business can be intense, and if you physically or psychologically are not up to the task, your business has little chance of success. If you thrive on pressure, then entrepreneurship may be your vocation. But if you want to crawl under the bed and hide in the face of uncertainty or a daunting array of tasks, then this may not be the career for you.

In order to assess whether you have the ability to manage the risk and stress involved in starting and running your own business, it is important to understand clearly the demands of the job. So now is a good time to ask: Am I ready for what is in store for me and my loved ones if I start my own business?

Knowing What to Expect

Starting your own business is not just a career change, it is a lifestyle change. You absolutely have to be aware of what this will entail, because if you are not ready for both the professional and personal demands of launching and running a company, then not only will the business not succeed, it may drag down other aspects of your life as well.

The reality of starting a new business is that it will entail:

- Long Hours

- Financial Insecurity

- Tremendous Pressure and Stress

- Accepting the Role of Decision Maker

- A Burden on Your Family

Long Hours

Starting a new business is not a 9 to 5 job, it is a 24/7 commitment. To begin with, you will find it is simply not possible to perform all of the necessary tasks during normal working hours. Much of that time will be taken up in meetings with employees, customers, suppliers, etc. The rest will be spent handling the details of running your business. As a result, you will find that the only time you have to spend reviewing, assessing, and strategically thinking about your business is when everyone else has gone home for the night.

In addition, no matter how much you delegate, at least until the time your business is up and running you will always be on call to answer questions and handle emergencies. Most likely, vacations will be put on hold for the foreseeable future, family obligations will be missed, and friendships will be neglected. In short, a new business is like a newborn baby—you always need to be there when it needs you, and it needs you most of the time.

Financial Insecurity

Unless you are independently wealthy, money will always be an issue when starting a new enterprise. You may be required to risk a substantial amount of your personal finances with no guarantee that they will be recouped. Most businesses are forced to run on a shoestring until they reach a level of sustained positive cash flow, and the personal income you are able to generate from the business may not be steady. Finding investors does not necessarily change that equation. Most investors will want to see you running your business lean and mean with their money.

Given all of this, you need to analyze your financial situation closely and make sure that you have enough funds to get by until your business is profitable, and that you are willing to make the sacrifices necessary to ensure that profitability becomes a reality, e.g. putting off buying that new car for a year or two. Do not make the mistake of many inexperienced business persons and find yourself out of personal funds before your product even reaches the market.

Tremendous Pressure and Stress

The effort and risk involved in starting your business will take its toll no matter how much you thrive in a stressful environment. You will be under tremendous pressure to perform, with family members, employees, customers, suppliers, and investors all relying on you. And the buck always stops with you—you will be responsible for making all key decisions and for the results that flow from those decisions.

If you cannot embrace this pressure and learn to handle it and channel it in a positive manner, then your own business will bring you down. So make sure you are in good health, both physically and mentally, because you will need your strength and will have no capacity for dealing with health issues during the critical early stages of your business.

Accepting the Role of Decision Maker

In running a business, it is simply not possible to keep all of the people happy all of the time. You have to be able to live with the fact that somebody is always going to be unsatisfied with every decision you make. Sometimes you will be required to make extremely difficult and unpopular decisions, such as the decision to lay off an employee. You can run your business like a family if you choose, but you have to be the parent.

A Burden on Your Family

One of the most important things to be aware of before starting a new business is that everyone close to you will be affected by the stresses and strains just described. It is simply not possible to insulate your loved ones from the commitment it takes to launch a new enterprise and the sacrifices that must be made as a result. Your family will also feel the financial strain and be required to make their own sacrifices so that available funds can be directed into the business. In addition, they will see you less often, and the person they do see will be someone who finds it very difficult to "leave problems at the office." This is not a judgment, it is just a reality.

Therefore, it is very important that your family members understand and support your decision to start a new business. If a loved one is rowing in the opposite direction, either your business, your relationship, or both will likely suffer.

The hard look in the mirror we've just walked you through was by no means intended to scare you into abandoning your dream of starting your own business. The purpose was to make sure you go into the process with eyes wide open, because this is absolutely necessary to give you the best opportunity for success.

Exotic Universe, Inc.

After reading this chapter, Cindy McKay closes the door to her home office, leans back in her chair, and ponders the questions we posed: Am I starting my business for the right reasons? Do I have the skills necessary to pull this off? Can I handle what's in store for me? Placing her motivations under a microscope, Cindy realizes that her primary reasons for launching her business would be to work closely with and help the local artists and artisans she has met on her travels, while at the same time making more money than her teacher's salary so she can pursue her dual passions for travel and art more extensively. Can she realistically achieve these goals? Taking a sober look back, she acknowledges that although she was always able to sell the art and handicrafts she shipped home, she was not always able to make a lot of money doing so. So if she wants to achieve her goals, she will have to develop a business model that will work—because if her business is not profitable and sustainable, she will not be able to help any artist or artisan, let alone herself. In addition, her dreams of future world travels may come in direct conflict with her dream of launching a new business. Most likely, there will not be time or money for both in the foreseeable future. Her relationship with the guy she just started dating may be at risk as well, unless he understands the demands on her time that her new business will require. And does she really have what it takes to make this work? After handling classrooms of unruly teenagers and tutoring in her free time to support her travel habit, Cindy thinks she can handle the pressure and long hours that her business will require. In addition, she has become a highly regarded instructor who commands the respect of both her students and fellow teachers, so she thinks she has the necessary personal skills and leadership qualities. But while she trusts her judgment in most matters, she has minimal business experience outside the small amounts of products she's sold over the last couple of years, and really doesn't know much about the ins and outs of running a company. She's also not entirely sure that her passion for art and travel will carry over into a passion for business. In any event, she understands that she has a lot of work to do simply to get up to speed on the technical aspects of starting and running a business, and that it may be a good idea to keep an eye out for a partner or adviser who possesses some of the skills that she lacks. For the first time, Cindy sees clearly that she will be giving up her guaranteed teacher's salary, benefits, and pension for a very uncertain proposition. She still wants to move forward, but decides not to hand in her resignation as a teacher until she's done some more extensive research into the business she intends to dive into.

CHAPTER 3:
WHAT'S MY LINE?

Chapter

3

CHAPTER 3

WHAT'S MY LINE?

Determining the Right Business for You

Now that you've determined that you have what it takes to be a successful entrepreneur, you need to nail down exactly what line of business is best for you.

Chances are you've already had a flash of inspiration and have a good idea of the product you would like to sell or the service you would like to provide. But even where this is the case, you may still need to refine your business idea to zero in on the specific needs of your potential customers. And now is the best time to do so—before you've committed a substantial amount of time, energy, and resources, and while your mind is still sufficiently open to allow you explore some of the other business opportunities that might be available to you.

So regardless of whether you are an entrepreneur in search of an idea or a person who believes he has already come up with the best invention since the microprocessor, you should go through the process of brainstorming. Not only will the process help you formulate new business ideas and recognize additional opportunities, it will help you narrow and prioritize your options and ultimately select the best one to pursue.

Brainstorming

Assuming that you already have a good idea for a business, are you certain it's the best idea you can come up with? Have you done a little brainstorming to see if your idea can be improved or even if you can think of something better? Sometimes initial insights turn out to be mere stepping stones that lead to even deeper pools of possibilities. So regardless of how attached you are to your original idea, be willing to set it aside for the time being, get creative, and see what else springs to mind. This is what brainstorming is all about.

While going through the brainstorming process, keep in mind that the ideal business to pursue will match your skills and interests with a product that fills a need for a large and growing target market. It will also be one that allows you to deliver that product to customers as part of a profitable business model.

Whatever business you ultimately select, in order to succeed at it, you will need to become an expert in the field and develop a passion for that line of business. It follows that you will be ahead of the game if you choose a business that you are already knowledgeable and passionate about. This doesn't mean you have to limit yourself to areas you are already familiar with, but at least explore these areas first to see what opportunities may exist.

You may find that by going through the brainstorming process you will discover a consumer need related, either directly or indirectly, to your current field of expertise. For example, if you are a master chef with no technology experience, in most cases it probably doesn't make sense for you to abandon your career to enter the software development business. However, if you have an idea for developing a software application that could be used by anyone to mix and match ingredients and create delicious new recipes, as well as the expertise to provide the necessary input to an experienced programmer, it may be worth pursuing even if you don't have the ability to write software programs yourself.

So turn on your laptop, or do it the old-fashioned way and pull out a pencil and paper, and write down what you do best and what you love to do the most. Then begin to ask yourself some questions related to these areas, focusing on consumer needs and demand, because that is the starting point of all successful new businesses.

To begin with, ask yourself:

- What product do I need and would be willing to buy that is currently not available?

- What product do other people need and would be willing to buy that is currently not available?

- Is there a product on the market that I could improve in order to meet an unfulfilled need?

- Is there excess demand for a current product that is not being met?

- Are there trends developing (such as new technology) that will provide new ways of filling existing needs or solving existing problems?

- Are there trends developing that will create new consumer needs and solutions?

- Is there a new business model available that would make a previously unfeasible business now possible?

First answer these questions with respect to your personal interests, areas of expertise, daily life, and work environment. Then expand your inquiry and ask the same questions of friends, family, colleagues, fellow entrepreneurs, and persons working in the field that you wish to enter. You never know, you may discover a hole in the market right in your own back yard that you are willing and able to fill.

An additional method of brainstorming is to browse, whether on the Internet or through traditional media such as newspapers, magazines, and trade literature. You may come across somebody that has successfully implemented a good business idea in another location, but does not have the ability to reach a market that you can service, i.e. you can duplicate a successful out-of-state, or even overseas, business in your locality.

As you can see, even if you started with a solid business idea in mind, asking yourself the right questions may help you come up with a better idea than you already had, or at least a new twist on your original idea that will generate more demand for your product. But there is another reason for brainstorming and developing several options that interest you—when placed under the microscope of market research and business planning, your initial idea might not stand up to scrutiny. Therefore, it's smart to have one or more additional options to fall back on.

So after you've brainstormed and come up with a list of start-up ideas, it's time to separate the wheat from the chaff and determine which ideas that you have for starting a new business are the best ideas to move forward with.

Narrowing the Field

From this point onward, you will need to put your business ideas through a series of tests to ensure that they are sound and that you are heading in a profitable and sustainable direction.

These tests will begin with a top-level overview of the ideas you came up with while brainstorming in order to narrow them down to a few options that you can select from and take to the next level of analysis. There, you will conduct more in-depth market research into your chosen business ideas to determine whether your number one choice is really worth pursuing. Having made that determination, and with market information in hand, you can create a full scale business plan to flesh out the strategy and goals for turning your idea into a profitable business.

In first narrowing down your list of business ideas and then selecting your preferred choices, ask yourself the following questions (with the realization that at this stage the answers will be educated guesses with limited hard data to back them up):

- What is the specific consumer need that my product will fill?

- Who is my target market? What are the characteristics of the customers who are most likely to buy my product?

- What is my value proposition? What compelling benefits will my product offer the target market that other products and services will not?

- How large is the target market? Is it growing, shrinking, or remaining constant?

- Can I cost-effectively reach these customers from a marketing, production, and distribution standpoint?

- Is this the right time to introduce my product? Is my product ahead of or behind its time?

- How strong is the competition and potential competition?

- Can I differentiate my product from those already on the market?

- What barriers to entry do I face? What are the main obstacles in the way of introducing my product and gaining market share?

- What sustainable competitive advantages would my business possess?

- Is there a viable business model for my idea?

  - What will be my sources of revenue?

  - How much will it cost to produce my product or deliver my service?

  - How will my product be priced?

  - Will I generate adequate gross and net margins?

  - What is my profit and cash flow potential?

- What amount of money will it take to start my business and run it until it is cash flow positive and profitable?

- Do I have the personal skills and resources necessary to execute on my idea?

- Am I passionate about this idea? Can I work around the clock for the next few years to make it work?

After having asked and answered these questions with respect to your best business ideas, it is likely that only a couple will become finalists. Now you need to make your first major business decision and select the idea you are going to pursue. It may be that one idea stands heads and tails above the others. But if not, go with the idea you feel most passionate about.

In other words, if all else is equal, choose the product that you really believe in—the one that you have a strong desire to provide to your customers because you believe it will benefit their lives. This is the idea that you will be willing to fully commit to going forward, and the one that will provide the most satisfaction when you succeed.

With your chosen idea in hand, it is time to put your instincts to the test of market research and see whether they stand up to consumer and industry scrutiny.

Market Research: Confirming Your Idea

Gut level instincts have their place in business, but whenever possible they must be supported by empirical evidence. This is especially true when starting a new business, because the failure to find hard data that confirms that your idea is solid could lead you down a time-consuming and costly dead end.

Regardless of how groundbreaking your idea might be, no business can survive without a market consisting of a sufficient number of customers willing to pay a minimum price for your product that will allow your business to be profitable. You could discover a cure for the common cold, but if the cost to do so requires you to charge an exorbitant price that nobody will pay, it has no meaning in the business world. In addition, you must also be able to gain and hold sufficient market share from whatever competitors currently exist or enter the market in the future.

In the start-up stage, you therefore need to perform market research with the goal of collecting and analyzing as much information as possible about the market for your product, your potential customers, and your competitors. In doing so, you will return to most of the questions you asked yourself in identifying what business idea to target. But this time you will gather outside data that either supports or refutes your initial conclusions.

The type of information you should seek to gather in your market research effort includes the:

- Size and nature of the overall market for your product

- Size and nature of the market segments within that overall market

- Demand for your product within each segment

- Growth potential of the overall market and each market segment

- Size and nature of the best target segment(s)

- Demographics, tastes, expectations, and buying habits of your target customers, such as:

  - ☐ Their personal characteristics, including age, gender, level of income, etc.

  - ☐ Their spending habits

  - ☐ Where they live and how you can get their attention

  - ☐ What product they want; when they want it; where they want it delivered; and at what price they will buy it

- Unique selling points that you can use to differentiate your product from the competition

- Price elasticity of your product

- Proven viable business models for profitably creating and selling your product

- Direct and indirect competition, including how they perform on all of these same questions

- Market share held by each competitor

- Barriers to entry

- Trends in the market and external trends that will affect the market

- Resources required to enter the market

- Strengths and weaknesses of your potential business, as well as the opportunities and threats you will face

To obtain this information, you should conduct both primary and secondary market research. Primary research is material that you directly acquire yourself or hire someone else to directly acquire for you. Secondary research is material that others have collected and published. Both types of research can be based on quantitative data or qualitative opinions.

Primary research will give you information directly from potential customers about such matters as who they are, what they like, what type of product they would be interested in buying, and what they would be willing to pay for that product. Secondary research will give you the information needed to analyze the market you are entering and the competition you will face, such as the market share held by companies already existing in the market, their marketing strategies, etc. If you want to open up a chain of coffee shops in your hometown, you better first know what Starbucks is doing and how you can effectively compete with them.

Begin with some secondary research, because that will give you the background necessary to properly formulate questions for your primary research and target the right subjects. Look to become as much of an expert on the line of business you wish to enter as possible. Gather and absorb all the information you can, particularly about the size of the market, the characteristics of your potential customers, and the competition. Then use this information to drill down and identify the best target segment to pursue and the product features that will convince consumers in that segment to buy from you.

Secondary Research

The purpose of secondary research is to learn everything you can about your industry, your market, and the competition. Sources of information can be found on the Internet and in local and university libraries, particularly business school libraries. Material can also be ordered from government departments, industry and trade associations, and business data providers. If possible, you should also obtain material from specialists who follow the industry, such as research reports written by analysts working for securities brokerage firms.

Here are some secondary research resources available on the Internet:

- Business.Com—www.business.com

- Fuld & Company—www.fuld.com

- Standard & Poors—www.standardandpoors.com

- Small Business Administration—www.sba.com

- Hoover's—www.hoovers.com

- Dun & Bradstreet Reports—www.dnb.com

- Thomson Research—http://research.thomsonib.com

- Value Line—www.valueline.com

- The U.S. Census Bureau—www.census.gov

- The U.S. Securities and Exchange Commission ("**SEC**")—www.sec.gov

- The Federal Trade Commission ("**FTC**")—www.ftc.gov

In addition, track down as many relevant business periodicals as possible, whether online or in hard copy, and look to resources such as: Dun & Bradstreet Industry Handbook; Encyclopedia of Global Industries; U.S. Industry and Trade Outlook; Handbook of North American Industry; Statistical Abstract of the United States; and Encyclopedia of Emerging Industries.

To locate a trade association that reports on your proposed business, look to the Encyclopedia of Associations (Gale Research) and the Encyclopedia of Business Information Sources (Gale Group). You should also seek out academics who are experts with respect to your industry and highly regarded professionals in the field.

At first glance, conducting market research among all of these dry sounding publications may sound like a dreary proposition. But not only is this a highly beneficial exercise, it is a test of whether you are truly passionate about your business idea and becoming an entrepreneur—because if you are, you will devour every piece of related information you can find.

As a starting point for all of this, you can perform simple Internet searches to gather information on similar products that are already on the market, the nature and number of potential competitors, and market niches that may be worth pursuing. Once you've determined who your competitors will be, visit their websites to gain information on their products, services, customers, pricing, and positioning.

Don't be satisfied, however, with performing online research as your only source of information on competitors. Get out and visit their stores, go to trade shows, and speak with their customers, vendors, and other people they do business with. Also look at their advertisements, which will reveal quite a bit about their business strategy.

Afterwards, using the secondary research material you have gathered as a base, you can turn to primary research and survey your potential customers to determine whether there will be a demand for your product, what particular product characteristics they value most, and at what price they are willing to buy.

Primary Research

Now it's time to speak to some actual human beings about whether they would buy your product, under what circumstances, and at what price. The keys to primary research are properly formulated questions and properly constituted survey, interview, and focus groups. If you ask the wrong questions of the wrong people, you will receive information that is worse than useless—it will form the foundation of bad decisions at the critical stage of starting your new business. As the old adage goes: garbage in, garbage out.

Primary research consists mainly of:

- Interviews

- Surveys and Questionnaires

- Focus Groups

Real-time interviews can be conducted in person, over the telephone, or online. Surveys and questionnaires may be closed-ended or open-ended. Closed-ended questionnaires provide users specific answers to choose from for each question—the old multiple choice we've all been familiar with since grade school—whereas open-ended surveys allow the participant to choose their own response, which is recorded and categorized.

Focus groups can be sophisticated and formal, conducted in a controlled environment by trained behavioral specialists, or unsophisticated and informal, consisting of an entrepreneur exposing family, friends, and business associates to a potential product, service, or message. One advantage of focus groups is that they are interactive. You can give participants hands-on experience with your product, give them your marketing pitch, throw out different product features or pricing options, and then observe and record how they react.

For example, if you've developed a new mosquito repellant, give it to a group of 20 people and ask them to track where and when they used it, and how effective it was. Then interview each of them about their experience, documenting exactly what they liked and didn't like about all aspects of the product. And that means all aspects. Focus groups allow you to discover the features, design, positioning, and marketing message that will best appeal to potential customers.

A key decision is whether to conduct the primary and secondary research yourself or hire a market research specialist to do the work. Good research firms and consultants do not come cheap, with the price escalating if more detailed, current, and local knowledge is sought.

As a business in the start-up phase, you will probably not have the resources to hire a professional outside firm to perform extensive and detailed primary research, so you'll need to get creative in order to gain an adequate sense of your target customers' characteristics, tastes, and buying habits. One possibility is to get students from a local university business school to help out. Another alternative is to hire a data collection firm that conducts the interviews and prepares, distributes, and collects the surveys and questionnaires, but then simply hands you the raw data to analyze yourself.

It may be the case, however, that you will be required to conduct your own primary research. For example, person-to-person surveys can be conducted at very modest costs by simply getting out and giving people a sample of your product and then asking them questions, or asking questions of people who have purchased a competing product.

You can also conduct online surveys. Many companies now provide the service of either conducting online research for you or providing the tools for you to conduct your own online survey.

Always remember, however, that you will be using your market research to make a decision regarding whether to launch a new business that will risk, at minimum, a substantial amount of your time and resources, and potentially your entire career and financial well-being. So if you're not going to hire a professional, make sure you do it correctly yourself.

When finished with your brainstorming, narrowing, and market research, all the time, effort and money that went into these three levels of analysis will pay off in three critical respects. First, it will tell you whether the business you chose is viable. Second, it will help you refine that idea so it has the best chance of success. And third, it will provide a substantial amount of data and information that will become the foundation of your business plan, which is the subject of our next chapter.

Exotic Universe, Inc.

After realizing that selling exotic art and handicrafts online would not be the easy proposition she originally anticipated, Cindy McKay is willing to explore whether other entrepreneurial opportunities may present a simpler and more straightforward first entry into the business world. But she decides right away that whatever business she enters, it has to involve her passion for art—she would rather remain a teacher than work entirely outside the art world. Cindy considers the possibility of forming a travel agency aimed at people who want to visit art destinations around the world as she had done. She also explores the possibility of combining her teaching experience with her business desires and developing interactive software that would allow students to travel in a virtual environment to meet artists and artisans from around the world. But she keeps coming back to her desire to expand the markets for the artists and artisans she has met in a manner that would be mutually beneficial to them and her. She is truly passionate about this possibility. So she decides to put her alternate ideas on the backburner, return to the original concept, and put it under the spotlight to see whether her idea holds up to scrutiny. However, when Cindy asks herself the questions posed in the section about "narrowing the field," she is confronted with the fact that she was not even aware of many issues involved in starting a business, let alone thought them through. Who is her target market? Her first reaction is the obvious one: people who love exotic art and handicrafts. But digging deeper, she considers the fact that she had previously sold to specialty retail shops within a 90 mile radius of her home, but now she's proposing to sell direct online. She actually has no idea if the characteristics of her potential customers would be similar to those who purchased at the shops, or completely different. How large is the market? Her instincts tell her that globalization has produced greater interest in products from remote places, but she actually has no factual basis for this conclusion. Is the market segmented? Come to think of it, she sold her jewelry and handbags to one type of store, and her paintings and sculptures to others. Can she successfully combine diverse products such as these on the same website? Will people looking for quality paintings feel like they'll find them on a site that sells cheap handbags? Cindy isn't really sure. Competition is another issue she's never had to think about. There was normally only one retail shop selling her type of products in each small and medium sized town where she pitched her art and handicrafts. But now she'll be selling online. How many other people are doing the same thing she's proposed?

With all of these unanswered questions and more, Cindy suddenly understands the importance of conducting some basic market research. She starts online, surveying all of the different companies that are selling arts and handicrafts produced in exotic locations. To her discomfort, she realizes she is not the first person to come up with this idea. In fact, she is one of many. Even worse, she discovers a number are offering the same type of handicraft products she wants to sell—although many of these companies' products seem more mass-produced, and of lesser quality, than the ones she has previously sourced. On a brighter note, Cindy comes across statistics and news articles about the online market for exotic art and handicrafts, confirming her instincts that this market is growing. In addition, after taking a closer look at her potential competitors' products and marketing strategies, she believes that her experience and contacts will allow her to differentiate herself by sourcing better quality, more unique products. With this information in hand, Cindy conducts her own informal primary research. She begins by speaking in depth with the retailers she had sold to previously, questioning them about what had sold well and what had not, as well as the demographic characteristics of their customers, pricing, etc. Then she puts together a survey and distributes it to all of her social network friends, those in the teaching and arts communities, etc. The feedback she receives about what products they would be most interested in, how much they would be willing to pay, whether and how they would look for and purchase products like this online, etc., was eye-opening. Among many other things, Cindy is surprised to learn that many of the items she liked best from an artistic standpoint were not always the ones potential consumers liked best and would be willing to buy.

After completing her research, Cindy comes away with two major conclusions. First, there is an online market for the products she wants to sell, and that market is growing. Second, nobody has developed an online business model for selling and delivering those products to the target market that is demonstrably profitable. Cindy still sees an opportunity, but she obviously has her work cut out for her.

CHAPTER 4:
DRAWING A BLUEPRINT FOR SUCCESS

Chapter 4

CHAPTER 4

DRAWING A BLUEPRINT FOR SUCCESS
Creating a Business Plan

To succeed in business, you need to give yourself the best chance for success right from the outset. And to give yourself that chance, you need to have a business plan.

A business plan is a blueprint for creating a viable, profitable, and sustainable business. A good business plan will help you to:

- Refine your business idea and precisely define the business that you will engage in, the consumer needs that your product will satisfy, the customers you will target, and the manner in which you will communicate with and sell to those customers

- Describe the competitive environment your business will operate in, how your products or services will be differentiated from the competition, and the competitive advantages and other key factors that will help your business succeed in the market

- Set goals and objectives for your business and for each key component of your organization, and lay out the strategy and tactics that your business will employ to achieve them

- Identify the strengths of your business and how they will be exploited, as well as the weaknesses of your business and how they will be overcome

- Flesh out the opportunities you foresee and how your business will take full advantage of them, and the threats your business will face and how it will combat them

- Identify the management team needed to implement your plan and drive the success of your business

- Forecast the financial outlook of your business and assesses what funds will be required to get it started, what funds will be required to achieve both a sustained positive cash flow and a sufficient level of profitability, and how those funds will be allocated within the business

The Importance of a Business Plan

The number one reason for writing a business plan is that it forces you to thoroughly analyze every important aspect of starting and running your business.

During the business planning process, you will inevitably discover flaws in your initial concept, business model, and strategy that need to be addressed. Finding flaws at this early stage allows you to make any required changes before they become problematic. You will also uncover opportunities that may otherwise have been overlooked, providing you the chance to take advantage of unfilled gaps in the market that may prove to be the difference between success and failure. In addition, your business plan will give you a good estimate of how much cash will be required to run your business until it can generate its own positive cash flow, so you don't run your ship aground before it ever gets out to sea.

Your business plan will also provide clear direction to everyone involved in running your business, so they are all operating from the same playbook and running the same plays. By having a global understanding of the direction and objectives of your business, you will make it easier to achieve management "buy-in" with respect to the goals and strategies you have set out for the business, thereby ensuring that everyone is committed to following your plan for success.

The business plan will provide practical benefits as well. The market research you perform as part of the business planning process will lay the groundwork for your all-important marketing plan. And your business plan's financial projections can be used as the foundation for creating your budget.

Last but not least, your business plan will be your company's primary marketing document when it comes time to raise money from investors, borrow money from lenders, hire key management employees, and enter into strategic relationships. As such, you need to tailor your business plan to your intended audience and make sure that it clearly and compellingly sells them on your business and answers all their key questions in a manner that convinces them to jump on board. For example, venture capital investors will want to see a clear "exit strategy," or manner in which they will be able to realize and pocket a return on their investment. Lenders, on the other hand, will be focused on the company's ability to generate enough cash flow to make the principal and interest payments on loans when due.

Getting Started: Vision, Mission, and Values Statements

One good way to start the business planning process is to sit down and express in concise written statements exactly what your business is about, what it intends to achieve and value it intends to provide its customers, and how it intends to go about doing so. This can be accomplished by writing a vision statement, mission statement, and values statement for your business.

Your "vision statement" signifies the type of business you intend to create, i.e. what you want your business to become. Think about the reasons you are going into your particular business and the primary goals you want to achieve. Then put those goals into a single sentence—or a few at the most—that encapsulates your vision.

One good example is Amazon.com's vision statement: "Our vision is to be earth's most customer centric company; to build a place where people can come to find and discover anything they might want to buy online."

The "mission statement" is customer oriented. Here you state precisely the benefits you will provide to your customers and the manner in which you will satisfy their needs.

CVS Corporation, which has thousands of retail pharmacy stores in the United States, boiled their mission statement down to one simple sentence: "We will be the easiest pharmacy retailer for customers to use."

Can you see how every aspect of their business can be focused on and built around this statement? Your goal should be to write a mission statement upon which you can do the same. Sometimes, by the way, companies combine their vision and mission statements into the same statement.

A "values statement" identifies an organization's core set of beliefs and the qualities that it prioritizes over all others. You can use your values statement to clearly identify the manner in which you want to realize your vision and accomplish your mission.

Most often, values statements will have both ethical and performance components, creating a corporate culture based on qualities that foster success, while at the same time setting ethical guidelines for accomplishing such success.

For example, the global pharmaceutical company Merck has adopted the following values statement:

"At Merck, we do business on the basis of common values. Our success is based on courage, achievement, responsibility, respect, integrity, and transparency. These values determine our actions in our daily dealing with customers and business partners as well as in our teamwork and our collaboration with each other."

Once your vision, mission, and values statements are finalized, shine every other aspect of your business through their collective prism in order to set your goals and strategies. By doing so, you will achieve the focus and coherence necessary for success. Then look for the best way to work these statements into your business plan.

In addition to these strategic statements of purpose and intention, every business plan should include certain key components. These are the elements that you and your management team must have a firm understanding of, and be able to communicate clearly and concisely, before launching your business.

What Every Business Plan Should Include

There are many ways to organize a business plan, and both the layout and content of your plan should be individualized so that it best highlights the most important aspects of your business and does not appear either "cookie cutter" or not thoroughly thought out. Regardless of the format you choose, however, all good business plans include the following categories of information and analysis:

- Executive Summary

- Description of the Business

- Business Environment—Industry Background, Market Analysis, and Competitive Analysis

- Marketing Plan

- Operations Plan

- Management Team

- Financial Plan and Projections

Executive Summary

The executive summary is the most important section of the business plan. It is not a "summary" as the subheading suggests—at least not in the classic sense of the word. The executive summary is a concise and compelling description of the business opportunity you have identified, the strategy and means you will use to capitalize on that opportunity, the resources you will require, and the potential payoff for those involved. It is the entire business plan condensed into 1-3 pages, and whoever reads it should come away with a very good understanding of exactly what your business is about and feel realistically excited about its prospects.

Therefore, your executive summary should zero in on the most important factors related to the success of your business. Ground the reader with some background on your company, but then hook them with your vision and/or mission statements. This should convey in a few sentences the type of organization you intend to build and the benefits that your business will provide to your customers, employees, investors, and the community. Afterwards, build the readers' understanding and excitement by offering a concentrated version of everything that will follow in the plan.

For example, use the executive summary to describe the factors that are most critical to your business, including:

- The market opportunity, i.e. the consumer need that your product will satisfy

- The product you will provide and the benefits your customers will receive

- The size and characteristics of the target market, as well as significant growth trends

- The competitive environment

- Your business's competitive advantages and product differentiation strategy

- The individual and collective qualities of your management team

- Your financial projections over the next 3-5 years

- Your capital requirements, including the amount of cash you are seeking to raise

- The return that you and your investors (if any) may realistically expect to achieve

The executive summary will force you to prioritize, and will reveal to the reader how you do so. It will also require you to be able to communicate clearly and concisely the strategy you will pursue with respect to those priorities.

You must convey your enthusiasm and get the reader to share it, leaving him or her chomping at the bit to read the rest of your business plan. If you do not achieve this in the executive summary, your business plan is destined to be tossed in the financier's "slush pile" where unfunded businesses go to die. On the other hand, a well-written and well-thought-out executive summary can be the seed from which your company springs to life.

Description of the Business

Now that you have hooked the readers and given them a targeted understanding of your business, you can walk them through a more detailed description of each component of your business plan, starting with the exciting business opportunity you have identified and the way you intend to take advantage of that opportunity.

Company Background

Begin by providing some background on your company, including when it was founded, where it is located and incorporated, and the current legal structure—just enough to give the reader some context about your organization.

Nature of the Business

Next, describe the nature of your business, your goals and objectives, and how you intend to satisfy those goals. In doing so, provide a compelling narrative about the line of business you are entering and your reasons for choosing that particular business. Begin with the opportunity that you have identified, i.e. the consumer problem you intend to solve or need you intend to satisfy. Then describe the products you will provide, and explain exactly how they will solve that problem and/or satisfy that need. Delineate how your product will be differentiated from others in the marketplace and what attributes will cause customers to choose your offerings over those of the competition.

Business Operations

Now describe the nature of your operations and how you will produce and deliver your product to the customer. Highlight the strengths and any competitive advantages you have in product development, distribution, sales, technology, intellectual property, etc. In addition, address any weaknesses you have identified and what you intend to do to strengthen your business in these areas.

Business Model

The next step is to describe how you will make a profit. As many entrepreneurs have discovered, even if you have millions of customers, if you don't have a good business model then you may soon be out of business.

A business model is the manner in which you will generate sufficient revenues to make a profit and produce positive cash flow. It identifies all of your sources of revenue—how you will get paid, how much, by whom, and when—and demonstrates that the revenue can be generated at a low enough cost to produce a sufficient net profit to create value in the business and the required return for you and your investors.

Funding Requirements

If your business will not generate sufficient funds to cover its initial cash requirements, then you need to identify what outside funds will be required, how you intend to raise them, how you intend to use them, and how the investors and/or lenders will be repaid. In this final respect, investors will be particularly interested in the growth potential of your business and the return on investment they can realistically expect.

Key Factors for Success and Milestone Schedule

Finally, investors will want to know the key success factors that will determine whether your goals and objectives can be achieved and growth targets met so they can obtain their desired return, as well as potential exit strategies for realizing that return. They will also want to know when they can expect to cash in on their investment, so you should include the key milestones you have set for your organization, as well as when and how you intend to meet them.

The Business Environment

This section is sometimes broken down into separate sections for its three components: industry analysis, market analysis, and competitive analysis.

The industry you will be competing in and the market for your products or services are not the same thing: an industry is a group of sellers, while a market is a group of buyers. It is possible for a market for a product to be attractive at the same time the industry supplying that product is not, and vice versa. For example, there may be a large market for a particular product, but the industry providing that product has substantial barriers to entry that only a few well established companies can overcome, all but precluding start-up businesses from gaining a foothold. So you need to understand both your industry and your market in order to assess the opportunities and challenges each present for your business.

Industry Analysis

An industry consists of sellers offering products or services that are similar or substitutable for one another. An industry can therefore be very broad, but it can also be divisible into sub-industries and sectors. The entertainment industry includes the sub-industries of film, television, radio, music, theater, dance, and literary publishing, each of which is a large industry unto itself. Businesses in each of these entertainment sub-industries compete for consumer dollars not only within their individual sector, but among all entertainment industry sectors, and their business strategies and marketing plans must take this into account in order to be successful.

It is important that you understand, and your business plan reflects, the size and characteristics of your overall industry and specific sector. Of particular importance are growth rates and trends, as well as current and future barriers to entry. For example: Is the development of new technology having an impact on the industry? Are products or services within the industry significantly differentiated? Do a small number of large companies dominate market share?

Market Analysis

A market consists of a group of consumers having the desire and ability to buy a product to satisfy a particular type of want or need. Take music, for example—the market for the music recording industry consists of everyone who wants to buy recorded music and will pay money to do so.

Clearly, however, even the largest companies in the music business would have trouble fulfilling the needs of every person who wants to listen to recorded music. In addition, within every market for a product, different consumers have different needs, get different benefits from the product, respond differently to marketing messages, are in different locations, etc. As a result, it would not be efficient to communicate with and sell to each potential customer in the same manner. It is therefore in the interest of every business to segment the market into manageable groups of people with similar needs that can be efficiently targeted.

Market segmentation is one of the most important concepts for you to learn and understand in starting a new business. In general, a market segment consists of a group of potential buyers of your product who have similar:

- Needs for the product

- Characteristics (demographic, geographic, behavioral, and/or psychographic)

- Responses to messages

Therefore, in performing a market segment analysis for your business plan, first determine whose needs your product will most satisfy. Afterward, identify the common characteristics of that group, focusing on those characteristics that are most related to the buying decision. Then further subdivide that segment into groups who will respond to similar marketing messages.

The goal is to develop a target segment that consists of the people most likely to buy your product who are within your marketing and distribution reach. Properly identifying this target segment will be the key to your business success. The reason is that if you understand who your primary potential customers are, what they want, and how and when they buy, then every component of your business— from product development to marketing to sales to distribution to customer service—can be geared towards satisfying their desires and convincing them to purchase what you have to offer at a price that allows you to make a profit.

Once you've identified your key segment or segments, you can also analyze and include in your business plan the size, growth potential, and barriers to entry with respect to your particular target segment. This will allow you to assess whether the number of people most likely to buy your product is large enough to support a profitable business.

Finally, identify and describe trends in your target segment. Is the pool of targeted consumers growing or shrinking, and why? Are they moving towards or away from your type of product? Will you be well-positioned to take advantage of their future needs? What about your timing into the market—are you going to be in the right place at the right time with the right product?

In addition, identify other factors that affect buying patterns and sales in your target segment, such as seasonality and cyclicality. And look at your business model and break-even calculations. Is there a critical mass of customers necessary to compete in this target segment, or can an even smaller niche be carved out that still has profitability and growth potential?

Competitive Analysis

An additional benefit of market segmentation is that it helps you identify and understand who your real competition will be. This includes companies that sell the same or similar products to yours within your target market, companies that meet the same needs as your product, and potential competitors doing either.

Identify the market share currently held by these competitors and the chances of your taking market share away from them, both now and in the future. Just as you've done with your own company, describe the strengths and weaknesses of your competitors and their product offerings. What competitive advantages do they hold? What are the key factors to success in competing with them? Most importantly, how will you differentiate your offerings from theirs?

These questions are the basis for the next, and possibly the most important, component of your business plan.

The Marketing Plan

Once you have completed your industry analysis, market analysis, and competitive analysis, you can use the results to develop a plan that allows you to communicate effectively with the consumers in your target segment, convince them to buy your product, and retain them as loyal customers.

Investors know that if you cannot explain how you will efficiently and effectively market your product, your business will not succeed. You can have the best product in the world, but if nobody knows about it or the people that do know cannot be convinced to buy, then the product has no meaning.

As we just described, market segmentation is crucial to developing an effective marketing plan. Dividing the potential market for your product into market segments, and targeting those segments that are most likely to buy your product, will allow you to achieve the greatest possible return on your marketing dollars and efforts.

This means you need to understand who, what, when, where, why, and how consumers buy the type of product you have to offer, and what they are really buying when they place their order. It also means you should focus not on what you are selling, but what needs you are satisfying and/or problems you are solving for your customer.

As such, your marketing plan should identify the factors that are most important to potential customers in choosing this type of product (for example price, quality, value, benefits, prestige) and gear your marketing efforts towards those factors. But more importantly, you need to identify the reasons why customers should buy *your* product—what unique value and benefits you can provide to them that differentiates you from the competition—and effectively communicate that difference to your target market consumers.

With this understanding and your knowledge of the demographics, geographic location, behavior patterns, and psychological characteristics of your target market, you can construct a strategy that effectively locates those consumers with the greatest propensity to buy what you have to offer, gets their attention, communicates with them about your product and its benefits versus those of the competitors, convinces them to buy, and garners their loyalty for future purchases.

The most effective marketing plan is comprised of the "Four Ps" of marketing: product, price, place (distribution), and promotion. As such, this section of your business plan should discuss the key features of your product, the pricing strategy you intend to follow, your distribution strategy and capability, and the manner you intend to promote your product through traditional and online advertising, public relations, and the like.

The Operations Plan

With respect to your business plan, "operations" consists of everything necessary to convert your idea into a product in your customer's hands. This includes product development, purchasing, manufacturing, packing and shipping, distribution, and accounting systems and controls.

In this section of the business plan, you should demonstrate that you have a firm grasp of the process necessary to develop your product and bring it to market in an efficient and cost effective manner that ensures the level of quality and profitability you desire. But the main value of this section, and the analysis that goes into it, is identifying the areas that must be concentrated on to succeed in your business—in particular those areas where you can gain a competitive advantage. Conversely, you need to identify the areas where you may currently lag behind the competition, and develop a plan for either getting up to speed or compensating for your weakness.

The detail required with respect to individual areas of product development and operations will depend on the nature of your business. If you are developing new software that has not been finalized, product development milestones and dates should be included in the business plan. If you will require a distribution partner in order to effectively access and distribute to your target market, your plan for obtaining such a partner, and the anticipated terms of the arrangement, should be laid out. If specialized machinery will be required to manufacture your product, then you should discuss whether you will purchase the equipment or outsource the entire process. Accounting systems and controls may seem like a very basic function of running a business, but if your system cannot effectively handle orders, collections, and payments, you may find a potential profit turning into a loss.

The bottom line is that you need to assure both yourself and your investors that you have thought through the entire process of running your business, not just the sexy part that revolves around marketing and sales.

The Management Team

When analyzing your company, investors will not only look to see whether you have a good idea and a large target market, they will closely assess whether you and your management team can execute on that idea and build a valuable business around it. They know that without the right people, even the best business idea will wither on the vines and their funds will go down the drain. Begin this section by providing background on each member of your senior management team, including their educational and employment history. Focus, however, on what their responsibilities will be in your business and what qualities they bring to the table that will help you succeed. Most plans also include an organizational chart to show who will be reporting to who in your company.

If you have formed a corporation, then also provide background on your board of directors. Highlight why they were chosen to sit on the board and any unique experience they have that will add value to your business.

Finally, identify who the business owners are and the percentage of the corporation or partnership they own. In the case of a corporation, show all outstanding equity, as well as all stock options or warrants, and describe the terms of any classes of preferred stock.

The Financial Plan & Projections

Last, but definitely not least, is a description of your financial plan. This is where you provide the projected financial results of putting your business plan into effect, and discuss the meaning and ramifications of those numbers for your business.

As with the rest of the business plan, the most important reason for putting together these financial projections is for your own internal planning purposes. They can serve as the basis for your budget, allow you to gauge how much extra cash you need to raise, and provide a measure of how you are doing with respect to your plan once actual results start to flow in.

In addition to becoming the primary barometer of your internal planning process, the financial projections you create for your business plan will allow potential investors and lenders to analyze whether your business idea, if properly executed, will provide them with a sufficient rate of return on their investment. If the business will not generate sufficient cash, reach profitability soon enough, or create enough value to make an exit strategy viable, they will wish you good luck and move on. But if your forecasted financial results will achieve these three goals, you may find yourself with a feeding frenzy of investors at your door.

The guts of your financial plan section will be pro forma income statements, balance sheets, and cash flow statements for the next 3-5 years, supported by a break-even analysis and relevant financial ratios. These are not financial accounting statements that reflect verifiable historical results. They are financial forecasts: an educated prediction of future results based on sales and expense forecasts, which in turn are based on a set of assumptions about your business, the market, the industry, and the economy.

These assumptions should be well thought-out and easily explainable and supportable. The most important of them should be communicated in your business plan. Once you have established your base assumptions, use them to forecast sales on a monthly basis for the first year, quarterly for the second and third years, and annually for the fourth and fifth. Take into account seasonality and buying trends in your industry. The most important thing is to be as realistic as possible—not overly optimistic and therefore not believable, but not overly pessimistic either.

From these sales forecasts—together with any other sources of income, amounts you plan to raise, and assumed taxes and expenses—you can create the required pro forma income statements, balance sheets, and cash flow statements.

Having completed your financial forecasting and pro forma financial statements, you should now have a detailed blueprint for starting and running your new business, and feel a huge surge of confidence because you can see before your eyes how it could all come together. Now it is time to take care of the nuts and bolts of organizing your company, and afterwards you will be ready to begin operations and put your business plan into effect.

Exotic Universe, Inc.

As a teacher, Cindy McKay always told her students: "Never be afraid to ask for help." So when it came time to sit down and write her business plan over the winter break, she calls in some experienced outside assistance. Her first recruit is her good friend Anne, currently the marketing director for a small line of children's clothes that are sold to specialty retail shops. Another friend, Roger, has his own website design business, and Roger recommends they add his friend Bill, an accountant who speaks fluent Spanish and previously worked for a consumer products company in Argentina. Cindy begins the first meeting with tremendous excitement, but as they dig deeper and deeper into the details of the proposed business, her concerns grow by the hour. Anne drives home the supreme importance of identifying the target *segment* and understanding their characteristics inside and out. She's not an online marketing expert, but she knows that to convert viewers into customers, you have to know exactly what they are looking for and how to speak to them. She also stresses the difficulties and expense involved in marketing to different segments at the same time. Roger then explains that constructing and maintaining a catalog-style e-commerce website like Cindy is proposing is not a simple proposition. And Bill presses her on the business model, specifically how she intends to source and distribute her products and pay her suppliers. For example, he asks whether the products Cindy sells will be purchased and held in inventory, or sold on consignment. Then, when Bill arrives at the second meeting with some preliminary financial projections and shows them to Cindy, she almost falls off her chair. It is going to take three times as long as she had anticipated to break-even, and she is in no position to fund the business for that long. Even if she could come up with the cash, there are many obstacles and threats to a successful launch of her business. "Sorry everyone, I guess I was just dreaming," Cindy says, and leaves the meeting resigned to sticking with her teaching career.

But the next day, Anne calls and asks Cindy to meet her friend Nancy, who successfully started two companies of her own. Over coffee, Nancy advises Cindy not to walk away from her idea, just to reduce her expectations and focus her efforts. "Build your business one step at a time," Nancy says. Then she asks Cindy a series of pointed questions: Which aspect of the business are you most excited about and best equipped to deal with right now? Which part most distinguishes you from the competition? Which could you implement most efficiently with the least cost? Cindy's answer to each of these questions is the same: selling quality paintings and sculptures created by unknown artists in exotic locations. This is Cindy's area of expertise, and the limited number of items that had to be sourced and shipped would make the logistics of the business much easier and less costly. In addition, while these items can be found online, there is no major competitor specializing in exotic artwork. However, there is a downside. The target market for artwork is much smaller than the market for accessories and home décor items, with lower prospects for growth. Yet once again, Nancy is encouraging rather than discouraging—finding opportunity in obstacles. With the spirit and vision of a true entrepreneur, she tells Cindy that once the website, marketing effort, business model, supply and distribution logistics, etc. for the business focused on exotic art are in place, they will be scalable into the other product lines/market segments that Cindy had originally contemplated. Hopefully, the business will have positive cash flow to invest at that point. And if not, it will have traction and a working business model, so will be more attractive to outside investors. The key, Nancy says, is to create a solid foundation that Cindy can build upon in the future.

By the time Cindy meets with her team of advisers once again, the business planning process has already served its primary purpose—it has fleshed out the business idea, exposed its strengths and weaknesses, provided the opportunity to make strategic adjustments, and saved Cindy from having launched a venture that she was ill-prepared for and would most likely have been a very expensive failure. Now, with a specific product line and target market in mind, the group once again thinks through the issues and re-crunches the numbers. When they have finished, it is apparent that they have identified an opportunity which can be turned into a profitable, and sizable, niche business that in the future could be scaled into something much bigger.

CHAPTER 5:
MAKING IT LEGAL

Chapter 5

CHAPTER 5

MAKING IT LEGAL

Choosing a Business Structure

Now that you've produced a business plan that provides a road map to success, you can simply open your doors and start doing business, right? Well, technically, yes. But in a vast majority of cases, it wouldn't be advised. First, you need to choose and implement the optimum legal structure for your business to operate under. This is not just a matter of compliance with the law; it is a matter of dollars and good business sense.

There are four basic types of business structures:

- Sole Proprietorship

- Partnership

- Corporation

- Limited Liability Company ("**LLC**")

There are also four main factors to take into account when selecting one of the above legal structures for your business:

- Taxation of the Business and its Owners

- Personal Liability of the Owners

- Ability to Raise Capital

- Ease and Cost of Formation and Operation

As you will see, each type of business organization is strong in some of these areas and weak in others. As a result, the structure you ultimately choose will be driven by the nature of your business and your future business plans.

Sole Proprietorship

A sole proprietorship is the default legal status of a business. If you simply begin selling products or providing services without a business partner, you will be deemed to be a sole proprietor and will be accorded the related legal rights and responsibilities.

From an ease and cost of formation and operation standpoint, a sole proprietorship is ideal: there are no corporate documents to create, no filings to be made or fees to be paid, no requirements for board or stockholder meetings, etc. From a tax perspective, sole proprietorships are also quite attractive. Since a sole proprietorship is not a separate legal entity distinct from its owner, your business profits will be deemed to be your own and will therefore only be taxed once in your name—and not separately in the name of your business. The profits will appear on your annual individual income tax return. You may even be able to set off initial business losses against other personal income, thereby reducing your personal tax bill.

However, when it comes to personal liability and the ability to raise capital, a sole proprietorship falls far short of where most business owners need to be. In particular, a sole proprietor (unlike the owner of a corporation or LLC) is personally liable for all of the debts and liabilities of his or her business. This means that if you head to the kitchen and start baking and selling those homemade ginger snaps that everyone raves about, and someone ends up getting food poisoning and filing a lawsuit against your business, you could lose your personal assets—including the very house that you were baking those ginger snaps in. For that reason alone, it is most often advisable to operate your business under a legal structure such as a corporation or LLC which shields you and your personal assets from liabilities incurred by your business.

Another big downside to having a sole proprietorship is that you are severely limited in how you can raise outside funds. Because sole proprietors have limited means by which they can provide ownership interests in their businesses to investors, their only real option for procuring additional funding is to take out a personal loan from either a financial institution or an individual willing to put up the money. However, as a lender will not benefit from any increase in the value of your business, it will seek to make its return on the loan by charging you interest. In addition, to ensure that it gets repaid, the lender will most likely demand that you provide it with security over your personal assets (including that house you want to protect) as collateral against repayment of the debt. If you fail to repay the debt, the bank can step in and sell the pledged collateral.

Partnership

According to the IRS: "A partnership is the relationship existing between two or more persons who join to carry on a trade or business. Each person contributes money, property, labor or skill, and expects to share in the profits and losses of the business."

And according to the Uniform Partnership Act: "The association of two or more persons to carry on as co-owners of a business for profit forms a partnership, whether or not the persons intend to form a partnership."

Therefore, if you start doing business with another person for profit, you may have formed a partnership whether you realize it or not. So be careful when you ask your buddy to give you a hand restoring vintage motorcycles out of your garage and then selling them, because if you don't put a formal partnership agreement in place then the provisions of state law will provide the terms for you, and you may inadvertently give your friend a right to half your profits. That being said, most people who enter into a partnership do so by choice, and there are two basic types of partnership to choose from:

- General Partnership

- Limited Partnership

General partnerships are relatively easy and inexpensive to form and maintain; all that is really needed is a partnership agreement spelling out the ownership and management arrangement between you and your partners. In particular, the partnership agreement should detail the ownership interests, how profits and losses will be allocated, how business decisions are made, how disputes are resolved, what is the authority and responsibility of each partner, what happens when one of the partners dies or resigns from the business, and how to handle a buyout.

General partnerships do not pay taxes. Rather, each individual general partner takes into account the allocated profits and losses on his or her tax return. Therefore, as with a sole proprietorship, there is only one level of taxation on profits (i.e. the individual partners pay tax, not the partnership itself) and the business owners may use business losses to offset other personal income. Keep in mind, however, that profits retained for use in the business will still be taxed even though they are not distributed to the partners.

In addition, as with sole proprietors, general partners are liable for the debts and obligations of the business. And even worse, each general partner is responsible for the liabilities incurred by the other general partners acting within the scope of their authority, which is basically anything related to the business. Therefore, if one partner incurs a debt on behalf of the business, all general partners are responsible for satisfying that debt.

This fact, among others, makes it very difficult to raise funds from outside investors using a general partnership vehicle. However, with a bit more effort and expense it is possible to form a limited partnership.

A limited partnership, which is usually established by filing partnership papers with the state, is more complex than a general partnership. It is a partnership owned by two classes of partners called general partners and limited partners. General partners manage the day to day running of the partnership business, contribute to the capital of the partnership, share in the profits of the partnership, and are personally liable for all of its debts. However, while limited partners contribute capital and share in the profits of the partnership, they have no rights to participate in the management of the partnership and their potential liability for the debts of the partnership is limited to the amount of capital that they have contributed.

However, in many limited partnerships, the general partner is often a corporation or limited liability company. This allows the people sitting behind a general partner to carry on the partnership business and be shielded from personal liability at the same time.

While limited partnerships are more flexible than general partnerships when it comes to raising finance, for the most part they are used as special purpose vehicles for tax related purposes and are not generally suitable for establishing new businesses. The vehicles of choice for forming new businesses are corporations and LLCs, each of which we discuss below.

Corporation

A corporation is a legal entity separate and apart from its owners. As such, it has the ability to enter into agreements and incur debt and other liabilities on its own behalf. The principal advantage of forming a corporation is that in almost all cases you and your fellow stockholder-owners will not be liable for the debts and liabilities of the business. Therefore, if you form a corporation which is unable to pay its bills, or is sued for an amount that insurance and company assets don't cover, your personal assets such as your house will be safe.

There are other significant advantages to forming a corporation, and chief among them is that a corporation is the best vehicle for raising funds from outside investors. Corporations can issue one or more classes of stock having whatever rights and preferences are set forth in the company's certificate of incorporation. Subject to federal and state securities laws, stock in a corporation is transferable, which investors typically require. This allows ownership and partial ownership of the business to be transferred in the event of the sale of the corporation, the exit of an owner, or the death of an owner.

In addition, subject to compliance with federal and state securities laws, a corporation has the ability to issue shares to a large number of investors in a public offering and have those shares traded on a stock exchange. This gives the company the ability to raise capital from a wide variety of sources, and at a higher valuation (shares that are not registered with the SEC and publicly tradable are discounted in value because they are not easy to sell). It also gives the company's initial investors and owners the ability to realize a return on their investment without selling the company in its entirety.

One downside is that a corporation is more expensive and difficult to maintain than a sole proprietorship or partnership. The certificate of incorporation (in some states called the articles of incorporation) must be drafted and filed in the state of incorporation, the company must be kept in good standing through annual filings and fees, board and stockholder meetings must be held, etc. In addition, stockholders by law are given certain rights that must be complied with, limiting in certain respects how much absolute control over the business the persons running it have.

The principal disadvantage of a corporation is the "double taxation" of corporate profits. A standard "C" corporation is required to file its own tax return and pay income taxes on its taxable profits. Afterwards, if the corporation distributes after-tax profits to its stockholder-owners in the form of a dividend, the individual owners are required to pay personal income taxes on the amount they receive—hence the term "double taxation."

If you intend to operate a small business and take most of the after-tax profits you earn out of your business in the form of dividends, then double taxation could result in a severe hit to the amount you put in your pocket as the profits will be taxed at both stages. However, if you are starting a company that you wish to grow into a larger organization in the future, then double taxation may be somewhat of an illusory problem. If you decide to pay yourself a salary, the amount of this salary will be deemed to be an expense which can be deducted from the corporation's profits. As such, when it comes to paying tax on those profits, there will be no need to pay corporate income tax on the amount of the salary as it's not counted for tax purposes. Instead, it's only taken into account for income tax purposes in the hands of the employee-stockholder. Any profits that remain in the corporation after expenses are deducted (i.e. pre-tax profits) are usually subject to corporate income tax in the normal way.

However, if a 'flow-through' entity is desirable, it may be possible to elect to have your corporation treated as a Subchapter S corporation under the Internal Revenue Code. With S corporation status, income and losses pass straight through to stockholders (almost like a partnership) so there is only one level of tax. At the same time, the entity remains a corporation in the eyes of the law, and therefore limited liability for its stockholders is preserved.

Unfortunately, S corporations must meet certain statutory requirements for the election to be valid. These requirements include having:

- Only one class of stock

- 100 stockholders or less

- Only U.S. stockholders

- Stock that is only owned by individuals, estates, and certain trusts and pension plans

- Profit distributions that are proportionate to shares held

Because venture capital and other investors are almost always not individuals and require a separate class of preferred stock, these restrictions virtually eliminate one of the primary advantages of incorporation: the ability to raise capital from outside investors.

However, if you do not intend to fund your operations with outside capital in the near future, it is possible to form a corporation, make a Subchapter S election, and later revert back to a C corporation when it is time to seek an equity investment.

Another possibility, similar but in important ways not identical to becoming an S corporation, is the formation of an LLC.

Limited Liability Company

In recent years, small businesses have increasingly chosen to operate as an LLC, an easily formed and maintained legal structure that combines some of the advantages of a corporation and a partnership. Like with an S corporation, an LLC is treated as a pass-through entity for federal tax purposes. In addition, the LLC structure shields the owners from personal liability for the business's debts and obligations, while at the same time allowing them all to participate in management.

All that is normally required to start an LLC is the filing of a set of articles of organization and the drafting of an operating agreement defining the company's policies and procedures. And whereas a corporation requires a board of directors, officers, and regular stockholders' and directors' meetings, an LLC is not required to observe such formalities. An LLC can be run essentially as if it were a limited liability partnership, but all members of an LLC may be directly involved in the company's management without jeopardizing their limited liability.

Advantages that forming an LLC have over an S corporation include:

- There is no limit on the number of members

- A corporation can be a member

- Members can decide on percentage distributions subject to IRS guidelines on partnership income distribution

Some disadvantages of an LLC include:

- There are no stock certificates; only "membership interests"

- Some states impose a 30 year limit on the life of the LLC

- The LLC dissolves when a member dies, quits, or retires

- Employee equity incentive programs are difficult if not impossible to implement

- There are limits on the ability to deduct employee benefits as business expenses

- Each member's pro-rata share of profits represents taxable income whether or not distributed to him or her

The biggest drawback to an LLC, however, is once again with respect to raising outside capital. In fact, most venture capital funds are prohibited from investing in an LLC or any other pass-through entity due to the fact venture capital funds operate as not for profit organizations and are not allowed to recognize business income. Therefore, for companies that wish to pursue venture capital and/or eventually pursue an initial public offering, the LLC is not an appropriate alternative to a corporation. And while it is possible to switch from being an LLC to a corporation, it is not as straightforward as discontinuing an S corporation. So don't assume you can begin as an LLC and then easily convert to a corporation when it is time to raise funds.

Exotic Universe, Inc.

With her business plan in hand, Cindy makes an appointment with a law firm recommended by Nancy that specializes in representing start-up companies. After reviewing this chapter, Cindy already realizes that her choice of what legal structure to adopt depends not only on the specific circumstances of her business as it exists at the outset, but also as it will exist in the foreseeable future. Therefore, when meeting with the lawyer, whose name is David, she specifically points out her intention to scale the business going forward. If all goes according to her business plan, Cindy will hire several employees and independent contractors almost immediately, launch her website in six months, generate losses for the following six months, and reach break-even in approximately one year. After that, the projected growth in profits and cash flow is substantial and she will begin to scale her operations into different product lines. However, it will not be possible to fund the first year cash requirements out of her personal savings, so she will need to raise money from some outside source. And when she scales her business after the first year, she will probably need to raise even more outside money. In addition, Cindy has already decided that her operation will be large and complex enough that she does not want to run the risk, and incur the stress, of potential personal liability, so she wants to form either a corporation or an LLC. It is tempting to go the cheap and easy route of the LLC, and this would allow her to offset initial business losses against the teaching income she has already earned this year. However, she wants to create the impression among potential investors that she is committed to establishing a professionally managed growth corporation, not just a small business. And in any event, she is committed to putting profits earned in the second through fifth year back into the business in order to expand the business and possibly find a buyer or strategic partner. So Cindy chooses a traditional corporation over an LLC. But should she make a Subchapter S election? The answer, she decides after speaking with David, is "yes." At least initially, in order to allow her to offset her teaching income against the business losses for the remainder of the year. But Cindy will make the election carefully and with the intention of converting back to a C corporation once she has established interest from outside investors. She believes she will be able to explain this strategy to potential investors and demonstrate her business savvy at the same time. "So how do I go about forming a corporation," she asks David.

CHAPTER 6:
LET'S GET INCORPORATED

Chapter 6

CHAPTER 6

LET'S GET INCORPORATED

Forming a Corporation

If you've decided that a corporation is the best legal structure for your new business, your next step will be to form a corporation in a state of your choosing. The laws and procedures relating to incorporation vary from state to state, so you will first need to familiarize yourself with the incorporation procedures and requirements in your chosen state, as well as its corporate and tax law.

In most cases, the steps involved in forming a corporation include the following:

- Decide when to incorporate your business

- Choose the state where you want to incorporate

- Select and reserve a name for your new corporation

- Prepare a certificate of incorporation (called articles of incorporation in some states)

- Prepare corporate bylaws

- Select a registered agent (if you are incorporating in a state where you do not have your own physical address and employees)

- File the certificate of incorporation with the appropriate state authority

- Appoint the board of directors and hold an initial board meeting

- Prepare restricted stock purchase agreements for the founding stockholders (called "shareholders" in some states)

- Issue shares of stock to the founding stockholders

Like many people focused on running a business, you may feel that some of these items are merely corporate housekeeping matters that don't warrant a significant degree of attention. However, it is critical that matters such as where to incorporate, the name of your corporation, the terms of the certificate of incorporation and bylaws, and the restrictions (if any) on shares of stock issued to founders are well thought out and the documents correctly prepared.

Failure to do so may result in difficulties that could have a serious impact on your business, such as being unable to obtain the required stockholder approval for certain important actions your company wishes to take in the future, being unable to secure financing from banks or investors, or even facing charges of trademark infringement or securities law violations. In other words, this may not be the most exciting thing you do in starting a business, but it will pay to take the time to get it right.

When to Incorporate

Many entrepreneurs hold off forming a corporation until the last minute, not wanting to expend the time and money necessary to incorporate until they are certain they will move forward with their new business. Often, however, they wait too long. This can cause numerous problems that have to be cleaned up by the new corporation, not to mention expose the founders to personal liability.

It is generally recommended that you incorporate before launching a product, taking on debt or other obligations, or undertaking any other activity—including hiring an employee or retaining an independent contractor—which could expose you to personal liability. In addition, if you are planning on raising funds from outside sources, early incorporation is recommended as it allows you to put some distance between the time shares of stock are issued to founders at a cheap price and to investors providing funds to the company at a higher price. If the stock issuances are too close together, the IRS may challenge the valuation of the founders' shares, which could have significant adverse tax consequences. Issuing stock to founders early on also starts the clock running on the capital gains holding period, potentially saving the founders a lot of money in reduced taxes when they sell their stock.

In addition, if you have more than one founder it is generally a good idea to incorporate as soon as possible. This forces you and your co-founders to focus on and decide what the equity allocation will be before spending a large amount of time and money on the business. If there are disagreements, it is better to hash them out sooner rather than later, as well as put things in writing so there is no future misunderstanding.

Incorporation is especially important if there is more than one founder and they are creating significant intellectual property, such as software code or inventions, for a new business. If a corporation is not formed, the intellectual property rights will vest in the founders personally. If that intellectual property is not assigned by the founders to the new corporation, then one founder could walk away from the business and either take the rights to use crucial intellectual property with him, or return later and claim an interest in the business. Having a "lost founder" pop out of the woodwork after the business becomes successful could be a very expensive problem. We'll discuss this in more detail in Chapter 15.

One note of caution, however, before you rush to form a corporation. If any founder is still an employee of another company, then that founder should take a close look at his or her current employment agreement and employee handbook, as well as state law, to make sure there are no potential issues that may affect the new business. For example, the intellectual property rights relating to software developed for the new business by an employee of another business could end up belonging to the other business.

Where to Incorporate

You don't have to form your corporation in the state where your business headquarters is located, or even where you are doing business. Technically, you can incorporate in any state. However, in most cases the two best options will be either (i) the state of Delaware or (ii) the state where your corporate headquarters or primary place of business will be located.

The decision as to where you ultimately incorporate will rest, among other things, on the nature of your business and how you intend to conduct it in the future. For example, if you plan on raising money from venture capital investors or by means of a public offering of stock, you should consider choosing Delaware, which has a sophisticated and flexible corporate governance regime and is the state where most professional investors prefer the corporations they invest in to be incorporated. In fact, a majority of all Fortune 500 companies and a vast majority of venture capital funded companies incorporate in Delaware.

The reasons to incorporate in Delaware include:

- A corporate law conducive to efficient corporate governance

- A corporate law that most sophisticated investors are familiar with and prefer

- A specialized court system geared towards quickly, efficiently, and effectively rendering informed decisions on corporate law matters

- A predictable and well-developed body of corporate case law

- Substantial protection for directors and officers against personal liability, including the ability of the corporation to indemnify its directors and officers in most situations

- The ability to have only one director

- No state corporate income tax for companies that are formed in Delaware but do not transact business there

- Stockholders, directors, and officers of a Delaware corporation are not required to be Delaware residents

- Stock owned by persons outside Delaware is not subject to Delaware taxes

Given all of these benefits, you might ask why any business would incorporate in a state other than Delaware. The first reason is to avoid Delaware franchise taxes, which can be substantial under certain circumstances. The second reason is to avoid having to comply with both Delaware regulatory requirements and those of the state where your business is actually headquartered and/or doing business.

If you don't intend for your corporation to attract venture capital investment or to become a publicly traded company, these reasons could be sufficient to lead you to incorporate in your home state. Don't assume, however, that you can do so initially and then easily reincorporate in Delaware in the future. While it may be possible to do this, you may incur legal and other costs that outweigh any tax and other savings you gained initially.

Choosing and Reserving a Name

When it comes time to choose a name for your corporation, you will have two sets of considerations: legal and business. You need to carefully select a name that can be registered in your state of incorporation and each state where you intend to do business, registered as a federal trademark, and then developed into a well-recognized and unique brand that reflects the image you want your company to project.

Legal factors to consider when selecting a name include:

- Is the name available as a corporation name in the state where you wish to incorporate, as well as in the states where you intend to do business?

- Does the name violate another person's or entity's trademark or trade name?

- Can the name be registered as a federal trademark?

Business factors to take into account include:

- Does the name reflect the image you want your business to project?

- Is the name unique and memorable?

- Will the name appeal to your target market?

- What are the connotations of the name?

- How does the name appear visually?

- Is the name available as a website domain name?

States also require corporation names to end with some designation that shows the corporate status of the entity, such as "Corporation," "Incorporated," or "Limited." Many states allow abbreviations of these words as well, such as "Corp.", "Inc.", or "Ltd."

Your chosen state of incorporation will not allow you to use a name that is the same or deceptively similar to one already being used. And if your name violates another person or company's trademark or trade name, you could find your business subject to expensive lawsuits and judgments, not to mention the potential of losing the ability to use the name at all. In selecting a name, you need to take the time to make sure that you don't waste a considerable amount of time, effort, and money creating a website and building a brand around a name that you ultimately have to change.

Therefore, your first step in selecting a bulletproof corporation name is to determine its availability in the state where you wish to incorporate and in all states where you wish to qualify to do business. In most states, you can provide the name to the state corporation office, which will check to see if the name is available and allowable. In addition, you should conduct a thorough trademark search and analysis, which we will discuss in detail in Chapter 15, to determine whether your chosen name can become a federally registered trademark. And finally, you should determine whether the name, or an acceptable derivative of the name, is available as a website domain name. We discuss procedures for clearing and obtaining a domain name in Chapter 13.

Once you have chosen a unique name for your corporation and determined its availability for corporate registration, trademark registration and protection, and domain name usage, it's a good idea to reserve the name until you are ready to file your incorporation documents. A reservation of this kind can normally be obtained for a small fee. In Delaware, the reservation lasts for 120 days, during which time no other person can form a corporation using the reserved name.

Be aware, however, that just because the state corporation office allows you to reserve a name, and subsequently form a corporation using that name, that does not mean that you automatically have any intellectual property rights with respect to your corporate name. It also doesn't mean that the use of that name will not violate the intellectual property rights of another person or entity. That is why the aforementioned business name, trademark, and domain name searches are so important.

Preparing and Filing a Certificate of Incorporation

In order to be officially incorporated and begin operating as a corporation, you must file a certificate of incorporation with the appropriate state authority. A certificate of incorporation is a public document that sets out specific details about the corporation. In Delaware, the certificate of incorporation must include the:

- Name of the corporation

- Business purpose of the corporation

- Total number of shares of stock authorized to be issued

- Description of the different classes of stock (if there is more than one class)

- Par value of the shares of stock

- Name of the registered agent and address of the registered office

- Name and signature of the person or entity forming the corporation

In addition to the items required to be included in the certificate of incorporation, there are many items that you might choose to include. In Delaware, the certificate of incorporation may contain any provisions relating to the management and conduct of the corporation's business, as well as provisions creating, defining, limiting, and regulating the powers of the corporation, the directors, and the stockholders (or any class of stockholders), if such provisions are not contrary to the laws of the state.

Keep in mind that some items you may want as part of your corporate governance regime are only valid if they are contained in the certificate of incorporation—one reason why you must carefully think through how you want your corporation to operate and be governed, and understand your options under the corporate law of your state of incorporation.

Examples of provisions you could add to your certificate of incorporation include those that:

- Increase the required number of votes for actions by stockholders and directors over the voting requirements under state corporate law

- Grant stockholders the preemptive right to subscribe to additional issuances of stock

- Limit certain liabilities and permit certain indemnification of officers and directors

- Create classes of preferred stock with specific rights and preferences separate from the corporation's common stock

Business Purpose

In most states, the business purpose for which a corporation is established can be very broad and may be phrased in generic terms. For example, in Delaware most corporations state in their certificate of incorporation that: "The purpose of the corporation is to engage in any lawful act or activity for which corporations may be organized under the General Corporation Law of Delaware." However, some states require a more specific description of the proposed purpose for which the corporation is being established. Where this is the case, you will need to make sure that the specific purpose given in the certificate of incorporation is sufficiently broad to enable the corporation to carry on the business for which it is being incorporated.

Authorized Shares of Stock

The authorized shares of stock are the total number of shares available to be issued by the corporation. This should not be confused with the number of "issued and outstanding shares," which means the number of shares that have been issued to, and are being held by, stockholders at any point in time. While the number of authorized shares can be increased by amending the certificate of incorporation, this will require stockholder approval. So when you file your initial certificate of incorporation it is a good idea to authorize a sufficient number of shares for the foreseeable future.

Your decision on the actual number of shares you decide to authorize may be driven by a combination of factors, including the nature of your business, your future financing plans, the need to retain flexibility for future share issuances, and state franchise tax concerns. For example, in some states such as Delaware, the number of authorized shares could potentially greatly increase the annual state franchise tax payments that must be made. This would argue for a low number of authorized shares. However, the number needs to at least be high enough to accurately allocate the percentage of equity to be held by the founding stockholders and any other persons that may be granted shares. Therefore, it is usually recommended that a minimum of about 2,000 shares be authorized.

However, some start-up companies authorize significantly more shares than this. In fact, many initially authorize between 10-15 million shares with a par value (the minimum price per share in order for it to be fully paid) as low as $0.001 or $0.0001 per share. The majority of these shares are issued to the founders, while 10-20 percent of the shares are earmarked for a stock option pool and the rest are reserved for future issuances. The high number of shares will normally allow for a future public offering of stock to be conducted without having to engage in a stock-split or reverse stock-split in preparation for the offering. But authorizing millions of shares is as much a function of human psychology as anything else—key employees feel better being granted an option to purchase 100,000 shares than 10 shares, even though the value may be the same.

What about the franchise taxes? Fortunately, Delaware has an alternative way of calculating such taxes based on the gross assets of the business. And since most start-ups have few assets, they can avoid paying high franchise taxes.

Classes of Stock

Before discussing different classes of stock, let's step back for a moment and define what "stock" actually means. A share of stock is a type of security that evidences a percentage ownership in a corporation and represents a claim against a portion of the corporation's earnings and assets. The claim against earnings comes into play when the corporation decides to make a distribution in the form of a dividend, and the claim against assets comes into play if the corporation is liquidated. In addition, subject to federal and state securities laws and any contractual agreement that may be in place, stock can be transferred, which is the principal way that many stockholders realize the value of their shares.

There are two basic forms of stock: common and preferred. But within these categories you can create different classes having different rights (such as voting rights) and preferences (such as liquidation preferences).

Common stock is the basic form of corporate ownership. The rights attaching to shares of common stock are governed by the laws of the state of incorporation, and in most cases state law will provide that each share of common stock carries one vote and common stockholders are entitled to their pro-rata share of dividends declared and distributions made by the corporation.

However, it is possible to create a different class of common stock having rights greater than the minimum rights guaranteed by state corporate law. For example, you could create a Class A Common Stock having 1 vote per share, and a Class B Common Stock having 10 votes per share. This would allow each share of common stock to have a pro rata financial interest in the corporation, while each share of Class B Common Stock would have much more voting power, and therefore influence in determining such matters as who sits on the board of directors. When the class of super-voting common stock is created specifically for issuance to the founders, it is often labeled Class F Common Stock, with the "F" standing for "founders."

Preferred stock is normally created to give certain investors a preferred position with respect to the common stockholders. For example, preferred stock may be given priority over common stock with respect to distributions upon liquidation of the company, a guaranteed yearly dividend paid from corporate earnings (if any), class voting rights on certain matters such as issuing additional shares, a sale of the corporation, the ability to elect a specified number of directors, etc.

Angel and venture capital investors almost always require preferred stock that can be converted into common stock at a specified conversion rate, along with other negotiated rights and preferences. Normally, every round of financing will result in a new class of preferred stock—e.g. Series A Preferred Stock, Series B Preferred Stock, etc. In each case, the specific rights and preferences of the new class of preferred stock are added into the certificate of incorporation by an amendment filed with the appropriate state authority.

Registered Agent

If you are incorporating in a state where you are not doing business and do not have any employees, you will need to have a "registered agent" and a registered office. The registered agent for a corporation is a contact person for your corporation residing within the state of incorporation. A registered agent receives important legal and tax documents on behalf of a business, including mail sent by the state (annual reports or statements), tax documents sent by the state's department of revenue, and service of process—sometimes called notice of litigation—which initiates a lawsuit.

Filing the Certificate of Incorporation

When it's time to file your certificate of incorporation, you will file the signed document with the appropriate state authority along with the appropriate filing fee. The certificate is signed by the "incorporator," which can be you or any person you designate. Once the corporation is formed, the incorporator then appoints the initial board of directors, and then his or her responsibilities are finished.

While the preparation of a certificate of incorporation is fairly straightforward, care must be taken to ensure that it is in the appropriate format for filing, because if not it will be rejected by the state authorities. States take different amounts of time to process and approve the certificate of incorporation, and in each state the amount of time may vary depending on the backlog of filings they have received. If you are in a hurry to incorporate, certain states have expedited processing available for an additional fee—Delaware will even process your certificate in one hour for $1,000. Once your certificate of incorporation is approved, you will generally receive a copy stamped with the effective date of incorporation. In Delaware, assuming your application is in good order, the effective date will be the date you delivered the certificate to the Division of Corporations.

Preparing and Adopting Corporate Bylaws

The corporate bylaws lay out the rules by which a corporation will govern its internal affairs. Delaware law allows a corporation's bylaws to contain any provision relating to the business of the corporation, the conduct of its affairs, or the rights or powers of its stockholders, directors, officers or employees, so long as the provision is lawful and consistent with the certificate of incorporation.

Normally, however, the bylaws set forth: the responsibilities of the directors and officers; the number of directors; the manner of calling meetings of the stockholders and directors (including the required notice); the maintenance of corporate records; the issuance of reports to stockholders; voting and proxy procedures; the rules regarding and procedure for the transfer of stock; procedures for the declaration of dividends; procedures for winding up the company's affairs; and other general corporate matters.

The best way to prepare your bylaws is to begin with a form document that contains a menu of provisions that makes you aware of your options, and then select the terms that will allow your company to govern itself in the legal manner that you desire.

Unlike the certificate of incorporation, the bylaws are not filed with the state. In Delaware, the power to adopt, amend, or repeal bylaws automatically rests with the stockholders entitled to vote. However, any corporation may also grant the power to adopt, amend, or repeal bylaws to the board of directors by stating this in its certificate of incorporation (doing so does not divest the stockholders of this power as well). Most corporations do this, and therefore the bylaws will generally be adopted at the first meeting of the board of directors.

Appointing the Board of Directors and Holding the Initial Meeting

The stockholders are the owners of a corporation, but it is the directors that manage its business. It is therefore the directors, rather than the stockholders, that will have the authority to determine your company's strategy, make major financial decisions, issue authorized shares, and control day-to-day operations. The role of the stockholders is limited to the election of directors and approval of certain important matters and large transactions, such as the authorization of additional company shares and the sale of the company through merger or asset transfer.

Your incorporator can appoint the initial board of directors by signing an "action of sole incorporator" document stating the number of initial directors and their names. The initial directors will then serve on the board until the first annual meeting of the stockholders, where a board of directors will be nominated and elected for the next term.

It's a good idea to hold an initial meeting of the board of directors soon after incorporation. Matters to be taken up at the initial board meeting include:

- Adoption of the bylaws (alternatively, the bylaws can be adopted in the action of sole incorporator document)

- Appointment of corporate officers

- Authorization of the issuance of stock

- Selection of a bank and approval of the opening of an account

- Approval of the official stock certificate form and the corporate seal

- If the corporation is to be an S corporation, the approval of the S corporation election

The actions of the board of directors should be recorded by the corporate secretary in the minutes of the meeting, which will be approved by the directors at the next meeting and placed in a corporate record book. The corporate record book will hold all of your corporation's important papers, including minutes of director and stockholder meetings and stock issuance and transfer records.

Issuing Shares

Although not legally required in most states, small corporations usually issue paper stock certificates. The basic process of issuing shares of stock is as follows:

1. Prepare restricted stock purchase agreements for each founder, which evidences the purchase of a stated number of shares of the corporation and the price that will be paid, and have the founders sign their agreement.

2. Collect the applicable purchase price for the shares from each founder and retain evidence of payment for the company's records.

3. Prepare the stock certificates and have each certificate signed and dated by the president and the secretary of the corporation. The appropriate "restricted stock" legends, which we will discuss in the Securities Law Compliance section below, must be on the back of the stock certificates.

4. Deliver the stock certificates to the founders, retaining a photocopy (front and back) for the corporate records.

5. Prepare a stock ledger to record the issuance of each stock certificate, including share amount, name of recipient, date of issuance, how much was paid, and the type of shares issued. Subsequent transfers and cancellations should be recorded in the same manner.

6. You may also have to file a "notice of stock transaction" if your state's laws require it.

Sometimes, a founder will want to contribute certain assets such as land, equipment, or intellectual property as part of the payment of his or her share purchase price. If this is the case, make sure you get professional advice to understand the tax ramifications of doing so, and the proper way to value the assets and structure the contribution.

Founders Restricted Stock Purchase Agreements and Share Vesting

If your company has multiple founders and/or will be issuing shares to key employees, one of the most important issues you will have to decide when issuing shares of stock is what, if any, contractual restrictions to place on those shares.

If each founder contributes a significant amount of cash or other valuable assets to the business, then normally some or all of the shares will be issued without contractual restriction. However, in many start-up companies, the founders pay a relatively small amount of money for their shares, with their main contribution to be their "sweat equity" going forward. In this situation, many corporations require that the shares "vest" over a period of time before they are owned free and clear by the holder, and such vesting provisions are included in each founder's restricted stock purchase agreement.

For example, if a corporation has three founders and each is issued 1,000 shares of common stock, the shares could be required to vest monthly over a four year period, with a one year cliff at the beginning. This means that each founder would vest 250 shares at the end of the first year, and then approximately 21 shares per month afterwards until the end of the fourth year. If any founder leaves before the end of the first year, all of his or her shares could be subject to repurchase by the company at the initial sales price (which is often a nominal amount). Similarly, if a founder leaves after the end of the first year and before the end of the fourth year, any unvested shares could be subject to repurchase at the initial sales price.

Venture capital investors almost always require founders and key employees to be subject to a vesting schedule for a majority of their shares. So if you plan to raise outside funds, then putting a vesting schedule in place at the outset is a good idea.

However, if you decide to adopt this structure, which many companies do, it is extremely important that you get legal and tax advice, because if a vesting schedule is not implemented properly the founders could be subject to severe tax consequences when their shares vest. All that it takes to avoid these consequences is to file what is called an "83(b)" election with the IRS within 30 days of the time the shares are initially issued. However, a founder's failure to do so may see him or her taxed at the ordinary income rate on the difference between the nominal issuance price for the shares and the fair market value on the date they vest— which could create a situation where the founder has significant tax liability, but no cash to pay it.

Other issues that you need to decide include whether shares that have vested should be subject to repurchase rights and/or other contractual transfer restrictions, and whether vesting should accelerate on certain events such as a change of control of the corporation or termination without cause. Often a corporation will want the right to repurchase even the vested shares at fair market value if a founder leaves the company or is terminated without cause. Conversely, if the company is sold, the founder often wants to be able to participate to the full extent of the shares he or she was originally issued.

Securities Law Compliance

The sale of stock in a private company, and the resale of such stock by purchasers, is subject to legal restrictions. Any time your business sells shares of stock, the offer and sale of the securities must either be registered with the SEC under the Securities Act of 1933 ("**Securities Act**") or meet the requirements for an exemption from registration. Fortunately, such an exemption is available for small businesses offering shares to a limited number of insiders and sophisticated investors.

Section 4(a)(2) of the Securities Act exempts from registration "transactions by an issuer not involving any public offering." This is the exemption sometimes relied upon when issuing shares to a limited number of founders who are familiar with and will be actively involved in managing the business.

However, if your corporation is going to sell shares of stock to outside investors (including friends and family who will not be actively involved in managing the business), either at the time of formation or any time afterwards, you should not rely on the vague standards of Section 4(a)(2) for such a sale, but rather should look to the safe harbor provisions of Regulation D under the Securities Act. The SEC has issued certain rules under Regulation D intended to provide clearer standards for what constitutes a private placement of securities that does not require registration, with the requirements set forth in Rule 506 being the safe harbor used most often by new businesses.

Rule 506 requires your company to file a Form D with the SEC, and the Form D requires you to publicly provide certain information about the offering and your company, such as the company's name, address, executive officers, directors, and the size of the offering. The Form D filings are easily accessible through the SEC's Edgar database.

In any event, before selling shares of stock to either founders or outside investors, get legal advice and make sure you fall squarely under one of the Securities Act exemptions. Also make sure you comply with any relevant state securities laws (one of the Rule 506 exemption's best features is that it works not just at the federal level, but also for each state). Failure to comply with either federal or state securities laws may allow a purchaser to rescind the purchase of securities and get his or her money back, as well as recover damages under certain circumstances.

In addition, you need to be aware that stock issued to a founder or investor pursuant to an exemption from the registration requirements is "restricted" by the federal securities laws and cannot be resold without another exemption. As a result, when the stock certificates are issued, they must contain a "legend" on the back stating that the securities may not be resold unless they are registered with the SEC or are exempt from the registration requirements. The main resale exemption is contained in Rule 144 of the Securities Act, which you should familiarize yourself with if you issue or hold securities in a private company.

Annual Reports and Franchise Taxes

Most likely, your state of incorporation will require an annual report and payment of annual franchise taxes.

- <u>Annual reports</u>

  Most states require corporations to file an annual report (sometimes called an annual statement), which allows states to track formed or qualified corporations. Other states require a biennial statement. In either case, states typically require that a fee be paid when statements are filed.

- <u>Franchise tax</u>

  Some states also have a franchise tax—a fee paid to the state for the privilege of operating as a corporation in that state. States employ different formulas, which may be based on business revenue or the number of authorized shares and par value, for calculating this tax.

In Delaware, the minimum franchise tax is $175 with a maximum tax of $180,000. The amount that is owed is the lesser of two calculations: one using the authorized share method and one using the assumed par value method.

Under the authorized share method, a corporation's franchise taxes are based on the number of authorized shares in the corporation's certificate of incorporation as of December 31:

- $175 for 5,000 or less authorized shares

- $250 for 5,001 to 10,000 authorized shares

- Plus $75 for each 10,000 authorized shares, or portion thereof, in excess of 10,000 authorized shares

This means that if you have 10 million shares authorized as we spoke about earlier, you would owe about $7,500 annually. Fortunately, however, the assumed par value method is calculated using the corporation's gross assets, and since most early stage companies have a low amount of gross assets, most do not pay much in Delaware franchise taxes.

If a corporation is sued and unable to show it met all corporate formalities and state requirements, a judge can rule that the company has been acting more like a sole proprietorship or general partnership, and the stockholders will lose their limited liability protection. In addition, if a corporation does not comply with a state's annual or ongoing requirements and therefore is no longer in "good standing," it may be subject to late fees and interest payments. Being out of good standing long enough may lead to administrative dissolution, in which all benefits of being a corporation are lost. It's therefore important to ensure that annual reports are filed and state franchise taxes paid.

Qualifications to Do Business

If your corporation will conduct business in a state other than its state of incorporation—i.e. have offices, resident employees, or a sales force—it must qualify to do business as a foreign corporation in that state. Therefore, if you incorporate in Delaware but are not located there, this means you must also qualify in the state where your corporate headquarters are located, as well as other states where you conduct operations. The types of activity requiring registration as a foreign entity and the consequences of failing to do so vary from state to state. Each state's office of the secretary of state and third-party service providers can assist you by providing information and assistance regarding state foreign qualifications.

Exotic Universe, Inc.

Cindy McKay was born and raised in Colorado, and tells her attorney David that she wants to form her new corporation in her home state. David listens to Cindy's reasoning, but then points to the section of her business plan that says the corporation will raise money from outside investors, and strongly encourages her to choose Delaware as the state of incorporation. It still sounds strange to Cindy that a small state like Delaware would be such a great place to incorporate, but when David tells her that a venture capital investor would most likely insist that she reincorporate in Delaware for sound business reasons, she goes along with his advice. Next on the agenda is to choose a name for the corporation, and this turns out to be much more problematic than expected. The name must serve three important purposes: it must be the company's trade name, principal trademark and brand, and domain name. Cindy's initial choice was ExoticArtisan.com, which a Google search two months earlier indicated may be available for all three purposes. But when her business model changed to focus at the outset on works of art, rather than handicrafts, the word "artisan" was no longer appropriate. Cindy thinks an easy fix would be to change the name to ExoticArt.com, but a new Google search reveals that it is already owned as a website domain name. The domain is available for sale, but David expresses reservations about whether this name would be protectable and federally registrable as a trademark (which we will get back to in Chapter 15). Afterwards, Cindy considers and discards dozens of potential names either because they were not available or not sufficiently protectable. Finally, she chooses the name Exotic Universe, Inc., and a thorough name, trademark, and domain name search reveals that "Exotic Universe" is available as a company name and trademark, and can be purchased cheaply as a domain name. So David has his paralegal reserve the name in Delaware. Afterward, he prepares a standard certificate of incorporation and bylaws appropriate for a Delaware corporation. Upon reviewing the document, Cindy asks why there are no classes of preferred stock, given that she intends to raise money from investors that will surely want preferred rather than common stock. David explains that it is common practice to negotiate the terms of the preferred stock with an investor first, and then file an amended certificate of incorporation afterwards to authorize a class of preferred stock having the agreed upon terms. David then files the certificate of incorporation with the Delaware Division of Corporations, and once the certificate of incorporation is approved he prepares the documents necessary to issue Cindy a stock certificate as the sole stockholder.

Up to this point, Cindy has been extremely pleased that all of the dreaded legal matters are going so smoothly. But when she meets with David to sign the initial corporate documents, she runs into a difficult issue she did not anticipate. Cindy tells David that when writing the business plan, she had mentioned to her team of advisers that she would like to repay them for their efforts by giving them shares of stock in her new corporation. When she informs David that this is what she intends to do, his grimace is highly noticeable. After pausing for a moment, he informs Cindy of the risks involved in simply passing out founder's shares to friends who may or may not be working with the company going forward. He explained that under Delaware Law, those shares come together with certain rights, and automatically place Cindy and any other company directors under certain fiduciary duties to protect the value of the shares. While under Delaware law directors are given quite a bit of leeway on how to run a corporation without being held liable for their actions (one of the reasons David recommended Delaware law, by the way), friendships do not always last forever, and unsophisticated dissident stockholders are not only annoying, they are very much frowned upon by investors. Realizing her mistake, Cindy puts the issue off for another day and puts the issuance of shares to her friends on hold. But she leaves David's office knowing that she has created an expectation in her friends' minds that in the future could cause personal friction, not to mention possible legal liability. Cindy has just learned her first lesson in treading the corporate waters very carefully.

CHAPTER 7:
BUILD OR BUY?

Chapter 7

CHAPTER 7

BUILD OR BUY?

How to Purchase a Business

As you can already see, successfully starting a business from scratch depends on many factors and involves quite a bit of risk. If you have a brilliant idea that addresses a clear opportunity, and you've secured enough cash to get you through the start-up phase, then by all means go for it. But if you really want to own your own business, yet lack confidence that your business idea will translate into a profitable operation, don't have the funding to start a new company, or simply don't want to start at the beginning, there is another option: you can buy an existing business.

Pros and Cons of Buying a Business

The advantages of buying a business versus starting one of your own include:

- Starting with a business that is already generating revenue and positive cash flow, thus avoiding the inevitable period of losses associated with most start-ups

- Knowing that the product to be sold by the business is actually something that consumers are willing to buy

- Acquiring a pre-existing customer base, brand, and business reputation

- Not having to hire and train an entire team of new employees

- Having relationships with suppliers, distributors, etc., already in place

- Having a business located in an established and proven location

- Acquiring in one transaction the full range of assets and equipment necessary to run the business

The main downside to buying a business versus starting one of your own is that you cannot start with a clean slate. Therefore, you cannot build exactly the type of organization—including culture, strategy, reputation, product mix, employees, external relationships, etc.—that you would like, because much of this will come part and parcel with the business you buy. While you can change these things over time, you cannot do so overnight.

This brings up another downside in buying a company—the transition from one owner-manager to another is nearly always a difficult process. You will inevitably find that your ideas about running a business will clash with those of certain employees who may have worked for the business for a long period of time. In addition, there will be the risk that you could acquire some hidden liabilities such as a lawsuit that had yet to be filed, or operating problems such as bad supplier relations, that were not uncovered during your due diligence process. While there are ways to manage or mitigate these risks, it can be hard to entirely eliminate them.

Deciding What Business to Buy

If you do decide to buy a business, you first need to determine what kind of business would be a good fit for you personally. Consider your skills, interests, and personality and select a type of business that you know you would be passionate about—that you know you would be willing to devote the time necessary to make a success. In addition, you will improve your chances of success greatly if you choose a business that you know and understand.

Once you determine the type of business you want, the next step will be to start investigating some potential acquisitions. In carrying out your preliminary investigations, ask yourself the same types of questions you would have to ask yourself when preparing a business plan for a new company in the same line of business. For example, ask yourself:

- Is the target market for the business's products growing or shrinking?

- What is the strength of the competition?

- What competitive advantages does the target business have?

- Is the existing sales and distribution network functioning effectively?

- Does the business have a solid reputation among customers, suppliers, and distributors?

- Are any of the assets or equipment of the target business obsolete and in need of replacement?

- What about the location — is it located in a place that you would have chosen to operate this kind of business from?

And of course there is the financial analysis. From a buyer's perspective, proven profitability, positive cash flow, and future earnings potential are the most attractive qualities in a potential business acquisition. Therefore, you should review the seller's audited financial statements for the last 3-5 years (if available), probe the financial statements and the health and prospects of the business by asking questions of the seller and his accountant, factor in research you have done about the industry and this particular business, and then ask yourself:

- Is the business well positioned to generate future earnings?

- Will the forecasted cash flow be sufficient to develop the business as you intend?

- Have revenues, cash flow, and profits been trending upwards or downwards?

- If downwards, what makes you think you can turn that around?

- If the financial results are healthy and moving in the right direction, do you think you can duplicate and improve on these results?

If the answers to these and other relevant questions have convinced you that a particular business is worth purchasing, then you next have to decide how much to offer for the business.

Determining How Much to Pay

Valuing a business is not an easy proposition, especially with small privately held companies, and is as much an art as a science. Therefore, if you lack the relevant experience in this area, you may want to hire a professional appraiser to help you perform the valuation. Such a professional can also assist you in negotiating the purchase price with the seller. Of course, the more involved an adviser becomes, the more you will have to pay him or her as well. However, choosing the right advisers can ensure that you don't overpay for the business and that you are properly informed of the pros and cons of buying the particular business in question.

Businesses are generally valued based on one or more of the following:

- A multiple of historical earnings

- Discounted projected future cash flows

- Value of net assets

- Comparable businesses and industry rules of thumb

Multiple of Historical Earnings Method

With respect to small businesses, one of the more common valuation methods is to use a multiple of average historical earnings for a chosen period of time. The first step in applying this valuation method is to decide what the term "earnings" means. Commonly, it will be defined as earnings before interest, taxes, depreciation, and amortization ("**EBITDA**"), with add-backs for certain discretionary expenses to arrive at a "normalized" earnings amount. The add-backs often include the owner's salary and bonus, and one-time discretionary expenses such as the large office party that the owner held with staff to celebrate his 50th birthday. The buyer and seller should understand and agree upon all of the adjustments to be made to the net income in order to determine the earnings amount used in the valuation. In addition, to avoid a skewed result based on one atypical year, you should either use an average, or weighted average, of earnings for the last 3-5 years. However, some appraisers also prefer to use a multiple of future earnings—if they can be adequately estimated.

Once you have determined the appropriate adjusted earnings amount, you then need to set the appropriate multiple. This will depend on the type of business and the amount of risk involved. Consider the fundamentals of the business, the years it has been around, its track record of profits and positive cash flow, the competition, the suppliers, the lease terms, the strength of the customers, the conditions of the assets, and importantly how easily the business will transition to a new owner — i.e. will customers continue to buy from a new owner, or are the current owner and the business synonymous. A professional appraiser will be able to assist you in determining the correct multiple for the target business.

Discounted Future Earnings or Cash Flow Methods

This approach requires projected earnings or cash flow for a number of years in the future, which can be tricky and is an inherently inexact process, as well as determining an appropriate discount rate. Each future year's earnings or cash flows are forecasted and then discounted by the appropriate discount rate, which is a function of the riskiness of the estimated earnings or cash flows— riskier businesses will carry higher rates; safer businesses will carry lower rates. The sum of the discounted values is deemed to be the estimated present value of the company.

Balance Sheet Methods

Balance sheet valuations equate the value of a business with the value of that business's net assets as reflected on the seller's balance sheet. For example, the value of the company can be calculated based on its book value, liquidation value, or market value of assets. The upside to this type of valuation is that balance sheet methods are generally less reliant on estimates and forecasts than the earnings based methods, and focus on actual assets and liabilities.

Conversely, the challenge with these methods is that asset-based valuations can over-simplify the process and neglect the value of the company's cash flow and earnings potential and goodwill. Many "asset rich" businesses do not generate much profit or cash flow, and many businesses with limited assets (such as service-based businesses) generate tremendous profits and cash flow. As such, asset-based valuations are commonly used in connection with the sale of defunct businesses and liquidations, but are not as common for companies that are doing well.

Rules of Thumb and Comparables Methods

In some industries, rules of thumb have been developed to serve as useful guides for the valuation of a business. In others, companies are often sold and so there are "comparables" available that help determine the value of a particular business. However, these methods can also be misleading because even if they look similar on the outside, no two businesses are exactly the same. For example, if using this method you would need to access whether the "comparable" company had the same future cash flow and growth prospects as the company you are looking to buy.

In addition, you have to be careful using a supposed "rule of thumb" revenue multiple for an industry, because this may represent a median multiple, with the actual acquisition multiples being widely varied. If a seller or broker suggests this method, make sure you find out the actual multiples used in specific transactions that were then used to determine the rule of thumb multiple.

As you can see, the value of a company can vary widely depending on the valuation methodology used. At the outset of any particular transaction, the buyer and the seller must first agree on which method is the most appropriate under the circumstances for valuing the business, which is no easy task because the best method for a particular business will depend on many subjective factors, and different methods will produce different valuations.

At the end of the day, however, the actual value of the business is the amount that someone is willing to pay for it. So once you have determined what you are willing to pay, and are happy with your initial review of the business, you can move ahead and make an offer at that price.

Making an Offer

To a large extent, the process of purchasing a company is the same whether you are buying a local Internet café or a national chain of office supply stores. The first stage usually involves a high-level review of information that is publicly available. Thereafter, if you feel that you have enough information to make an initial offer, you can approach the owner of the business and make an offer subject to carrying out a subsequent due diligence investigation. If you are interested in the acquisition but it feels like you need more information, which is most often the case, you may approach the owner, express an interest, and then ask to receive additional information such as audited financial statements, tax returns, and material contracts. You will normally need to sign a confidentiality agreement before the seller will let you have the information.

Approaching a business owner who is not publicly shopping the business must be handled with tact and care. Once a purchase price is agreed to in principle, you may want to sign a "letter of intent," which is a preliminary agreement in which you agree to buy and the seller agrees to sell subject to a clean due diligence investigation, good faith negotiation of a purchase and sale agreement, and receipt of all necessary company and regulatory approvals. The letter of intent will most likely contain a confidentiality provision that says neither party will disclose the fact that negotiations to buy the seller's business are taking place, because if word leaks out that the business is for sale it could have an impact on both your company's and the seller's business operations by raising concerns with employees, lenders, customers, and suppliers. It could also have an adverse effect on the price you ultimately pay for the business.

There may also be an exclusivity period in the letter of intent, during which the seller agrees not to solicit or negotiate the sale of its business with anyone else. As a buyer, you will want this provision included because you will be spending a considerable amount of time and money investigating the seller's business and negotiating the purchase and sale agreement. In return, the seller may request a break-up fee if you decide to walk away from the deal without good cause. You may also want a break-up fee to cover your time and expenses should the seller cancel the deal.

Conducting Due Diligence

Your initial valuation of the seller's business will often be based on the assumption that everything shown in the seller's financial statements is materially accurate and there are no issues or liabilities that are not reflected in those statements which could adversely affect the value of the seller's business. However, this is seldom the reality. As such you will need to make sure that what you think you are purchasing is in fact what you actually purchase.

For this reason, the next step in buying a company is to thoroughly investigate the seller's business in what is known as a "due diligence" investigation. This consists of financial due diligence and legal due diligence, which go hand in hand with each other.

Financial due diligence typically involves a review of the historical financial results; current financial position; forecasted financial results; working capital requirements; financial risks and opportunities; tax exposure; and all financial information used in arriving at a valuation. Financial due diligence is intended to confirm the validity of the financial information provided by the seller. Therefore, the person conducting financial due diligence will investigate the systems and controls, policies, and assumptions underlying the seller's historical financial statements and future projections to make sure the statements and projections can be relied upon.

Keep in mind that financial due diligence does not only look to the past. It also investigates all matters that could affect the company's balance sheet, results of operations, and cash flow going forward. In fact, financial due diligence is most concerned with the future—e.g. whether the historical earnings and cash flow levels can be maintained following the acquisition.

Legal due diligence consists of a thorough review of the company's books and records, contracts, title to assets, intellectual property, potential claims or lawsuits, and the like. The goal is to determine whether the seller owns what it purports to own, has the right to transfer its assets or shares of stock, contracts, and property, and is not subject to any liability, or potential liability, that is not disclosed on the seller's financial statements.

If the due diligence investigation turns up any previously unknown facts that change the assumptions you made when valuing the seller's business, you can either renegotiate the purchase price or walk away from the deal. These are much better options than you would have if you skipped due diligence, crossed your fingers, and discovered a hidden liability such as an undisclosed lawsuit after the fact.

Structuring the Acquisition

Buying a business presents an entirely new set of issues from starting a new business, including how to structure the acquisition and what form of continuing relationship you will have with the seller after the deal is done.

The optimal legal structure will be driven by many considerations, including tax liability and planning, accounting concerns, and whether you wish to purchase all or only a portion of the target company's assets and liabilities. Professional accounting and legal advice is a must at this stage, because the issues can be very complicated and choosing one structure versus another can lead to vastly different financial outcomes.

Possible deal structures for the purchase of a business include the purchase of all or a portion of the shares in the target company, a purchase of all or a portion of the assets of the target company, a direct merger between the buyer and the target company (if they are both corporations), or a merger between a subsidiary of the buyer and the target company.

In addition, you and the seller will also need to agree on how and when the purchase price will be paid. For example, will the purchase price be paid all at once on the closing of the sale and purchase, in fixed installments over a period of time, or "earned out" depending on the business's future performance? The consideration to be paid doesn't need to consist exclusively of cash. It can include cash, stock, warrants, debentures and/or any combination of these.

However, the tax and accounting implications of using the different forms of consideration need to be thoroughly understood by both you and the seller.

How to Buy a Company's Shares

The most common way to purchase an ongoing business is to acquire all of the outstanding stock of the corporation that owns that business. In most cases, the acquisition can be completed by means of a straightforward purchase of the shares owned by the selling stockholder or stockholders in the target company. Alternatively, the acquisition can be completed by means of a merger of the buyer and the target company, or a merger of a subsidiary of the buyer and the target, although this last form is more common in acquisitions of companies with many stockholders (to avoid the need for approval from each stockholder).

Concurrent with the financial and legal due diligence review, the buyer and selling stockholders and/or target company will draft and negotiate a stock purchase agreement or merger agreement. This agreement will establish the:

- Consideration to be paid by the buyer to the selling stockholders

- Mechanics of payment

- Representations and warranties to be made by the selling stockholders and target company about the target business

- Consequences for breach of those representations and warranties

- Actions necessary to close the transaction and the obligations of each party to take those steps

- Conditions to each party's obligation to close the transaction

- Covenants by the selling stockholders and target company as to how the target company will run its business prior to the closing (if there is a time gap between signing the deal and actually closing it)

- Rights and procedures for termination of the deal, including any break-up fee that must be paid

The representations and warranties section of the stock purchase agreement or merger agreement includes a series of legal assurances given by the selling stockholders to the buyer about the target business and the selling stockholders. For example, the selling stockholders will represent and warrant that all of the shares being purchased in the target company have been properly authorized and issued; that the selling stockholders have the right to transfer those shares; that all consents and approvals necessary for the sale of shares have been obtained; that the financial statements accurately reflect the business's financial results for the periods stated; that the business has no outstanding issues with its key suppliers and customers; that there is no undisclosed litigation or threat of litigation; that all necessary tax returns have been filed and that there is no liability for unpaid taxes; and so forth.

Negotiation of the representations and warranties often center on whether the selling stockholders will guarantee that a particular representation and warranty is absolutely true in all respects, is true in all material respects, or is true to the best of the selling stockholders' knowledge. The strength of the warranty given will normally depend on risk allocation and the negotiating leverage of the parties.

The stock purchase agreement or merger agreement must also address what happens if any of the selling stockholders' representations and warranties turn out not to be true following the closing. Normally, the selling stockholders are required to indemnify the buyer for any losses or damages incurred as a result of the breach of a representation or warranty. For example, if an undisclosed lawsuit surfaces after the closing of the acquisition, then the selling stockholders would have to indemnify the buyer for the amounts of any damages the buyer has to pay as a result of the legal action, as well as any attorney's fees and other costs of defending the suit. However, there is often a minimum threshold amount of collective damages, called a "basket," that must be reached in order for the selling stockholders to be liable for breaches of representations and warranties. In addition, the selling stockholders most likely will ask for a "ceiling" as well, i.e. a cap on the total amount of indemnification the seller is liable for.

To ensure that the selling stockholders indemnify the buyer as required, a portion of the purchase price will often either be held back by the buyer or placed in escrow for a negotiated period of time. If no breaches occur within the relevant time frame, the payment will be released to the selling stockholders. If a breach does occur, the purchase price will be deemed to have been reduced and the buyer will keep the money or part of it.

In addition to making representations and warranties as to the status of its business, if there is a delay between the signing of the purchase agreement and the actual closing of the sale and purchase of the target business, the selling stockholders and target company will normally be required to covenant that they will run the business in the ordinary course until closing. This is to assure the buyer that the business it has signed up to purchase will not change before the deal is completed. The selling stockholders and target company will also covenant to use their best efforts to obtain any necessary consents to the deal, such as bank consents and waivers for change of control provisions in material contracts, as well as all necessary stockholder and regulatory approvals.

When the acquisition closing date arrives, there will also be a list of conditions that must be present for the buyer and selling stockholders to be required to go forward with and complete the sale and purchase. The selling stockholders and target company will be required to repeat the representations and warranties given when the agreement was signed, certifying that they are still true and correct in all material respects on the closing date. If they are not, then the buyer will be able to terminate the agreement, negotiate a reduced purchase price or other more favorable terms, or proceed to the closing.

In addition, the selling stockholders and target company will be required to represent that there has been no material adverse change in the business, operations, earnings, prospects, assets, or financial condition of the target business. For example, a material adverse change will probably be deemed to have occurred if the target company's leading customer terminates its contract or indicates that it intends to do so, or if the main factory burns to the ground. Once again, if such a material adverse change has occurred, the buyer can walk away from the transaction or renegotiate the terms of the deal.

Assuming all is on order, however, the closing day will arrive and the proper documents and certificates will be delivered, along with the purchase price payable on that day. In addition to the main stock purchase agreement, the documents may include opinions of counsel, audit letters, the target company's minute books and stock ledgers, signed copies of required consents, waivers and approvals, and a host of other documents. Most importantly, the selling stockholders will deliver the stock certificates, along with stock transfer forms, to the buyer.

There are several manners in which the purchase price can be paid on the closing date. If the purchase price is to be paid in cash, it will often be placed in an escrow account maintained by the buyer's lawyers, with the lawyers awaiting instructions to release the funds to the selling stockholders on the signing of all of the relevant documents and completion of the sale and purchase. Other times, the purchase price is paid by wire transfer of funds from the buyer's account to the selling stockholders, or the delivery of a certified or cashier's check.

Once all of the closing documents are confirmed to be in order, the buyer will release the purchase price to the selling stockholders. At the same time, new share certificates in the target company will be issued in the name of the buyer. At that point, the buyer will be the official owner of a new company.

How to Buy the Assets of a Business

While a stock purchase described in the previous section is the most common method of purchasing an existing business, it is often the case that a purchase of a business's assets is the optimal method of buying an ongoing business, and in some cases the only means available.

The instances when it will make both legal and financial sense to purchase the assets of a business include situations where:

- The target business has not been incorporated and is being operated as either a sole proprietorship or a partnership

- You wish to purchase less than all of a company's assets—such as a single retail store rather than the entire chain

- The target company has specific liabilities that you wish to expressly exclude from the purchase, such as historical tax liabilities or pending lawsuits

In many respects, buying the assets and liabilities of an ongoing business is much the same as buying the outstanding shares of a company. The due diligence process is almost identical and an asset purchase agreement contains many of the same terms as a stock purchase agreement. But there are certain issues that must be attended to that are unique to asset purchases.

For example, in the legal due diligence process, particular attention needs to be given to the identification of contracts of the seller that cannot be assigned or transferred to another person without the consent of the other party to the contract. In addition, it will be critical to identify all of the assets necessary to run the business you are purchasing and list them in the asset purchase agreement to ensure that they are transferred as part of the deal.

Equally important is to list the liabilities that you agree to assume with respect to the business that you are purchasing, and to exclude all other potential liabilities from the deal. Otherwise, your company could be on the hook for these liabilities. In addition, the indemnification provisions in the asset purchase agreement should cover all excluded liabilities. That way, if your company is required to pay for an excluded liability, it will be entitled to make a claim against the seller for reimbursement of the amount paid.

Financial due diligence can also be more complicated in certain asset purchase transactions. For example, in the case of sole proprietorships and partnerships, the seller's financial statements may be less complete and less reliable than those of a corporate seller. In fact, if purchasing less than all of the assets of a company, financial statements for that particular section of the business may not be available at all. As a result, pro forma financial statements may have to be prepared in order to value the business being acquired.

The representations and warranties in the asset purchase agreement can also take on added importance, because the seller must warrant (guarantee) that it has title to and ownership of all of the tangible assets and intellectual property being transferred, and has also obtained the consent necessary to assign to the buyer all licenses and contracts necessary to operate the target business. Similarly, the covenants and closing conditions in the purchase agreement will have provisions specific to an asset purchase. For example, if key employees are to come along with the deal, the buyer may require each to enter into employment and non-competition agreements before being obligated to close.

The closing of an asset purchase will take place in a manner similar to that of a stock purchase, again with certain exceptions. The board of directors of each company will have to approve the transaction, with resolutions to that effect being adopted, signed, and delivered. However, whether stockholder approval from either company will be required depends on the circumstances. For example, the buyer may not require stockholder approval for a cash purchase of assets, while it may require stockholder approval if shares are to be issued to the seller as consideration for the purchase of the business. The seller, on the other hand, may not require stockholder approval for the sale of a division of its business, but may require stockholder approval for the sale of substantially all of its assets. In every asset purchase and sale, the certificate of incorporation and bylaws of each corporate party, as well as any existing stockholder agreements, should be consulted to determine what approvals are required.

Exotic Universe, Inc.

Given her lack of resources, the possibility of buying an existing business had never occurred to Cindy McKay. But her new friend Nancy, the successful entrepreneur, has many contacts in the venture capital community, and it just so happens that one of them is an investor in an online company selling exotic handicrafts and home décor items. The company is struggling due to poor management, the related inability to implement a successful business model, and poor relationships with its suppliers. And although the owners are not publicly shopping the company, Nancy has been told that for the right price it is definitely for sale. Nancy believes that with the proper business model and a good person managing supplier relations, the company could be turned around. She has been impressed by Cindy and believes that with enough support she can be successful in her chosen line of business. So Nancy approaches Cindy and says that she's willing and able to put together a group of investors to buy the existing company if Cindy is willing to join the team. Nancy outlines a proposal where she would be CEO and Cindy would be president and head of product procurement, i.e. choosing the art, handicrafts, and home décor items to be sold. Nancy would receive a 40 percent stake in the company, the other investors 40 percent, and Cindy 20 percent. At first, Cindy is overwhelmed. A few weeks ago she was an art teacher aspiring to start a new business, and now she has a chance to be president of an international corporation with a good salary and the resources she needs to help local artists. Also, she would be surrounded by people having the business expertise she lacks.

It seems like Cindy's dream has come true, but try as she might, she cannot bring herself to get excited about buying and running this existing company the same way she was while putting together her own business plan. In the original scenario, she would found and shape her own business the way she had envisioned. Here, she would be a member of a management team inheriting a struggling company with many unhappy employees and suppliers and a business model that needs a complete overhaul. In addition, a top-level due diligence review reveals that there may be legal problems with a couple of the company's foreign subsidiaries. Given the company's poor management, there's no telling what other issues the due diligence investigation might turn up, or what liabilities might slip through the cracks and then pop up after the acquisition is closed. Upon further investigation, Cindy also discovers that the company in question is not known for aiding local artisans, but for exploiting them, and that most of their products are mass produced copies of local artisan products. Nancy tries to convince Cindy that all of these concerns could be remedied. In the end, however, after going back and reviewing the reasons she wanted to get into this line of business in the first place, Cindy decides that she is willing to pass on what could be a great opportunity. She wants to start from scratch and follow her own vision.

CHAPTER 8:
PRIMING THE PUMP

Chapter 8

CHAPTER 8

PRIMING THE PUMP

Financing Your New Business

Starting a new business involves an inherent tension between two famous adages: "Run your business on a shoestring" and "You have to spend money to make money."

Regarding the first adage, it's important that you run your new business lean and on-budget, making every dollar count until you have achieved sustained profitability and positive cash flow. This is important not only from a current cash flow standpoint— but also because it sets the right tone for running your business successfully in the future.

On the flip side, cash generally fuels business growth. If you don't inject enough cash into achieving the key milestones that your business must hit to be successful, your business could either stagnate or fail—with better capitalized competitors simply passing it by.

So it is vital that you determine at an early stage how much cash your start-up will need to get to a sustained level of positive cash flow from where it can finance itself through revenues generated by sales. Once you know how much you need, you should then plan how you will raise the necessary funds to get the business to this self-sufficient level. This will involve either funding the initial operations with your personal assets, raising debt financing from lenders, or having investors contribute equity capital to your business.

To develop such a plan, you can begin by asking yourself five basic questions:

- How much cash does the business need?

- Should I raise money from outside sources?

- Who should I raise money from?

- How much money should I raise and when?

- What ownership interest should I give, if any, to equity investors?

How Much Cash Do I Need?

The one phrase a business owner never wants to hear is: "We're out of cash." Fortunately, if you've prepared a business plan you already have a strong idea of how much cash your business will need to achieve a sustained positive cash flow, as well as how you will obtain that cash. So you should never hear those words unless something unexpected happens. If you haven't prepared a business plan, you now have one of the best reasons to do so, because having a firm grasp of your business's current and future cash needs is one of the most important aspects of successfully running a business, and having a handle on your business's cash needs is extremely difficult without having considered those needs properly.

To determine how much cash your business will need in excess of that which it is likely to generate from sales, and when you will need it, look at your business plan and compare your cash flow projections with your milestone schedule. By doing so, you will be able to determine how much additional cash you will need in order to achieve all of your major milestones up until your business has become cash flow positive.

In addition, check your monthly and quarterly cash flow forecasts to make sure that you will not run out of cash at any specific moment in time. For example, if you can foresee abnormally high negative cash flow during a certain period, perhaps because your business is seasonal, or because it will need to make a large capital expenditure for equipment, then you may need to secure additional funding to cover the shortfall during that period.

Finally, it is important to include a buffer in your cash flow projections. If your product launch or business opening is delayed a couple of months and you run out of cash as a result, or if the economy takes a downturn just when you projected your business would take off, it could be disastrous. So it's a good idea to add a minimum of a twenty percent—and up to a fifty percent— cushion to your expected cash needs for the next two to three years.

Should I Raise Money?

The answer to this question depends first on whether you have the ability to self-finance your business, and secondly on the nature of the business itself. If you can swing it, then self-financing your business allows you to maintain absolute control over your operations and gives you the maximum amount of flexibility in the future. This, however, requires you to take a close and clear-eyed look at your personal financial situation and the assets you have available, or can leverage, to contribute to the business.

Just as you don't want your business to run out of money, you don't want to personally run out of money either. Both could have a drastic effect on your new business and your life. Therefore, manage your personal finances the same way you manage your business, and start by creating a personal balance sheet and cash flow forecast in order to see clearly what assets and liabilities you have and what your monthly personal cash needs will be for the foreseeable future.

Make sure you have enough cash or other liquid assets to pay your living expenses until the time that your business can contribute regularly to your income. At a minimum, you probably want to be able to cover one year's worth of living expenses, with a buffer for unforeseen circumstances. Unless you are independently wealthy, it will almost certainly be necessary to cut many corners during your start-up period, but try not to add the stress of not being able to pay your own bills to the already stressful situation of starting a new business.

Even if you personally have the cash necessary for your business to get started, depending on the nature of your business and the industry in which you will be competing, you may want to raise money from outside sources. This is especially true in high growth businesses, where additional cash may help scale the business much more quickly and successfully, and in industries where competitors have more capital resources and can spend their way to market share.

However, if you are contemplating going this route, ask yourself whether you are prepared for the implications of raising money from outside investors. The most obvious implications are that you will give up a percentage ownership interest in your new company and perhaps some control as well, with investors likely gaining a seat on your board of directors or at least looking over your shoulder to protect their investment. Their goals may not always be the same as yours, and you may find yourself in a position of having to compromise on the type of organization you want to create.

Raising money from outside investors may also affect your ability to raise money from other sources in the future, or to exit the business as and when you would like. For example, taking a $20 million offer to buy your business may seem like a dream come true to you, but your investors may block the deal in hopes of a much bigger payoff down the line. Conversely, you may wish to hold onto a business that you have built from the ground up, but your investors may want to force a sale to cash out on their investment.

If you do decide to raise money from outside sources, you should thoroughly understand the process and have a long-term fundraising strategy in place before you take the first dime.

Who Should I Raise Money From?

Who you raise money from will be highly dependent on the nature of your business, because the nature of your business will dictate your options. Most angel investors and all venture capital investors will require the possibility of very high rates of return on their investment, so if your business does not have high growth potential leading to an exit strategy for the investor in 3-7 years, then angel and venture capital money will not be an option. For less scalable businesses, a loan may be a possibility. But most banks will require the proven ability to cover the loan payments and hard assets as security, so new businesses without a track record and significant assets may not be able to secure a loan.

Depending on the type of new business you are starting and the point at which you need to raise money, your basic financing sources will include:

• Friends and Family

- Angel Investors

- Venture Capital Investors

- Banks and other Lending Institutions

- Small Business Administration Loans

- Crowdfunding

Friends and Family

If you cannot finance your business yourself, then friends and family can be both your best and worst sources of funds. On the positive side, you may be able to borrow money from friends and family on favorable terms without having to give up much (if any) equity or control. But if your business goes sour and you are unable to repay the money you borrowed, or the equity in your business loses its value, it could harm some of the most important relationships in your life.

If you have no choice but to borrow money from friends and family, or if other options are not palatable for one reason or the other, the key is to do so professionally. Handshake deals are the primary recipe for disaster. Therefore, treat whoever is providing the funds as an arms' length lender or investor, providing them with your business plan to analyze, answering their questions, and drawing up legal documents that make clear whether the money is being provided as a loan or an investment, as well as the exact terms on which that money is provided.

Creating the proper expectations is the key to maintaining the relationship that led to the money being handed over in the first place. This applies whether your business succeeds or fails.

Angel Investors

Angel investors are typically high net worth individuals who provide funding to businesses at very early stages in exchange for a share of that business. Many angels have started, ran, and sold successful businesses of their own, and are now investing in other start-up companies. Often, angel investors form groups, where they pool their resources and spread their risk by investing small amounts in many start-ups.

Angel investors may be the best option when you need a limited amount of capital, anywhere between $20,000 and $1 million, and are still at the stages of developing your concept and proving it will be viable in the marketplace. However, most angel investors will expect the possibility of a very high return on their investment in exchange for the high degree of risk they are taking with their money. They may also seek significant levels of control over your business.

Venture Capital Investors

Venture capital investors are distinguished from angel investors by the amount of money they invest, where their money comes from, when they invest, and the manner in which they invest.

Venture capital funds raise large amounts of money from institutional investors and high net worth individuals, and then "manage" that money by investing in high growth companies. Venture capital investors typically invest at an early stage, but not as early as an angel investor. Normally, they require a higher degree of certainty that the product will actually be brought to market and have a strong probability of success.

Venture capital investors will normally want to invest between $2 million to $10 million, and even beyond, in today's market. They will not make smaller investments because they require the potential of a very large return on each investment. In addition, they require a more hands-on approach with their investments than an angel investor, and therefore do not want to spread either their financial or human resources too thin.

Banks and Other Lending Institutions

It is notoriously difficult for a small business to get a loan from a traditional bank, especially in a poor economic climate. Banks typically receive no equity upside to the money they lend, and are therefore interested solely in whether the new business can repay the principal and interest on the loan. Because a much higher percentage of new businesses default than do established businesses, in general start-up businesses are not considered a good risk for a bank. This is true even if the borrower can provide adequate collateral, because banks do not want to be in the liquidation business.

The best way to secure a bank loan is to have a historical record of positive cash flow that would cover the loan amounts due, as bankers are much less interested in projections than are equity investors. In addition, either your business will need asset coverage of the loan, which is unlikely in a start-up situation, or you will have to pledge your personal assets in order to secure the loan. In most cases, it will probably need to be both.

As an alternative to a loan, it may be possible to secure an overdraft facility with your bank— which is a credit agreement allowing you to use or withdraw more than you have in your account up to a maximum negative balance. This can help cover short term cash flow deficiencies. But once again, this will probably require a personal guarantee.

SBA Loans

Another potential financing option is to borrow money via the U.S. Small Business Administration ("**SBA**") loan program (http://www.sba.gov/loanprograms). These loans are normally accessed through your local bank, credit union, or non-profit financial intermediary, and often require a personal guarantee. The three most relevant SBA loan programs are the Basic 7(a) Loan Program, the CDC/504 Loan Program, and the 7(m) Microloan Program. The 7(a) and 504 programs are restricted to small businesses with less than $7 million in tangible net worth and less than $2.5 million in net income.

Basic 7(a) Loan Program

The 7(a) is the SBA's most popular loan program. Start-up companies who qualify can get up to $750,000 from their local 7(a) lender. 7(a) loans are typically used for working capital, asset purchases, and property improvements. Personal guarantees are required from all the business owners holding an ownership stake of 20 percent or more in the borrowing company.

CDC/504 Loan Program

The 504 loan program is intended to supply financing for major fixed asset purchases, such as equipment or real estate. The asset purchase is normally funded by a loan from a bank or other local lender, along with a second loan from a certified development company ("**CDC**"). The CDC loan is funded with an SBA guarantee for up to 40 percent of the value of the asset. Personal guarantees are also required from company owners for 504 loans.

7(m) Microloan Program

The microloan program provides loans of up to $35,000 that can be used for a broad range of purposes. The loans under this program come directly from the SBA and are provided to business owners via non-profit community-based intermediaries. All new businesses are eligible to apply for the microloan program.

Crowdfunding

Crowdfunding is the process of raising capital from many individuals who each make a small contribution towards funding a project or new business. In order to raise money in this manner, entrepreneurs normally select a crowdfunding platform, establish fundraising goals, create a page on the platform's website describing the business or project being funded, and then use social media and other means to publicize the campaign and raise the money. There are two main types of crowdfunding—donation-based and investment-based. The concept began and first caught fire on the donation-based model, where funders donate money to finance a project in return for products or rewards. Investment-based crowdfunding, on the other hand, is where businesses seeking capital either sell shares in their company or take money in the form of a loan. In this model, individuals who fund become stockholders or lenders and have the potential to make back more than their original investment.

There are hundreds of crowdfunding platforms available, but the vast majority of funds are raised through the most popular sites such as Kickstarter, Indiegogo, and Crowdfunder. All platforms are not the same, however, so compare them carefully before making a choice. For example, some platforms only support donation-based crowdfunding, not investment-based, and some require you to make your fundraising goal or the funds must be returned.

A crowdfunding platform also serves as an excellent marketing tool and provides a forum from which you could receive valuable feedback about your product. However, be aware that crowdfunding exposes a new business idea or product to the public early on in the development stage, creating the possibility that a better capitalized competitor will take the idea and beat you to the market.

Until recently, there were significant securities law restrictions on the ability of new businesses to raise money from large numbers of investors in the form of crowdfunding. However, in 2012 the Jumpstart Our Business Start-ups Act (the "**JOBS Act**") came into effect, changing the start-up fundraising equation. The JOBS Act provides a new securities law exemption allowing start-ups to sell shares to a large number of investors through investment-based crowdfunding, so long as the offering meets the criteria set forth in the JOBS Act and any rules and regulations promulgated thereunder. Before getting started on an investment-based crowdfunding strategy, make sure you familiarize yourself with this new law.

How Much Money Should I Raise and When?

If you do have a business with the growth potential necessary to raise money from angel and/or venture capital investors, you should be aware that most companies in your position raise money in stages rather than all at once, and become familiar with how the process normally works.

The stages of financing, named after the series of preferred stock that are typically issued to investors, are:

- Seed Capital

- Series A Round (First Round or Start-up Stage)

- Series B Round (Second Round or Expansion Stage)

- Series C Round (Third Round or Later Stage)

During each of these stages, entrepreneurs typically only raise a portion of the total amount they will need to raise during their company's first 3-5 years of existence. The reason is that the earlier the stage they raise money, the larger the equity percentage they will have to give away per investment dollar because of the higher degree of risk involved. Therefore, most start-up companies will raise enough to achieve a significant milestone, and then raise another round on better terms for subsequent milestones, and so on.

Despite the fact that your business is at its initial stages and may be several years away from the prospect of multiple rounds of financing, it is important to understand the process, because how you raise money at the early stages affects how and whether you raise money at later stages.

Seed Financing

Typically, seed financing helps a start-up company hire its first few employees, develop the product it intends to offer, plan for the product's introduction, fine-tune the business model, and possibly launch the first product in the marketplace. A seed financing round typically raises anywhere from $10,000-$2 million, but for high growth start-ups the amount is normally in the range of $250,000-$750,000. The investors are usually angels and early stage venture capitalists.

Series A Round

Once your product has been developed and you are either preparing to launch or have already gained some traction with the target market, a Series A round can be raised for purposes of successfully rolling out your new product, increasing your marketing reach in order to significantly grow sales, capturing additional sources of revenue, and hiring senior level management and prime technology talent. The amount typically raised used to be $2 million to $15 million, with a median of $3 million to $7 million. But Series A round financings have risen dramatically in recent years, and the $7 million to $15 million rounds have become more common. Venture capital investors typically lead a Series A round.

Series B Round

At this point, you should be generating steady revenues under a working business model. The funds raised will normally be for the purpose of developing follow-on products, further expanding sales and marketing efforts into new territories, supplementing operations, and the like. Sometimes a Series B round is used to raise funds to buy other companies as well. The round normally raises anywhere from $7 million upwards. Often the Series B round is led by the same venture capital investor who led the Series A round, but at this stage the company also may attract investors who focus on later stage deals.

Series C Round

The Series C round is often used by a company for big ticket items such as acquisitions, major capital expenditures, international expansion, development of new product lines, etc. that will give the company the additional revenues necessary to become IPO (i.e. initial public offering) ready. The amount raised can range from tens to hundreds of millions. At this stage, the venture capital investors may wish to step aside and allow an investment bank or other later stage financier to lead the round in preparation for an IPO or strategic merger.

At each stage of financing, there is a tension between the inclination to "raise as much as you can, while you can" and the desire to avoid undue dilution. In any event, however, you should at least try and raise enough cash to get you through a couple of major milestones, plus a cushion of six months or so that would allow you to close the next round at a much higher valuation than the last.

What you want to avoid is attempting to raise money when running out of cash, because then all the leverage you gained by accomplishing the last milestone may fly out the window. And you definitely want to avoid a rushed "bridge" round that plugs a cash gap but can be very expensive and send a bad message regarding your cash management capabilities. This means, once again, that you must have a firm grasp of your future cash needs and stick to your budgeted amounts to avoid running dry prematurely.

The other thing you want to avoid is a "down round," i.e. a round of financing at a valuation lower than the last. This introduces yet another tension — that between wanting to obtain as high a valuation as possible from your investors and not overvaluing the business so that future financings become more difficult.

What Ownership Interest Should I Give to Equity Investors?

The amount of equity that you give away will be tied to the valuation of your business. However, even though valuation techniques are used to value the business, it is the market conditions, the lead investor's experience, and the amount of interest in the company that ultimately dictates the terms of investment and equity levels sought. As a business owner it's important to be familiar with how this process works so you don't end up giving away more than you need to.

As discussed in the previous chapter, there are many valuation techniques, and the technique or combination of techniques an investor uses will depend on the nature of your business and its stage of development when the funding occurs. These techniques include the discounted cash flow method and market and transaction comparables method. However, the discounted cash flow method does not work well for early stage companies because accurately predicting future cash flows without the benefit of historical sales is too difficult, and because the model is extremely sensitive to the discount rate chosen.

In fact, valuations at the "seed stage" are driven in large part by subjective factors, because the company at that time is either at or just past the concept stage, with no proven results of any kind. These subjective factors include the abilities of the CEO and management team, value and strength of the company's intellectual property, how long it is expected to take for the company to launch a product, how long it is expected to take for the company to be profitable, estimated capital needs and burn rate, and volatility of the particular industry. In post-seed investing, achieving milestones such as demonstrating proof of concept will factor strongly in valuation determinations. After a company launches a product, more quantifiable data on revenue and cash flow is available and can be used to value the company.

Taking all of this into account, what many venture capital investors do in valuing an early stage company is the following—or something similar thereto:

1. Estimate the future exit value of the company based upon comparable companies that have done an IPO or been sold.

2. Determine the rate of return that the investor requires based on the degree of risk of the investment compared to other possible investments.

3. Determine the amount of money to be invested in the current and future financing rounds.

4. Determine the ownership percentage the investor needs to receive in order to realize the desired rate of return.

Most venture capital investors will require a rate of return that will give them a minimum return of 10x cash on exit, or a compounded rate of return of approximately 38% per annum.

All of these calculations are done through financial modeling based on certain assumptions, and then tweaked to take account of the market conditions that the target business is operating under in order to gauge the probability that a lucrative exit will actually be achieved.

Needless to say, you need to negotiate a high value for your business so that you end up selling as little equity as possible. But come armed with good arguments and be careful of what you ask for, because if investors cannot achieve the required target returns they will simply walk away and invest in another opportunity.

Exotic Universe, Inc.

Right now, Cindy McKay has a shell corporation and a business plan, nothing more. In order to begin building her business and implementing her plan, she needs to come up with a significant amount of cash. According to her business plan, Cindy will need approximately $250,000 to start and run her business for one year until it starts generating positive cash flow.

Therefore, her goal is to have $350,000 in liquid assets available to get her through that period. Then, after establishing her exotic artwork business and getting it to the point of profitability, if necessary she can look to raise a larger amount from outside investors in order to scale into new product lines and expand into different geographic regions of the world. Previously, Cindy felt she had two options for coming up with the required funds. The first is for her to borrow from her 401(k) and for both her and her parents to take out second mortgages on their houses. This would put a significant financial strain on everyone involved, as well as place her family's homes and security at risk if the business doesn't succeed. The second option is to borrow money from Cindy's rich Uncle Steve, who owns a successful chain of men's clothing stores. Steve is willing to provide the full $350,000, but is asking for a large portion of the investment to be in the form of a convertible note that would provide some protection on the downside and give him considerable equity if the business succeeded. He also wants to be named chairman of the board of directors with significant veto power over how the business is run. Although he claims he would be mostly hands off, his old school personality doesn't give Cindy much confidence that would be the case. Despite the large financial risk involved, Cindy and her parents are just about to take the plunge when Nancy once again calls her and asks to meet for a cup of coffee.

Cindy is surprised to hear from Nancy, figuring the successful businesswoman had written her off as a pie-in-the-sky novice after she rejected the offer to be a partner in buying the existing business. But it turns out that the opposite is the case. Nancy says she now respects and trusts Cindy even more, so much so that she would like to come on board as an angel investor. As usual, Nancy doesn't mince words, laying everything out on the table. She will require a significant equity percentage in the company, as well as a seat on the board of directors. She also wants to have a say in the initial hires Cindy makes to ensure she is surrounded by the right people. Most importantly, Nancy needs an exit strategy. Cindy must commit to her plan of eventually scaling the company into higher growth markets, which has the potential to lead to a public offering or lucrative sale of the company. This may at some point conflict with Cindy's altruistic goals, Nancy admits, but that is the reality of raising money from investors who want a healthy return. However, Nancy says she understands and shares many of Cindy's goals, and believes that a business could be both profitable and socially responsible at the same time. Although Cindy has some of the same reservations she had when considering the acquisition, Nancy has become her business mentor and Cindy welcomes the fact that she would sit on her board of directors. And given Cindy's intention of honing the business model, website, and supply chain, as well as attracting venture capital investors when it is time to scale the business, Nancy will provide an invaluable source of contacts and advice when it comes time to raise that money. Finally, Nancy has been where Cindy was, developed two successful businesses, and maybe just as importantly, failed at one other. This is exactly the type of adviser Cindy knows she needs. Therefore, she decides that the percentage of the company Nancy is asking for is well worth what Cindy would receive in return. Nancy is now on board and, if Cindy is able to prove to Nancy that she is committed to making her business work at a high level, will be her first investor.

CHAPTER 9:
PULLING A TEAM TOGETHER

Chapter 9

CHAPTER 9

PULLING A TEAM TOGETHER

Hiring Skilled Management

No business person can be an island unto him or herself. While everyone knows the legends of those famous companies that had their beginnings as one individual with a great idea working out of a home office or garage, the reality is that the founders of those businesses had to assemble teams to help them turn their initial ideas into profitable realties. Just like the Bill Gates and Steve Jobs of this world, you too will need to build your team.

Whether you put your management team and board of directors in place all at once or over a number of years will depend on the trajectory of your business plan and the specific circumstances you encounter while trying to implement that plan. But even if you put your team together over time, you need to have a hiring strategy in place so that you compile a cohesive group that includes individuals who collectively possess the mix of skills and traits that will best contribute to the success of your business.

Management Team

In forming a management team, it is important at first to take a step back and visualize how your organization can run most effectively in the future. In doing so, you should review your personal strengths and weaknesses, keeping firmly in mind the values, vision, and mission you foresee for your business, and then identify the key success factors that will make or break your desired outcome.

In visualizing your future business operations, place in the foreground the fact that you will, by necessity, have to let go of the reins at some point and manage your team rather than perform even the most important tasks yourself. Even if you can perform a particular task better than anyone else, it will most often be less efficient overall for you to do so rather than delegate. This means that you must have complete faith and trust in every manager you hire.

In addition, there will be many areas of the business where you can hire somebody to perform and manage the tasks better than you could yourself. In these situations, you must be secure and confident enough to hire the best and the brightest you can find and afford, even if they know more about a particular area of expertise than you do. As the leader of the organization, you want to assemble a team that brings more to the table than you personally have to offer, and are willing to voice their professional opinion rather than simply agree with whatever you say.

That being said, you also want to look for team players that have genuinely bought into your vision and mission for your new organization, and the values you want that organization to represent. While you will want to secure independent thinkers who take the initiative and can manage their functional areas without constant oversight, you also need to avoid hiring mavericks that refuse to follow strategic direction and operate without regard for the success of the business as a whole.

There is also a tension between the need to get a management team on board in a timely manner and making sure you hire the right people. While you want to have your team in place early enough to capture the business opportunity you have identified, do not compromise on your management hires just to have a warm body overseeing a particular area of your business. It is critical that every manager has the skills and experience to meet the needs of your business. As with every team, if one member is unable to perform his or her role adequately, the entire group falls apart.

Finally, look closely at the roles each member of the management team will play in the business and try to assemble a team with a diverse mix of backgrounds that complement each other. What you want to create is a synergistic environment where putting people with different experiences and skill sets together leads to a high level of creativity in determining and implementing the strategies, goals, and objectives of the business.

Ultimately, your team will most likely include managers overseeing sales, marketing, product development, technology, operations, finance and accounting, human resources, and possibly business development and legal matters. At the beginning, two or more of these areas may be managed by a single individual, and some may be handled by outside professionals, but as the business grows they will most likely require a designated vice president, or at least someone at the management level. The priority of these hires will depend on the specific needs of your business and the timeframes included in your business plan.

Sales

In most successful businesses, the person running the sales department is treated like royalty. This is for good reason. Even if you have the best product in the world, the only way your company will make money is if enough people buy that product at the right price, and it is the sales manager's responsibility to get them to do so.

Everyone knows the stereotypical slick salesperson, but the best are those that are focused like a lazar on closing the deal with the customer at a price that earns the best possible profit. Remember, however, that what you need in a sales manager is not just a good salesman, but a good manager of people and accounts, and a good strategic thinker that understands how his team fits in with the rest of the organization. If you find that person, he or she will be worth their weight in gold—and will probably demand it in salary and incentives.

Marketing

While sales and marketing go hand in hand, they are by no means synonymous. And while from a cost standpoint you may combine sales and marketing under the same manager when your business is in its infancy, eventually it is a good idea to have separate management for the two functions. This is true first of all because the skill set required is not the same, and second because it is good to have a healthy tension between the two departments so that they push each other to greater heights.

More so than any other member of senior management, your marketing manager should be able to help you understand, analyze, and think strategically about how to capture the business opportunity that you started your company to capitalize on. He or she will be responsible for building the brand, differentiating the product, and getting the message out to potential customers in a manner that makes the sales team's job as easy as possible. In many cases, marketing will also drive product development by identifying the benefits consumers want and working with the development team to incorporate features into your product that provide those benefits.

Product Development

The product development manager has the difficult and unenviable task of making sure the product works perfectly and contains all the features that marketing and sales need to sell the item, while at the same time ensuring that the development timetable is met and there are no cost overruns. This means that the best developer does not always make the best product development manager, the same as the best salesperson does not always make the best sales manager.

You do need someone that understands the technology, otherwise it can become easy for the development team to pull the wool over the manager's eyes as to whether milestones will be met on time or not and whether or not key product features can be incorporated to meet the requirements of the marketing team. However, in addition to understanding the technology, it's just as important to have a good manager in place; someone that can motivate the development team to meet the equally important goals of quality, timeliness, and cost effectiveness.

Technology

In today's economy, there is hardly any business that gets by without the use of technology. Therefore, someone in your organization will need to have the competence to manage and implement your technological requirements.

One difficulty with start-ups is that the company often can't afford the technology managers that it really needs, and often end up making hires whose capabilities are soon outgrown by the pace of business innovation and development. The key to managing this process is thinking through the short, medium, and long-term technological needs of your business, recognizing that this bridge must likely be crossed down the road, and preparing the organization for the transition from an initial technology manager to a top-level chief technology officer and/or chief information officer.

One of the keys in doing so will be to create a specific job description for this position, both now and in the future. This will allow you to determine what skills the technology manager must bring to your organization during its early stages and what skills you might look for in a technology manager a little further down the road. The specific requirements will depend on the nature of your business and your organization. Companies whose technology needs are mostly internal may hire a chief information officer to be responsible for the technology necessary to run the company in the most efficient and profitable manner. Companies who sell technology-driven products may also be in need of a chief technology officer, who will be in charge of developing technologies for commercial purposes.

In preparing the job description for a chief information officer and/or a chief technology officer, keep in mind that your chosen person will be a member of your management team and will therefore need to be able to think strategically as well as technically, having the ability to understand the dynamics of the business and the competitive environment in which it operates.

Finance and Accounting

If you don't have much experience in business, it is easy to fall into the trap of believing that all you need in this position is a bookkeeper—someone to make sure the accounts are kept in order. At the very beginning this may be true, but as your business grows the person in charge of finance and accounting will become a key strategic member of your management team.

From a practical standpoint, the person you hire must have the experience to be able to put in place systems and controls that produce accurate records and ensure your accounts will meet the highest level of scrutiny. At the next level, your finance and accounting officer will take on the essential role of financial forecasting and budgeting, which will affect every aspect of your business's decision making process, especially your cash flow needs, and serve as the benchmark for whether your business is progressing as planned. A good finance officer will help make sure that costs do not exceed budgeted amounts and every dollar you spend in every area of your business produces a good return on its investment.

Finally, this person will be your point person on dealing with lending institutions and investors, helping them understand the financial statements and projections, and reassuring them that the financial foundation of your company is solid and its goals are attainable. If investors and lenders don't have faith in the person in charge of your finances, they will not have faith in your business.

Human Resources

Even more so than finance and accounting, it is easy to be lured into thinking that human resources is simply a recordkeeping function. But a good human resources manager can be the person that fuels your organization by recruiting talented new hires, keeping those hires happy by effectively resolving grievances and managing benefit programs, and protecting you from unwanted distractions such as lawsuits. The right human resources manager can be the glue that holds your company together and keeps everyone motivated to achieve its goals.

Board of Directors

A well-assembled board of directors can be a great asset to your business, providing you with experienced practical advice and strategic direction, as well as with valuable contacts in the commercial world. A dysfunctional board, however, can be a company's worst nightmare, resulting in deadlocks and tensions that can drag your business to a standstill, or worse. So take your time and put together a board of directors that both adds value to your business and can work well together amongst themselves and with your senior management team.

As with putting together a management team, the assembly of a board of directors should be driven by the needs, challenges, and opportunities of your business. The key is to find directors with complementary experience, skills, and perspectives who can work together as a group. But the tricky part is to find members who are sufficiently independent so that they challenge you and your business to perform at the optimum level, while at the same time supporting the vision that you have for your business.

From an experience standpoint, look to enlist a couple of people who have already been where you want to go and done what you want to do, i.e. built a start-up company into a sustainable and profitable enterprise. They will have faced the same challenges you are about to face, understand your needs as an owner-manager, and be able to offer specific advice about how to grow the business and overcome threats and obstacles.

Also look for people who have an in-depth understanding of your business and industry. They will likely be able to provide insights into the market you are entering and the competition you will face, and provide related strategic advice that goes beyond the experience level of you and your management team. They may also be able to provide contacts in the industry and help you recruit talented managers, employees, and strategic partners from within the industry.

If you obtain financing from venture capital or angel investors, they will almost surely require seats on your board of directors. This is not a bad thing, because most will bring a breadth of experience of working with start-up companies and will be highly aware of the factors that lead to success or failure. They will also force you to keep your eye firmly on the goals of profitability, positive cash flow, and return on investment. However, their priorities may not always be the same as yours, and you will also want some independent directors that can bridge any tensions between you and your investors, as well as give you a sense of whether you are on or off track in the arguments you are making when those tensions arise.

Another practical consideration in selecting board members is their availability. Someone running a large company and sitting on multiple boards may seem appealing, but they may not be able to devote enough time and attention to your business to give you more than superficial advice. In addition, you may find yourself in a logistical nightmare trying to arrange board meetings that fit their schedule, if they are available to attend at all.

Finally, take into account personality types. Persons who are bullies or overly dominant tend to shed more heat than light on an organization and inhibit good advice from other board members. On the flip side, even if you think it would be nice to have a rubber stamp board, if you go this route you will have missed a great opportunity to gain strategic advice and obtain a helpful gauge as to whether you are heading in the right direction.

Generally, you should think in terms of a three to five member board. For obvious reasons, you will want an odd number to avoid a stalemate in the decision making process. That being said, a board consisting of three members will run the risk of two people always taking sides against the other. However, that is something that you may need to contend with and manage at the outset. In most cases, it is best to start with a three-person board and increase it when you raise money from investors who require board seats, or as you grow and can attract new and better qualified candidates.

Exotic Universe, Inc.

When Cindy first assembled her friends to write a business plan, she hoped that she was sitting around the table with her new management team. Unfortunately, she told them all just that, as well as making other promises about flexible hours, working at home, and shares of stock in the company. As a result, Anne has already started putting together her home office, Roger is working on a website design, and Bill is talking to her about the high number of stock options he would require to leave his current lucrative position. When Nancy gets wind of all this, however, Cindy sees her frown for the first time. Nancy then goes on to emphasize two points: Cindy does need a core management team consisting of the *right* people to launch her business; but at the same time she needs to run lean and mean to minimize her cash burn rate. The key is finding the proper balance. With respect to finding the right people to form her initial team, Cindy needs to identify exactly what is required *before* she offers jobs to anybody, let alone her friends. Not doing so is a recipe for disaster, both for the business and for the friendships. A case in point is Anne, who is a good friend of both Cindy and Nancy. Anne is very good at her marketing job, but her company sells to retailers, not directly to consumers. They have a basic website, but have not really kept up with the age of the Internet. Nancy emphasizes to Cindy that Exotic Universe, Inc. is in the Internet marketing business as much as it's in the exotic artwork business. So the most important skill-set that Exotic Universe, Inc. needs is someone with Internet marketing experience who knows the best ways to attract potential customers' attention online, drive them to the website, convert them into customers, and get their repeat business. Nancy has serious doubts about whether her friend Anne is the right person for that job. With respect to Roger, there is no doubt that the company needs a top-quality website and that he can deliver that for them. But the question is whether once he has done so, would the company need his advanced web design skill-set to maintain and update the site. Possibly not, and so it makes more sense to bring him on as an independent contractor at the beginning, maybe with a monthly retainer for a set number of hours of work going forward. When it comes to Bill, this is a tougher decision than the other two. He is highly experienced in international accounting and business matters, which the company needs. And as he had explained during the business planning sessions, there will be many issues involved in setting up the company's accounting systems and controls, and good financial planning will be a key success factor. But even so, he is over-qualified for what Exotic Universe, Inc. needs in the accounting/finance position now, and will be way too expensive in terms of salary and equity to bring on board. He would make a good consultant, and maybe the future CFO when the company grew into the position. But what the company needs at this point is a sound controller with some international experience, not a high-powered CFO. Finally, as an investor Nancy is not willing to give away shares to all of Cindy's friends, both for the reasons her attorney David had mentioned when the corporation was formed, and because of the dilution involved. A stock option pool will be created, and most if not all employees the company hires will be allocated options, but persons who are neither employees nor investors should not become minority stockholders. Therefore, Cindy has some damage control to do, especially with Anne, who probably will not be offered any position with the company and yet was counting on one the most. So Cindy's initial management team will consist of herself, a marketing manager with significant Internet marketing experience, a controller, and one other member that Cindy realizes she needs—a director of international operations who can oversee the relationships with suppliers around the world and the logistics of delivering orders to customers. Other than that, Cindy knows she can rely on Nancy and Bill for top-level advice and direction for the time being, and can layer in other management members when the time is right.

CHAPTER 10:
STAFFING UP

Chapter

10

CHAPTER 10

STAFFING UP

Hiring Employees and Independent Contractors

A business is only as good as the people who perform its operations. However, the critical task of finding, hiring, training, and retaining good people is one of the most difficult and time consuming responsibilities of an entrepreneur.

Before embarking on a recruitment spree for your new business, you first need to identify the business operations that need to be performed by people, both now and in the future. Once you have identified those functions, you will then need to assess whether they should be undertaken by a full-time or part-time employee of the business, or whether it is better to retain an independent contractor to do the work. In doing so, you should analyze whether the service is an integral part of operating your business that will be required for the foreseeable future, or whether it is a temporary need either to get your business up and running or improve its operations.

For example, if you own a designer clothing store and have little technological expertise, you may want to hire a website designer and/or developer to launch your website and teach you how to update the site, but you may not need those services going forward. In this situation, it will perhaps make more sense to enter into a short term service agreement with the website designer/developer, rather than hire him or her as an employee. However, if you intend to sell your designer clothes exclusively online, and will depend on your website as your primary marketing and sales vehicle, you may want to hire that person as a full-time webmaster to ensure your website maximizes its sales potential and functions efficiently and smoothly at all times.

Hiring an employee versus an independent contractor raises more than just practical business concerns. There are important legal and financial ramifications as well. In the ensuing sections, we'll start with an overview of the employment process, including recruiting and hiring. Then we'll look at outsourcing alternatives, including the proper way to bring independent contractors on board when it makes commercial sense to do so.

Recruiting an Employee

In your search for talented employees, you'll want to cast as broad a net as possible in order to have as wide a selection as possible. At the same time, however, you need to target your efforts and screen out applicants so that you don't waste time reading inapplicable resumes and interviewing people who are not qualified for the job.

The first and most important step in the recruitment process is to assess the needs of your business and create a job description that defines what the roles and responsibilities of the person you wish to hire will be. This job description is just as important for your business as it is for the person being hired, because the last thing you want to do is to hire somebody and realize afterwards that the job actually requires different skills than the person you just employed.

In addition, you need to think not just of your current business needs, but future needs as well. What will be the requirements of this position as the business grows? Can the person you hire grow along with the position? Also, think through exactly how the position you are creating will fit within your business organization, and define exactly who the person being hired will report to and how that job will interrelate with other positions within the business. To hire the right people and operate your business efficiently, you should have a clearly defined organizational structure.

Once you have a job description, you can create a job listing that highlights the most important aspects of the job and the necessary qualifications for the candidate you are seeking. Then target job listing resources that will give you broad visibility with the type of person you wish to hire, without wasting time and money on unqualified or disinterested job seekers.

The listing resources you may want to consider include:

- Online Job Sites

- The Classified Ad Sections of Print and Online Newspapers

- College and University Placement Centers

- Personal Networking

- Job Fairs

- Employment Agencies

- Search Firms and Headhunters

- Industry Trade Press

- Social Media

In most situations, posting a job opening online is more cost and time effective than print advertisements. Normally you can post more information for a longer period of time, and screening candidates is easier using this method.

If you're looking for top-level technical, sales, financial, or management talent, then a search firm (sometimes called a "headhunter") may be worth the considerable fee it will charge to find the right employee. Personal networking can also be an important tool when recruiting key employees and often leads to the best results. Candidates obtained through networking are often referred by someone you know personally who can vouch for the skills, experience, and accomplishments of the candidate.

When recruiting new employees, you also need to make sure any application form you use conforms to Equal Employment Opportunity Commission ("**EEOC**") guidelines and that your hiring decision is not based on discriminatory criteria in violation of federal and state laws and regulations. This means you cannot ask about or make your hiring decision based on age, sex, race, color, religion, national origin, disabilities of any kind, date and type of military discharge, marital status, etc. Go to the EEOC website at www.eeoc.gov for more information. In addition, keep your file on all applicants, whether you hire them or not, for at least six months after the hiring decision has been made.

Hiring an Employee

Bringing a new employee into your business may seem like a very simple proposition. For example, if your software business needs a customer service representative, you simply interview candidates and give the best one the job. But the decision to hire a new employee raises a series of important questions that must be answered, such as whether to hire the customer service representative on a full-time or part-time basis. In addition, hiring even one employee brings your company under the vast umbrella of laws and regulations governing the employer-employee relationship, which you must understand in detail in order to avoid being subject to claims brought against your company by employees, as well as potential government fines for non-compliance.

There may be many reasons to hire a part-time employee—the job involved may not require full-time work, a good worker may not be available full-time, your company may not be able to afford a full-time worker, etc. But do not think that by hiring workers part-time you will avoid the legal responsibilities and protections afforded your full-time workers. In fact, almost all of the laws that apply to full-time employees apply to part-time as well. However, you are not required to provide part-time employees those employee benefits which are not required by law, but which you provide your full-time staff on a voluntary basis.

Employee Benefits

One of the most important decisions you will have to make regarding your employees is what benefits to offer them in addition to their salary or hourly wage. Employee benefits can make up one of your company's biggest expense items, often adding 30-40 percent to the cost of an employee. But in order to recruit talented employees and keep them on-board and motivated, most companies provide some type of benefits package, especially as the company matures and hires a larger staff.

There are certain employee benefits that are mandated by law, and it is extremely important that you become familiar with them. For example, the law requires that you comply with all workers' compensation requirements such as minimum wage under the Fair Labor Standards Act, pay your own portion of FICA taxes (which fund retirement and disability benefits for your employees), pay state and federal unemployment taxes, and comply with the federal Family and Medical Leave Act.

You are generally not required by law to provide a retirement plan, health insurance, life insurance, paid vacations, or sick leave. However, most employers offer some combination of paid holidays, vacation, and sick leave, and many put together some form of retirement plan and health insurance coverage to be competitive in hiring qualified employees and to keep them happy and motivated. If you are going to provide these types of major benefit plans, it is crucial that you do so properly, because mistakes and bad decisions can add greatly to their cost.

The most important laws you need to be aware of with respect to certain of your benefit plans is the Employee Retirement Income Security Act ("**ERISA**"), which establishes minimum standards for retirement, health, and other welfare benefit plans. ERISA's rules also cover the federal income tax effects of transactions associated with employee benefit plans, and include standards that qualified plans must follow to make sure that plan fiduciaries do not misuse its assets.

ERISA does not require an employer to provide employee benefits, or that plans provide a minimum level of benefits. But once an employer decides to provide benefits that are subject to ERISA, the plan's operation is regulated by ERISA, and the benefits must be detailed through a written plan document.

Retirement Plans

With respect to retirement plans, some of the most popular options include:

- Traditional 401(k) Plan

- Payroll Deduction Individual Retirement Account ("**IRA**")

- Savings Incentive Match Plan for Employees ("**SIMPLE**")

- Simplified Employee Pension ("**SEP**") Plan

- Profit Sharing Plan

- Defined Benefit Plan

Banks and independent financial advisers can help you set up a plan that meets your compensation needs and has the added advantage of providing your company and its employees with various tax benefits. For example, if your company establishes a retirement plan that meets the requirements of ERISA and the Internal Revenue Code, it will receive a tax deduction for the contributions it makes on behalf of its employees. It is very important, however, to comply with government regulations with respect to these plans, particularly ERISA. Failure to do so can result in the loss of these tax benefits and, in some situations, other penalties such as fines.

Medical Plans

Up until present day, the decision about whether to provide health insurance to employees has always been optional, and it still is. However, beginning in 2014, the failure to provide health insurance for employees will result in a significant price to pay for some businesses.

The Patient Protection and Affordable Care Act ("**Affordable Care Act**"), otherwise known as "Obamacare," enacted comprehensive health insurance reforms that will most likely have an impact on your business at some point in time. Implementation of the Affordable Care Act occurs in stages, with many of the reforms and requirements taking effect in 2013 and 2014. The affordable care act has the biggest effect on businesses with more than 50 employees.

In brief, starting in 2014, the Affordable Care Act requires, subject to certain exceptions, every person to either have a "minimum essential" level of health insurance coverage or to make a "shared responsibility payment" when filing a federal income tax return. Also beginning in 2014, employers with 50 or more full-time employees that do not offer affordable "minimum essential" health insurance to their full-time employees (and dependents) may be required to pay what amounts to a fine. A full-time employee is one who is employed for an average of at least 30 hours per week.

Under the Affordable Care Act, all employers are required to provide employees with a standard "Summary of Benefits and Coverage" form explaining what their plan covers and what it costs, and penalties may be imposed for non-compliance.

If you are going to offer health insurance to your employees, the types of plans available include:

- Traditional Indemnity Plan

- Managed Care

- Health Savings Accounts

Under a Traditional Indemnity Plan, employees choose their own doctor and the insurance company either pays the doctor directly or reimburses employees for the amounts covered by the plan.

Managed Care plans are those offered by Health Maintenance Organizations ("**HMO**") and Preferred Provider Organizations ("**PPO**"). Under an HMO, employees are required to use doctors from hospitals approved by the HMO. Under a PPO, employees choose doctors from an approved list and then pay a prescribed amount per office visit, with the insurance company picking up the rest of the tab.

Health Savings Accounts ("**HSAs**") allow workers with high-deductible health insurance to make pre-tax contributions to cover healthcare costs and use these amounts to pay for most medical expenses not covered by the high-deductible insurance. Employer contributions to HSAs are tax deductible and not subject to employment taxes.

ERISA generally applies to all employer-sponsored group health plans. It is very important that any health insurance plan you offer is in compliance with ERISA, which sets minimum protection standards for individuals participating in most employer-sponsored group health and benefit plans. Be aware that individuals who manage a plan (and other fiduciaries) must meet certain standards of conduct under the fiduciary responsibilities specified in the law. If your business's health insurance plan is ERISA qualified, it may obtain certain important tax deductions.

Employee Stock Option Plans

Employee stock options give employees the right to buy shares of a corporation's common stock at a specified price, called an exercise price, which is normally the fair market value of the stock on the date the option is granted. Stock option plans allow the company to compensate employees without a significant outlay of cash and motivate them by giving them an interest in the company. This is typically accomplished through the creation of an equity incentive pool in which 10-20 percent of the company's initial authorized shares are reserved for issuance to employees. In order to comply with IRS rules and for other corporate governance reasons, only the company's board of directors (or a designated committee of the board) should be authorized to approve stock option grants.

Stock options are normally exercisable for a 5-10 year period as long as the employee remains with the company. However, the options are typically made to vest over a period of 3-5 years, meaning that a percentage of the options become exercisable at certain intervals during that period. If an employee leaves the company or is terminated, he or she loses options that have not vested, and has a specified period of time to exercise those that have. In order to limit a company's stockholder base to persons connected to the company, many option plans include (i) a company repurchase right (generally at fair market value) over shares issued upon exercise of options in the event such stockholder's service to the company terminates and (ii) a company right of first refusal over transfers of shares issued upon exercise of options.

The value of a stock option lies in the potential that the company will increase significantly in value and conduct an initial public offering of its stock, allowing the employee to exercise his or her options, sell the shares, and make significantly more money than would have been possible through normal compensation plans. However, for this to happen, the company must both be successful and either register its shares so they are publicly tradable, or sell the company in a transaction that allows option holders to receive value for the underlying shares.

There are two basic types of employee stock options: incentive stock options and non-qualified stock options.

Incentive Stock Options

Incentive stock options can only be granted to employees and must be granted in accordance with a written plan approved by the stockholders. The option price must be no less than the market value of the stock at the time of the grant, and it must require exercise within 10 years from the time it was granted. In addition, the market value of the stock for incentive stock options exercisable in any year is limited to $100,000 for any individual. Options in excess of this limit are treated as non-qualified options (see below).

The main benefit of receiving an incentive stock option versus a non-qualified stock option is the potential for favorable tax treatment. The employee recognizes no income when the options are granted or when they are exercised—taxes are only imposed when the underlying stock is sold. If the stock is sold after it has been held for at least two years from the date the option was granted and one year from the date it was exercised, the difference between the market price of the stock when the option was exercised and the price for which it was sold is taxed at long-term capital gains rates, which are lower than ordinary income rates.

Non-Qualified Stock Options

Non-qualified stock options can be granted to employees, directors, and even independent contractors, and there are no limits on the number or value of options that can be granted. Non-qualified stock options are taxed at the time they are exercised and transfer restrictions on the issued shares have been lifted. At that time, the difference between the exercise price and the fair market value is considered ordinary income.

Under federal law, it is now very important for companies granting employee stock options to set the exercise price of the underlying shares at or above the price that can be shown by a reasonable valuation method to be fair market value ("**FMV**") at the time of grant. Companies can establish a defensible FMV by using an IRS-approved valuation method.

If the options are issued at less than FMV, the option holders can be severely penalized by the tax law. Section 409A of the Internal Revenue Code requires the holder of an option having an exercise price below FMV at the time of grant to recognize taxable income equal to the spread between the exercise price and the FMV of shares as they vest. Thus, the option holder will be taxed on income the option holder does not actually receive, from shares that may not then even be saleable. Further, in addition to regular federal income and employment taxes, an additional 20 percent or more federal tax will apply.

In addition, any non-public company granting stock options, or other compensatory equity awards to employees or consultants, needs to be familiar with Rule 701 under the Securities Act and comply with it. Remember, you can't sell stock or issue stock options without either registering the securities with the SEC or availing yourself of an exemption from the registration requirement. Rule 701 is the federal securities law exemption for compensatory equity issuances. You also have to worry about state securities law exemptions with regard to stock options or other compensatory equity award issuances.

Rule 701 is a broad exemption. There are no forms that need to be filed with the SEC, or any fees that need to be paid to the SEC, but Rule 701 does have significant conditions and limitations and if you run afoul of them there can be very onerous consequences, including potential personal liability for a company's officers and directors.

One other federal law you need to be aware of with respect to employee stock options is Section 6039 of the Internal Revenue Code, which establishes requirements that employers must meet each year when an employee exercises an ISO, including the requirement that employers must file information statements about these transactions with the IRS.

Hiring an Independent Contractor

Every business has certain tasks that need to be performed where it does not make sense to hire an employee to do the work. This can be because the specific skills will be required for a limited period of time or because it would not be cost-effective to engage a new employee to perform the task. For example, you may want someone to design your company logo, or landscape the property surrounding your office building, or give you legal advice on buying an additional business. In these types of situations, you will probably want to hire an independent contractor to perform the tasks at hand.

However, when hiring an outside contractor, you need to be extremely careful not to inadvertently turn your contractor into an employee having all of the rights, benefits, and protections provided by federal and state law.

In determining whether an employer-employee relationship has been established, the IRS and the courts will look at the totality of the circumstances. The general rule is that a person is an independent contractor if the company retaining that person only has the right to control or direct the end result of the work, but not how the independent contractor actually does that work. What matters is whether the employer has the legal right to control the details of how the independent contractor's services are performed. Therefore, while you can agree with your independent contractor on the specific task to be performed, the independent contractor gets to determine exactly how it will be accomplished.

Another factor that is taken into account is whether the person performing the services can do similar work for other businesses, or will work exclusively for your company. If the independent contractor clearly has his or her own business, which provides its own work materials, hires its own staff, and is subject to its own financial risk, then it is safe to say no employment relationship will have been established. In addition, the longer the period covered by the agreement, the more likely it will be considered an employment agreement. Some of the many other factors include the nature of the payment scheme, whether the work is for a set number of hours per week, and the place the work will be performed.

In order to clearly document that an independent contractor relationship is intended to be established, as well as to provide a clear understanding of the rights and responsibilities of each party, a services agreement should be signed each time you hire an independent contractor to provide any services to your business. The amount of detail contained in the agreement, as well as in each provision, will depend on the nature of the services to be performed.

The services agreement should include provisions to cover the following:

- Services to be performed

- Timetable for performance of the services

- Payment amount, procedure, and schedule

- Payment of certain expenses

- Penalties, if any, for late performance

- Duration of the services and the contract

- Confidentiality obligations

- Ownership of intellectual property

- Ownership of work product

- Indemnification

- Force majeure

- Dispute resolution

- Termination

It is very important that the description of the services to be performed is clear and sufficiently specific so that both parties understand what is required of the project. If the services are not clearly identified and a required end product or result not specified, there is a risk that a dispute will arise between you and the contractor. The contractor will argue that any additional work required by you is outside the scope of the original work and will most likely require further payment. On the other hand, you may argue that it was intended to be within the agreed scope of work. So to avoid misunderstandings about what constitutes completion of the job, make the services agreement very clear. You may also want to include specific performance benchmarks along the way, so that everyone is satisfied that the job is going as expected.

In relation to payments, the agreement should clearly set out the amount of each payment required and when it has to be paid. It is often useful to state that payments will be contingent on the achievement of certain milestones before they become payable to the contractor. The agreement should set out whether any taxes are payable by the employing party and whether the employing party will be responsible for expenses incurred by the contractor.

If the contractor generates written material or software code, or delivers patentable goods, the service agreement should be explicit about who will own the work product and the rights relating to it. In some situations, the contractor may insist on ownership so that he or she can use the material for other jobs. You, however, will want your business to have ownership of all copyrights and patent rights developed in the course of the project and to have those rights assigned to it or, at minimum, to have the contractor grant a perpetual license of those rights to your business that can never be terminated.

This ownership of intellectual property rights will have to be negotiated between your company and the contractor. The outcome of those negotiations will depend on the nature of the work being performed, as well as the nature of your business and that of the independent contractor. On a related note, you will also need to ensure that when your business deals with an independent contractor that it takes appropriate steps to protect the ownership and confidentiality of any intellectual property and trade secrets it provides to the independent contractor in connection with the performance of the required services or duties under the services agreement.

An independent contractor may also have certain duties of its own to provide a safe and healthy work environment for is personnel, and the service agreement will need to ensure that if the services are to be provided at your company's place of business that those standards are met. From your business's perspective, it may also require the independent contractor to maintain its own insurance to cover job-related accidents and other events. In addition, the service agreement may require the service provider to indemnify your business for certain unauthorized actions it might take, and should specifically state that the contractor is not an agent of your company authorized to enter into agreements on your company's behalf, unless or course this is intended.

Hiring a Consultant

Regardless of whether a business is run by an experienced management team or a sole proprietor just getting his feet wet in the commercial world, it may be necessary at times to hire a consultant to provide specialized advice. Fortunately, consultants come in every shape and color, and can be found for almost any area that your company lacks the necessary expertise.

For example, your business can hire a consultant to advise you on setting up your information technology system, on establishing an employee benefits plan that complies with the law, on putting in place proper accounting systems and controls, and on developing a marketing strategy designed to best reach your target audience.

One of the primary difficulties in hiring a consultant, in contrast to a service provider, is that the arrangement is often vague and deliverables are hard to define. In many cases, it is also difficult to determine the impact a consultant's advice actually has on your business results. For this reason, before hiring a consultant you should assess clearly why the consultant is being retained, what exactly you want him or her to do, and how you believe the relationship will help your business.

For example, hiring a management consultant without specifically defined tasks and deliverables could result in your paying a lot of money and generating nothing but endless meetings and vague advice. It can also result in disagreements over when and whether payment is due. This is not a good result for either your business or the consultant.

A major step in overcoming the problem of ill-defined duties and deliverables is to prepare a consulting agreement that sets out as many specifics as possible. For example, the agreement can provide for the number of hours the consultant will spend on your project each week, how much time will be spent at company locations, the frequency of meetings with company management, reports that must be delivered and the contents of those reports, and the follow-up assistance that the consultant will provide in implementing the advice given.

Because most consultants will have developed a body of work that they tap into for each client, the company and the consultant will have to discuss who will own any work product developed by the consultant. Another issue that must be considered is whether the consultant is allowed to work for competing businesses, which could lead to conflict of interest situations. In general, a consultant will not want to be limited in the customers it can work for, but may agree not to consult with directly competing customers for the term of the agreement.

In addition, it must be kept in mind that a consultant is actually a form of independent contractor, and so both in the consulting agreement and in the manner that the relationship actually occurs, care must be taken that the consultant is not deemed to be an employee by relevant government agencies.

Exotic Universe, Inc.

Having sorted through what was needed from an initial management standpoint, Cindy McKay sits down to put together a full-blown organizational chart, including all expected future hires over the next twelve months. During the business planning stage she had performed a similar exercise, so she wasn't shocked at the results—but it did confirm once again that the business she has chosen is much more complex than she had originally anticipated. With respect to product development/procurement, she will need local staff or service providers who are in direct contact with the artists to procure the artwork, handle the shipping, make the payments, and take care of any country-specific rules and regulations, including customs, that have to be dealt with. Some of the artists may become full-time independent contractors as well, creating artwork exclusively for Exotic Universe, Inc. In addition, unless she can find a way to clone herself, Cindy needs to move quickly on recruiting her director of international operations to manage all of this. This position will be difficult to fill, and the job description will be critical in doing so—she needs someone experienced in dealing with and making things happen in other cultures. From a marketing and sales standpoint, in addition to her director of marketing who will devise and run the internet marketing program, Cindy will need a mid-level person to refresh content and maintain the website once Roger gets it up and running. Cindy will also need at least one customer support person to handle phone and e-mail enquiries. In addition, she will have to find a photographer/independent contractor to provide professional shots of the artwork and artists for the online catalog. And in the second half of her first year, she plans on developing a stable of outside sales agents to directly pitch art galleries and dealers with her highest quality pieces to create an additional revenue stream. Cindy also realizes that the technology that will be required to handle the orders, shipping, tracking, customer database, etc. as the company grows will entail far more than basic website design. So while she may hire Roger as an independent contractor to work in tandem with her director of marketing to design the initial website, and she will undoubtedly purchase an e-commerce hosting solution providing many of these features, she will at some point want to start recruiting a chief information officer who can manage the required technology as the company grows. Then there is finance. Her controller needs to be recruited and hired and she needs to speak to Bill about a possible consulting role for himself. The question is whether the controller will need a staff person to handle order processing and basic bookkeeping functions. Despite the fact that Cindy intends to invest in high-quality accounting software, the answer is most likely yes. Finally, Cindy knows she needs at least one administrative assistant.

When she has finished with her organization chart, Cindy creates a salary and benefits spread sheet, which leaves her slumped in her chair. Just adding the director of international operations and customer service rep, positions she had not accounted for in her original business plan budget, will cost Cindy money that was already ear-marked to cover a couple of months of start-up expenses—a fact that Nancy is not pleased to find out about, since it will be her money and she had based her investment commitment on Cindy's financial projections, which are turning out to include significantly higher monthly expenses than expected. As a result, Cindy has her first lesson in what it means to have a watchful board member/investor looking over her shoulder. But Cindy knows that Nancy is right, and once again lectures herself to always think through the issues that can be thought through, and save the unpleasant surprises for matters outside of your control. In that respect, Cindy sees from her organizational chart and job descriptions that she needs to be very careful when hiring her several independent contractors. Because most of them will work significant hours, she has to make certain they don't cross the fine line and become employees; otherwise her budget will explode even further. This raises yet another issue—the cost of employee benefits. As a teacher, Cindy has become accustomed to the significant benefits negotiated by her union. But now as the employer, she sees how expensive these benefits actually are. She is determined to provide her employees with health and dental coverage, which will constitute a huge expense for her small business. But she can't afford much more, so other benefits will have to wait. To compensate for this, Cindy instructs her attorney David to prepare a stock option plan. An employee stock option pool is then created and each position on the organizational chart assigned a range of shares to be issued according to the experience level of the hire. All shares will vest over a four year period, and will be subject to repurchase if the employee leaves the company. With all this in mind, Cindy sits down to devise her recruiting plan.

CHAPTER 11:
A COMMERCIAL LEASE ON LIFE

Chapter

11

CHAPTER 11

A COMMERCIAL LEASE ON LIFE

Finding and Leasing the Right Property

According to the famous axiom, the three most important rules in business are location, location, and location. This holds true whether you are in the retail, restaurant, manufacturing, or almost any other line of business. Most companies in the start-up phase will find it impossible, impractical, or inefficient to purchase property in the right location, so almost all end up leasing commercial space to meet their business needs.

Normally, a commercial property lease will comprise one of the largest single operating expense items of running a small business. As a result, the choice of where, for how long, and at what price to lease commercial property is one of the most significant start-up decisions you will make. It is therefore critical to think strategically about your long-term business plans before signing a lease, taking into account both the current and future needs of the business.

Choosing the right property is a difficult proposition, and one of the trickiest aspects of this decision is the length of the lease. If you sign a long-term lease for more commercial space than you presently need and your business does not "grow into" the space as expected, then the burden of the lease could collapse the entire business. However, if you sign a short-term lease and/or lease property that is insufficient to meet the future needs of your business, you may end up spending important capital on improving a property that you don't use for long and paying brokers' fees and moving expenses for a second time in quick succession—not to mention confusing your customers by changing location.

Ideally, you would rent sufficient space to meet your current needs, at least for the initial two years, with adjacent space available that you can expand into when your business grows in the future. But of course this type of space is hard to come by in a good location, so at the beginning you may need to either rent more space than you initially need, or sign a shorter lease with a plan in mind for moving to a larger space in the future. Much of this will depend on the nature of your business—the key is to have a plan.

Along with location and term, price is the other most important factor in deciding what property to lease. In determining how much you can afford, look to what percentage of your annual revenues the rent will entail. If it's more than 10 percent, it's probably too much. But remember, for many businesses it is worth paying more for a better location that will drive higher sales. Check the rents on comparable properties in the area to get a feel for whether a particular property is over, under, or at market price. Keep in mind, however, that many factors can impact the rent, and hidden costs may be involved, so look closely before making any judgment.

In searching for an acceptable property, first identify the best general location and then analyze each available property within your price and term range, weighing all of the important factors that can make or break a particular location.

Choosing the Right Location

Issues to consider when analyzing a commercial space include the following—note that the majority of them deal with location in one form or another:

- Nature of the desired property and neighborhood—retail, commercial, or industrial

- Condition and appearance—are major repairs required?

- Layout conducive to your business

- Adaptability: can leasehold improvements be made that meet your needs?

- Availability of additional space for future lease

- Proximity to and ease of access for target segment customers

- Proximity of complementary businesses that attract your target customers

- Proximity to and ease of access for pool of employees

- Proximity to and ease of access for suppliers

- Location of competition

- Zoning restrictions and other applicable ordinances

- Site image, history, and reputation: Is the location consistent with the image you want to maintain?

- Neighborhood safety and building security

- Parking for customers, visitors, and employees

- Sufficiency and cost of utilities—electric, plumbing, heating and air-conditioning

- Availability of municipal tax and other incentives

- Does the site allow you to meet your business goals?

Property Lease

Once you have identified the right location at an acceptable price, you need to look carefully at the terms and conditions of the lease. Remember that renting commercial property is in effect a "buyer beware" proposition. The type of consumer protections available to persons who lease residential property will not protect those who lease commercial properties. On the contrary, it will be assumed that a business owner is sophisticated enough to understand the provisions of the lease, and if not will retain a professional adviser. So if the base monthly rent seems much lower than for comparable properties, look carefully at the details of the agreement, because the deal you've been offered might in fact be too good to be true.

For example, some commercial leases make the tenant responsible for the full maintenance of the property. As a result, an unwary tenant used to residential leases could budget only the base rent amount, but then get stuck with having to make expensive repairs to the building, the cost of which far outweighs whatever was saved on the reduced rental price. Similar care must be taken with respect to other lease terms which could affect the actual price your business will end up paying for the property, as well as its value to the business. In any event, before signing a long-term lease, you should have an expert thoroughly inspect the property—the same as you would if purchasing the property.

Bear in mind that the initial terms of a commercial lease almost always favor the landlord. Everything, however, is subject to negotiation, so don't hesitate to bring up issues that are important to you. How much success you will have will be determined by the market conditions, the location, and the nature of the property.

A commercial property lease typically includes these provisions:

- Description of Leased Premises

- Term

- Option(s) to Renew

- Rent

- Rent Increases

- Utilities and Other Expenses

- Taxes

- Maintenance

- Insurance

- Condition of the Property

- Security Deposit

- Tenant Improvements

- Landlord Improvements

- Permitted Use of Property

- Landlord Access

- Guarantor

- Termination

- Assignment and Sub-leasing

Lease Term and Renewal Options

As mentioned above, deciding how long a lease to commit yourself to involves balancing between stability and flexibility, and depends on the nature of your business, the condition of the property, and the desirability of the location. For example, if you foresee spending a lot of money to improve the property, you'll probably want a longer lease. But if you are an e-commerce business that just needs limited generic office space for the first year, after which you plan on significantly ramping up your hiring, then you should sign a short-term lease (and begin searching for your next space relatively soon).

Commercial property leases can span anywhere from 1-25 years. You should assume, however, that you will not be able to get out of the lease until the term is complete, and once it is complete you will have to vacate the premises if you don't have an option to renew. This assumption will help you think clearly about your business needs and negotiate an appropriate term.

While a 5-25 year lease is the norm for established businesses generating predictable cash flow, the best option for a new business is to sign a shorter term lease, between 1-3 years, with several options to renew for additional terms. Keep in mind, however, that you will pay a price for both the shorter term and the options to renew. Landlords are often less willing to grant incentives and concessions on short-term leases, and this could increase your overall annual costs. In addition, there may be fees or higher rents associated with the grant and exercise of the options to renew.

Despite the higher annual costs, if the needs of your business unexpectedly change, there is an economic downturn, and especially if you are required to personally guarantee the lease, it's good not to be locked into a long-term lease, at least until you've established a stable business with consistent and considerable positive cash flow. If you do go the route of a short-term lease with the option to renew, get as many renewal options as possible, and definitely try and lock in the parameters of any rent increase on renewal—you don't want to find yourself effectively evicted by a landlord who raises the rent to a price you can't afford.

Rent and Rent Increases

Most commercial leases have several financial components that must be negotiated and allocated between landlord and tenant—base rent, property taxes, insurance, utilities, and maintenance and repairs. Base rent is typically calculated on a square-foot basis, so you need to understand exactly what space you are renting and how the landlord measures that space. For example, are the hallways and rest rooms included in the calculation?

But the base rent is only a portion of the real cost of renting commercial space. You also need to negotiate and agree on how the other cost components will be calculated and allocated between the landlord and tenant. In this respect, you should be aware of these principal types of commercial lease:

- Full Service Lease

- Gross Lease

- Net Lease

- Percentage Lease

In a "full service lease," you pay a single amount to cover the base rent and all of the costs of operating and maintaining the property, including taxes, insurance, maintenance and repairs, and utilities. In a "gross lease," the tenant pays a single amount for everything except utilities, which are billed separately. These forms of lease give your business the advantage of stability and predictability of monthly property expenses, at the cost of sometimes paying more than the actual costs involved.

With a "net lease," there is a base rent and then the landlord bills the tenant separately for the exact amount of taxes, insurance, maintenance and repairs, and utilities. One particular expense item to be aware of is common area maintenance, which landlords charge for taking care of the parking lot, lobby, restrooms, and stairwells. Get an itemized list of the expenses the landlord proposes to bill you for and make sure that inappropriate items are not being passed along. Also make sure that you are paying a prorated percentage of the space your business rents versus the entire space available in the building, and not just that part of the building that is occupied by you and other tenants. Otherwise, if a large tenant leaves the building, you may see your business's common area maintenance costs skyrocket.

With respect to maintenance and repairs, some landlords attempt to hold tenants responsible for everything, others for anything other than the roof, exterior walls, and parking lots. This means that if there are problems with the electrical system, plumbing, heating and air-conditioning, etc., you could find your business facing enormous cash outlays at a time you can least afford it. Therefore, this is an issue to pay close attention to, and depending on the nature of your business and the space you are renting, one to negotiate heavily.

On the other end of the spectrum, utility costs are normally and properly borne by the tenants, the question is just how they are to be determined and billed. Some buildings have separate meters, but often in office settings the utility costs are allocated based on square footage.

As you can see, a net lease can result in unpredictable swings in monthly expenses, but has the advantage of accuracy with respect to actual costs. If you do go with a net lease, try and negotiate caps or limits on the various expense items. If you cannot, then it may be better to pay a higher amount for a gross lease.

However, be aware that most full service and gross leases often include an annual increase in the rent amount that takes into account increased landlord expenses relating to the property and other factors. Some call for fixed increases, others for adjustments based on the consumer price index, and others are calculated based on the actual increased costs of operating the property. Once again, especially in the latter case, try to get a cap on the amount of each year's increase. The failure to negotiate these caps could be the difference between a profit and loss, positive and negative cash flow, for your business.

One additional way to calculate rent is through a "percentage rent clause," under which tenants agree to pay a base rent plus a percentage of their gross revenues over a certain threshold. These types of leases are called "percentage leases." While under a percentage lease the rent is not predictable with respect to the total cash outlay, it is predictable as a percentage of sales. It is still a good idea, however, to negotiate a percentage rent that doesn't kick into effect until you have consistently hit the threshold for a period of time, possibly even 12 months in a row. You may also want to negotiate a provision allowing you to break the lease if your gross revenues don't hit the threshold for a stated period of time.

If you are in the retail business, one other commercial lease clause that you should be aware of and negotiate is a "co-tenancy clause." Co-tenants are typically the anchor tenants in a mall. They are the large, popular stores that attract increased traffic that spills over to other stores in the same location. You can negotiate a provision stating that if an important anchor tenant leaves, your business can pay lower rent or can itself terminate the lease and leave.

Tenant Improvements and Incentives

If you intend to conduct business operations that go beyond basic office activity, it is likely that you will want to "build-out" the space you rent in certain ways to make it suitable for your business. So it is critical that your lease allows for such improvements, because you don't want to find out after signing a lease that you cannot use the space as intended, and in an optimal way for your business.

You can also allocate tenant improvement costs. Because landlords are in competition to attract good long-term tenants, they often agree to either share or pick-up tenant improvement costs as an incentive. Sometimes these incentives will come in the form of a dollar amount per square foot of the space being leased.

Especially when demand for commercial space is low in the area you are considering, you may be able to negotiate other financial incentives from the landlord as well, such as free rent for the first several months. If you don't need a significant build-out, ask for this in the alternative.

Personal Guarantee

Landlords often ask the principal owners of a start-up company to guarantee the rent. Such a guarantee will obviously put your personal finances at risk, and so the terms and the ability of the landlord to act on the guarantee should be reviewed carefully. When a personal guarantee is present and there is no ability to terminate the lease early, the right to sublease becomes even more important than usual.

Sublease

Most commercial leases in the United States do not include the right to terminate prior to the end of the lease term, and when they do significant financial penalties for early termination will be included. This is especially true when the landlord provides incentives such as paying for tenant improvements or offering a reduced base rent for a long term lease.

Therefore, try and negotiate the right to sublease the property—at minimum with the consent of the landlord, not to be unreasonably withheld. This will offer at least some protection from financial disaster if for some reason your business takes a drastic downturn and you cannot afford the rent; or some flexibility if you desire to move to another location.

In addition, make sure you have the right to assign/transfer the lease to a third party purchaser if you decide to sell your business.

Termination

It is extremely important that you understand how and on what terms your landlord can terminate your lease. Just as the landlord wants to lock you in, you want to make sure the landlord cannot pull your lease out from under you. So make sure that where the landlord has the right to terminate if your business breaches a provision of the lease, that (i) there is a cure period that allows your business to remedy the breach (usually 30 days) and (ii) that the landlord's right to terminate is limited to material defaults under the lease and not to trivial matters.

Broker

Unless you have a significant amount of experience in shopping for commercial real estate, it's a good idea to use a qualified real estate agent. Whether you are buying or leasing, an agent can help by prescreening properties, which saves you time, and by negotiating on your behalf, which can save you money. Typically the landlord pays the agent's commission, which may raise some questions in your mind about loyalty of the agent. However, keep in mind that the agent doesn't get paid until a deal that satisfies you both is negotiated.

Lawyer

You should also hire an experienced real estate lawyer to review the lease agreement. Remember, your commercial lease will constitute one of the most significant costs of running your business, and you will need to make certain that you can use the property the way you intend. Hidden costs and restrictions buried in a legal document can do serious damage to your new business. It is worth the upfront cost of retaining an attorney to make sure this does not happen.

Exotic Universe, Inc.

When Cindy McKay first put together her business plan, one of the things she was most excited about was finding a building in downtown Boulder that could serve both as an office and an art gallery where she could display some of the paintings she sourced from overseas. This was included in her business plan and financial projections, but with her human resource budget being blown out of the water by two unanticipated hires, she now has to make some tough choices to find that lost money. The gallery is a "nice to have," not a "need to have" for the business. So Cindy decides, begrudgingly, to put that plan on hold until she can afford it. The first question she has to ask and answer is how big of a space to rent. Initially, she will only have a handful of employees, but once she begins scaling her business after the first year, she will have to increase her staff as well. She decides once again, however, that she needs to stay small until she is certain her business is ready for the next phase. So she decides to look for a one-year lease in an office big enough for herself and six full-time employees. In theory, this seems like an easy proposition, but it turns out to be more difficult than expected. Most of the suitable office space she finds in this category is either far from her home or not in a safe location for working long late hours. In addition, some landlords want a much higher monthly rent for a short-term lease. Finally, she hears about a company which has had to downsize in the bad economy and has an entire floor available in a building with a long-term lease. They are willing to rent space to Cindy for a year, and she is just about to sign the lease when she talks to the owner of a neighboring business and learns the company she wants to sublease from may go out of business soon. If they lose the lease, she will lose her lease as well, not to mention her deposit and any expenses she incurs fixing up the space. Feeling like she dodged a bullet, Cindy continues to hunt for office space. She sees a small house in her neighborhood with a "for rent" sign and thinks that may be a perfect short term option and a cozy place for her team to work. The neighborhood, however, is not zoned for business, and once again she doesn't want to take a risk when just starting her business. Finally, Cindy stops by a friend's gallery in downtown Boulder for an art opening, and over a glass of wine she tells her friend her dilemma. It turns out that the top floor of the three story building is empty, and Cindy's friend would be willing to rent it out on a year to year basis. In addition, if the paintings Cindy brings back are up to the gallery's standards, her friend would be willing to host an Exotic Universe launch party, complete with a one month showing of the best exotic paintings and sculpture. Cindy considers herself lucky, but in business you make your own luck by creating opportunities where good things can happen. She has always felt it was important to maintain good relations with people in the art community, and this approach has now paid off—hopefully for the first of many times.

CHAPTER 12:
HITTING THE TARGET MARKET

Chapter

12

CHAPTER 12

HITTING THE TARGET MARKET

Creating and Executing a Marketing Strategy

If you asked a group of small business owners whether they have a marketing program, many would reply, "Sure, we place ads online and in our local paper, hand out flyers at the supermarket, stuff like that." But marketing is not simply advertising. Marketing is the process of finding out what a sizeable group of people want or need; developing a product that satisfies their desires; getting their attention and communicating with them about how your product will add value to their lives; motivating them to buy; delivering the product to them at a satisfactory place and time; and retaining them as customers in the future, all while maximizing long term profit and cash flow.

If that sounds like a large chunk of your operations, it's because it is, and the best way to make all this happen is to develop a comprehensive marketing plan for your business and then execute that plan. The steps involved in putting together a good marketing plan include:

- Conducting Market Research and Analysis

- Setting Marketing Goals

- Developing Strategies and Tactics to Achieve Marketing Goals

- Budgeting

- Measuring Effectiveness and Return on Investment

As you can see, the marketing plan is an integral part of your business plan. It must therefore be developed to work in tandem with all aspects of your business and help achieve the overall goals of your organization.

Market Research and Analysis

Good business decisions depend on good information, and your market research efforts should be designed to give your management team the information it needs to make good decisions when setting marketing goals and strategy.

Therefore, your market research should be focused on identifying your target market, identifying the category of persons in that market most likely to buy (i.e. your target segment), and understanding the people your target segment is comprised of—including who they are, what they want, and how to attract them and convince them to buy. In addition, you want to understand clearly the strengths and weaknesses of your product and your organization, as well as the opportunities and threats that are present in the marketplace.

But business is not conducted in a vacuum, and therefore market research should not be as well. It's just as important to collect information on your competition, and to identify and understand trends in the market and forces external to the market—such as government regulation or the introduction of new technology—which may have an impact on your ability to sell your product.

As a new company, you will undoubtedly be constrained by what you can afford. But regardless of whether you have money to spend on formal studies performed by outside consultants, or are limited to informal surveys of potential customers and publicly available information, it is very important to collect as much information as you can using the resources that you have.

In conducting market research, you can use whatever primary and secondary methods described in Chapter 2 that you feel are appropriate and affordable for your business. If you have already put together a business plan, much of this research may already be completed. However, at this stage you may want to drill down even further, concentrating in particular on:

- The size and nature of the market where demand for your product exists

- The size and nature of the market segments within the overall market

- The size and nature of the market segment where demand for your product is highest and target customers are most likely to buy (your target segment)

- What product features and benefits your target segment want and value the most

- Where, when, and how your target segment want the product delivered

- The demographics and buying habits of your target segment

- The tastes and expectations of your target segment with respect to the type of product you wish to offer

- The price elasticity of your product within the target segment

- The direct and indirect competition, including how they perform on all of these same questions

- The value proposition/unique selling proposition that you can offer to differentiate yourself from the competition

- The SWOT components: the Strengths and Weaknesses of your product, as well as the Opportunities and Threats you will face in the marketplace

Determining and analyzing the market segments within your target market, and then selecting the best segment or segments to target, is one of the most important roles of marketing, especially in a start-up business. You will have limited resources to communicate with potential customers and convince them to buy, so you need to make sure you are targeting the most likely customers that will give you the largest market share and generate the highest profit. It may be that you choose more than one segment to target, but choose carefully and don't overreach.

Once you have selected what segment(s) you will target, you can use your market research to analyze and understand the persons who make up that segment: who they are, how they act, what may motivate them to purchase your product, and how, when, where, and at what price they would buy. This will allow you to determine what features to include in your product, how to position your product with respect to the competition, how to find and communicate with potential customers, the best price to offer your product at, and where to offer your product. In other words, it will allow you to create a set of marketing goals, as well as strategies and tactics to meet those goals.

Using the market research to perform a SWOT analysis is also important to good decision making. SWOT stands for Strengths, Weaknesses, Opportunities, and Threats.

In analyzing the strengths of your product, you want to determine what it is about your product, as well as other aspects of your business, that customers value the most and make you distinctive from the competition. You need to understand your value proposition and unique selling proposition in order to set a strategy that attracts customers and differentiates you from the competition. Conversely, understanding the weakness of your product and other aspects of your business, especially vis-a-vis the competition, can help you either improve what you have to offer or develop a marketing strategy that convinces customers to buy regardless.

Remember that strengths and weaknesses relate not only to product attributes such as features, quality, and price, but also to customer service aspects of your business such as delivery time, warranties, and customer support.

You can't take advantage of opportunities you don't know about, and you can't defend yourself against threats you're not aware of. So it's important to analyze your market research data and determine whether it reveals profitable possibilities you hadn't previously considered, as well as lurking competitive or external dangers that you need to address.

For example, your surveys may show customer dissatisfaction with some aspect of a competing product, and if you design your product to address that dissatisfaction, you may be able to capture market share from your competitor. Your research may also reveal that a large company which previously did not compete in your market is about to enter the fray, and therefore allow you to design a strategy that differentiates your product not only from existing competitors, but such new competitors as well.

In any event, your market analysis should include a thorough understanding of the competitive environment. This will include the number of players in your target segment and the market share they currently hold, the strengths and weaknesses of those competitors and their products, and their strategies and tactics. This understanding will play a large role in how you develop and position your product and company to effectively compete in the marketplace.

Once you have finished your market research and analyzed the information collected, you should have a solid foundation for determining the goals of your marketing program and the strategies and tactics you will use to meet those goals.

Setting Marketing Goals

Your initial instinct might be to say that the goal of marketing is to generate as much revenue and make as much profit as possible. In the long run, this may be true. But the path to realizing those goals may not be a straight line. Focusing on other goals such as building a brand and gaining market share may result in lower profits in the beginning, but ultimately lead to a more profitable and sustainable business.

In addition, keep in mind that your marketing goals should mesh with the goals embodied in your vision, mission, and values statements, pointing not only towards profits, but also towards the type of reputation you wish to build in the marketplace and the community. In the long run, this will also add value to your business.

Therefore, in addition to generating cash flow and producing a profit, the goals of a marketing program can include:

- Brand Building

- Product Positioning

- Market Share

- Market Penetration

- Customer Loyalty and Retention

- Return on Marketing Investment

At the end of the day, you will always want to establish a brand, properly position your product, gain market share, develop customer loyalty, get a good return on your marketing dollars, generate cash flow, and make an acceptable profit. But in marketing, focus is important. Different goals may involve different, and sometimes conflicting, strategies and tactics. And as a business in the start-up phase, you will likely have limited marketing resources. So concentrating on one or more goals at a particular point in time is often the best way to efficiently allocate resources and achieve all of your goals in the long run.

For example, your market research and analysis may indicate that you are among a number of new entrants in a high growth business, so establishing market share and brand awareness are initially more important than profit margin. As a result, you may focus on these goals at the outset and adapt strategies and tactics—such as pricing your products lower than you otherwise would and spending a higher percentage than you otherwise would on marketing and sales—that may cost you profits in the short run but allow you to win the competition for a critical mass of customers and outlast your competitors.

Branding

A brand is a name or symbol that uniquely identifies a business's product in the market, and establishing a well-recognized and respected brand will touch upon every aspect of your marketing plan. As a new company, you will be starting from scratch with respect to your brand. The question becomes how much of your resources you want to allocate towards actively building your brand, and the answer will depend on the nature of your product and the resources you have available. If you have limited cash resources, it may be that the best way to build a brand is simply to sell as much of your product as possible and let the customers' experiences drive the reputation of your brand. This is fine, because unless you're selling a mass-market consumer product and willing to spend millions on advertising, it is your products that will ultimately create your brand.

188 | ENTREPRENEUR'S GUIDE TO STARTING A BUSINESS

However, in every tactic you adopt for your marketing program, you should always take into account the reputation you want your products and business name to acquire in the minds of your customers and the market in general. That way, as awareness of your brand grows, you can capitalize on this reputation and "brand equity" in your future marketing programs and pricing strategies.

When launching, building, and managing a brand, think about what makes your product and business distinctive. What distinguishes you from the competition? What is your value proposition that sets you apart from the rest? The answer to these questions is what you can begin to build your brand around. Strive for consistency in image and reputation in every aspect of your marketing program, so viewers get a clear and persistent message of who you are and how your product will add value to their lives.

Determining the Marketing Mix

Your marketing mix consists of the strategies and tactics you will use to accomplish your marketing goals. Traditionally, a company's marketing mix has been centered on the Four Ps of Marketing: Product, Price, Place, and Promotion. These are the aspects of marketing that are within a company's control, as opposed to external factors such as the tactics of competitors that can be addressed and managed using the Four Ps but cannot be controlled.

Over the last decade, marketing strategies and tactics have been revolutionized by the Internet, which allows companies to get their message out to a large number of people at a relatively low cost. The impact has caused many marketing managers and experts to reassess the applicability of the Four Ps to today's technology-driven economy. However, in one form or another most businesses must still pay attention to the original Four Ps, and work to integrate their traditional promotions with those available on the Internet for a comprehensive marketing program that combines traditional marketing and new marketing strategies and tactics.

So let's first take a more detailed look at the Four Ps and then get an overview of what marketing on the Internet entails.

Product

On the surface, product development and marketing have a bit of a chicken and the egg relationship—it's hard to tell which function drives the other. But at the end of the day, it does not make sense for a business to develop any product unless marketing has identified a need or desire for that product in the marketplace. And once you know what your target market wants and needs, it does make business sense to develop and produce a marketable product that contains features that satisfies the desires of your target segment while differentiating you from the competition.

Therefore, in designing and developing your product, it is critical to keep in mind your value proposition. Simply put, this is a concise statement of why a consumer should buy a product. The statement should address what it is the customers are really buying, what benefits they will receive from your product, and why your product will add more value to their lives or better solve their problem than what the competition is offering.

Branding will also be an important consideration in product development, because you want to develop products that are consistent with the brand reputation you want to build, and vice versa. Other important elements of the interrelationship between product development and marketing include the selection of features, the product's look and feel, and development of related product lines.

Price

Pricing a product is a delicate balance between generating revenue and maximizing profit margins, while at the same time realizing your other marketing goals. A low price may increase sales, generate higher revenues, and increase market share, but at the expense of profits. A high price may increase profit margin and help establish you as a premium brand, but at the expense of customers unwilling to pay that price.

Pricing will also be impacted by forces outside your control, such as how competitors are pricing their products and general economic conditions. Your market research effort should collect information on the price points of competing products and what target customers are willing to pay, as well as their price sensitivity. This will give you a sense of the price range you can charge depending on the goal you want to achieve. Taking all of this into account, you should price your products at a point you think will best help you achieve your marketing and business goals.

Place

Place involves where and when your customer will purchase your product, as well as where and when you will deliver it to the customer. Your marketing strategy must determine whether your customers wish to purchase directly from you or from wholesalers or retailers, whether they will place orders online or otherwise and have them shipped, or take possession of the product at its point of sale. The first key is to determine where your potential buyers will expect to purchase your product, and make the purchase available to them in that location. The second is to determine how, when, and in what quantity your customers will expect to have the product delivered to them, and devise an efficient and cost-effective manner of doing so.

Promotion

Promotion is what most people typically think of when they hear the term "marketing." It is the communication of information to your target market in an attempt to get them to buy your product both now and in the future.

The four major types of promotion typically integrated into a marketing strategy are advertising, publicity, sales promotions, and personal selling. Your promotional mix should be designed to reach as much of the target audience as possible in a manner that gives you a good return on your investment of money, time, and other resources—i.e. best achieves your marketing and business goals.

The key to a successful advertising campaign is to assess which mix of vehicles will reach the greatest number of likely buyers at a time and in a place where it is possible to influence their behavior. Each vehicle available for advertising entails its own set of goals, strategies, and tactics that must be understood and integrated to be effective.

Advertising vehicles include:

- Internet

- Print Media, such and newspapers and magazines

- Broadcast Media, such as radio and television

- Direct Mail

- Brochures, Flyers, and Postcards

- Catalogs

- Newsletters

- Billboards

Publicity, or public relations, entails the use of free media—such as feature articles about a company or product in a magazine, or related interviews on television talk shows—to spread the word to the target audience. Public relations-oriented promotions, for instance, may be more effective at building credibility within a community or market than advertising, which many people see as inherently deceptive.

Public relations vehicles include:

- Articles

- Events

- Press Releases

- Grand Openings

- Networking

- Trade Press

- Industry Analyst Coverage

Sales promotion allows the business owner to target both the consumer as well as the retailer, which is often necessary for the business to get its products stocked.

Sales promotion vehicles include:

- Free Samples

- Coupons

- Contests

- Rebates

- Point of Sales Promotions

Personal selling, which refers to face-to-face or telephone sales, usually provides immediate feedback for the company about the product and instills greater confidence in customers. Personal selling also allows the business owner to collect information on competitive products, prices, and service and delivery problems.

Internet Marketing

The Internet provides businesses with the ability to reach large numbers of target customers in an interactive, real time, collaborative online environment. As a result, Internet marketing will allow your new business to combine mass marketing, public relations, sales promotions, and personal selling into one promotional forum.

The first step in establishing your Internet marketing program will be to design and create a website, which we will cover in detail in Chapter 13. A basic website will contain information regarding your business, a description of the products you offer, and promotional material related to those products. With a more advanced website, you can optimize your Internet marketing potential by providing informative content such as articles and blogs. And if you wish to engage in e-commerce, which we will also cover in Chapter 13, your website will include an online shopping store as well.

Once your website is established, you need to create an online promotional mix that reaches your target market, attracts their attention, draws them to visit your website, and converts them as customers. Reaching your target market involves determining which websites they visit regularly, when they visit, and how they use the sites. Once you've found where your potential customers reside online, however, they have to find you.

The techniques for getting the attention of your target customers and drawing them to your website fall into one of two categories: "inbound marketing" and "outbound marketing." Inbound marketing vehicles such as content creation and social media engagement take human effort and cost money to produce and maintain, but no unaffiliated third party is paid. With outbound marketing vehicles, you pay a third party for placing an advertisement, sponsored link, or the like on their website.

Inbound marketing is also called "earned" marketing. It is a manner of drawing visitors and generating leads through a combination of content and links to your website. While inbound marketing is free of media costs, there are significant organizational and human resource costs to executing this strategy successfully. It takes significant effort to create, publish, maintain, and refresh content that gets the attention of a large number of quality viewers and draws them to your website. That being said, in the long run the cost of drawing visitors to your website using inbound marketing techniques tends to be less than using paid outbound marketing techniques.

An inbound marketing strategy will take longer to put in place than simply paying for sponsored links and advertisements on other sites, which can be launched very quickly. It takes time to build interesting and informative content, establish and grow social networks, increase website authority, and acquire high quality links. Once created, however, your online content will have a much longer life than traditional promotional material and draw higher quality visitors—i.e. those visitors most likely to be converted into customers— to your website. And unlike outbound marketing methods, which disappear once you stop paying for them, inbound marketing content will remain available online for a long time.

Inbound marketing methods include:

- Website Content

- External Online Content

- Social Media

- Referrals (Links)

- E-Mail

- Public Relations

- Online Customer Service

Content is king in today's Internet marketing environment. The method of content marketing has been around for a long time, but it has exploded as more and more people look to the Internet as their primary source of information on products and services they want to buy.

Content marketing is a method of getting "found" by your customers, promoting your products, and creating brand awareness indirectly without a direct sales pitch. The idea is to create informative content that is highly ranked by Internet search engines, so people who are looking for that information will find either content located on your website, or content that you have created and placed on another site with links back to your website. The goal is to build product and brand awareness and reputation with your content and generate sales by enticing a large number of high quality visits to your website. High quality content also develops valuable customer relationships, establishes credibility, and builds a trustworthy reputation.

Types of inbound marketing content include:

- Articles

- Blogs

- Social Media

- Video

- Podcasts

- Research/White Papers

- Forums

- Q&A

- Webinars

- Infographics

- Newsletters

- Press Releases

- Public Relations Placements and Mentions

- Online Business Directories

You can create content such as articles, blogs, forums, white papers, and Q&A for your own website, but don't stop there. To give you the optimum opportunity to get found by potential customers, place high quality content you have created on other websites, and link that content back to your own website.

Social media networking has become a key ingredient in the Internet marketing strategy of many businesses. Sites such as Facebook, Twitter, Tumblr, Pinterest, Instagram, LinkedIn, Google+, and Digg provide a platform both for placing your content and interacting with your target market. Video hosting websites such as YouTube or Metacafe have also been a benefit to little known businesses. Creating a video that goes viral can make millions of people aware of your business in a very short time.

All of your sources of content can interact with each other through links and search results, and should be coordinated as such.

The key to all of this, however, is that your content must be discovered by your intended audience and drawn them to your website. The best way to ensure that happens is to rank high in Internet search results. And the best way to get a high ranking is employ search engine optimization ("**SEO**") techniques such as keywords and tags and creating quality relevant content that is regularly refreshed.

The other important SEO technique is to place and generate as many high quality links to your site and content as possible, because the more such links you have and the higher quality they are, the higher you will rank in the search engine results. So the more links the better, especially from sites relevant to your business.

When you create your own content, you can embed links in whatever you create, whether it resides on your website or that of a third party. But you also want to generate what are known as referrals, which are links on third party sites and embedded in content created by third parties such as articles, product reviews, and discussion forums. You can seek free links at news sites, industry-related sites, local business directory sites, and the like.

Links can also be paid for, as can search results, and this is where you enter the realm of outbound marketing.

Outbound marketing techniques include:

- Pay Per Click

- Display Ads—Banners and Pop Ups

- Google Adsense

- Sponsored Search Results

- Sponsored Links

- Affiliate Links

- Retargeting

- Classified Ads

- Rich Media Video

One important thing to keep in mind when adopting an Internet marketing strategy is that if you go down this road, you need to pay close attention, keep your hands on the wheel, and keep your vehicle finely tuned and up to speed. First of all, if content is not continuously refreshed and new links are not generated, all your initial efforts could go to waste because your search rankings will nosedive into a ditch. In addition, Internet marketing is a dynamic environment in which the techniques, platforms, and technology change rapidly, so you need to keep abreast of what is going on in order to take full advantage of the opportunities available.

Budget and Analytics

One of the most difficult parts of creating a marketing plan is setting a budget. It is very easy to get carried away and spend too much, resulting in paying for promotions that do not give you a good return on investment. But it is also easy to short shrift the importance of marketing by spending too little, resulting in missed opportunities to sell your product, gain market share, and build your brand.

There are two key aspects to setting a marketing budget: how much money to spend and how to allocate those funds.

How much you spend will be determined by the resources you have available and the nature of your business. If your resources are limited, don't abandon marketing as a priority, just educate yourself on all of the less expensive marketing opportunities available to you, such as some of the Internet marketing techniques we just discussed, and take advantage of them as much as possible. If you do have adequate resources, see if you can get information on the percent of revenues that companies in your business typically spend on marketing. You may, however, need to spend a higher percentage than your competitors at the outset, until your business and products become known by your target market.

When you're coming up with an annual figure for marketing costs, don't forget about related expenses such as market research, attending functions and trade shows, training yourself and others, and hiring experts to help you with special projects. And always allow a bit extra for the unexpected.

The key is to get the biggest bang for your marketing buck, and in order to do so it's important that you track and measure how successful your marketing programs have been.

At the beginning, it will be difficult to predict exactly the return on investment you will receive from each promotion. You can make an educated guess by looking at industry related material. But once your product is launched, the key to a successful ongoing marketing plan will be to gather information about the effectiveness of the marketing dollars you are spending.

You've probably been often asked, and sometimes annoyed, about how you found out about a certain business. But knowing how a customer discovered your business is a key component to judging the success and cost-effectiveness of your marketing program. So try and gather this information from customers however you can.

Once you have information about which promotions are driving the most customers to your business, you can adjust your marketing plan accordingly. If you're getting more customers through your content-rich website, or more people are reading your blogs and following your tweets, keep spending your time and/or money on those efforts. If more of your ideal customers are finding you from a print ad in a local magazine, or because they heard about you on the radio, then run with those vehicles. Spend more there, and less on the disappointing channels. Your ability and willingness to change on the fly can be a huge competitive advantage with all the available avenues to promote your business today.

Exotic Universe, Inc.

When Cindy McKay conducted market research prior to writing her business plan, she assumed it was the last time she would have to do so for quite a while. But she thought wrong. The initial market research she collected was geared towards her original business idea and focused in large part on the market for exotic artisan handicrafts. Now that she will launch her business as an online seller of exotic art, saving the handicrafts for phase II, she needs to understand that focused target segment inside and out before creating a marketing plan. So Cindy starts fresh and collects as much information as possible regarding the type of person who buys art online, the reasons they purchase art from any venue, how much they are willing to pay, where they reside online, where they physically reside, etc. She also collects information regarding her online competition for artwork. Her efforts in both areas begin with simple Google searches to see who is selling art online—and she is highly discouraged by the results. There are hundreds of websites selling paintings and sculptures online, ranging from artists hawking their own wares to sites acting as virtual galleries for many artists to high-end auction sites. Exotic Universe, Inc., she feels, is sure to get buried in this avalanche of websites. But as she digs more deeply into the sites and looks at what they specifically have to offer, she sees that very few of them concentrate on artwork from exotic locations around the world, and those that do either offer paintings from one country only, or don't have the quality artwork she is sure she can source. With that knowledge in hand, Cindy creates a survey for the purpose of ascertaining the level of interest in the artwork she wants to offer, on what terms the respondents will be willing to purchase from an online dealer, the motivations behind their purchases, and the type of artwork they will be most interested in. This time, the results are extremely encouraging. Cindy finds a high level of interest from middle to upper-middle income households in buying high quality paintings from undiscovered artists. The people she surveys indicate they would be very likely to buy art that they feel would become a "talking piece" in their home—a high quality painting or sculpture that is guaranteed to be unique and come with its own "identity" and sense of connection to another part of the world. As such, they want to learn as much about the artist as possible, even expressing interest in communicating with their artists via email, chat, or even Skype calls. On a similar note, in her follow-up interviews Cindy discovers a high degree of interest in commissioned works from the type of artists she has met overseas, and an offshoot of her business model is born.

These research results provide the genesis of Cindy's first marketing plan. Her goal is to position her product line as "high quality exotic art by high quality exotic artists." In other words, she wants to differentiate herself from the scores of companies offering cheap art and prints online. This goal does not only relate to her initial line of artwork—it will be her branding strategy going forward as well. She wants the brand Exotic Universe to be associated with quality, so in the future people will come to her site looking for her jewelry, furniture, etc. that fit within the same motto. Cindy wants her website to be the place where people can find the real deal, not cheap knockoffs or mass-produced items. In order to do so, however, she needs to offer high quality items that people are willing to buy at a price that both her target market will accept and will allow her the required profit margin to make her business model work. This will be one of her key challenges, especially since her target market will be buying primarily for decorative rather than art collecting purposes. The reason there is a gap in the market, Cindy feels, is because of the difficulty in developing a profitable business model selling high quality art online. This is a huge barrier to entry—but it is also an opportunity.

CHAPTER 13:
SITE SPECIFICS

Chapter

13

CHAPTER 13

SITE SPECIFICS

Creating a Website

Websites have become an integral part of running almost any line of business in today's technology-driven economy. Although it may still be possible to do business the old fashioned way based on print and broadcast advertising, as well as word of mouth, it is almost guaranteed that a properly conceived, established, and managed website will deliver a good return on the time and money invested. For that to be the case, however, the website must be created and operated in the right way, or the beneficial results you anticipated could be reversed.

The first step in establishing a website is the same as the first step in starting a company—you have to select a name and then take the right measures to secure the use of that name. The name of a website, which also acts as the primary portion of its Internet address, is called the "domain name." Every domain name must be registered and placed in an international database. Unlike trademarks, where the same mark can apply to different types of products, every domain name is unique.

Simultaneous with selecting and securing a domain name, you can be designing the layout and user interface that will make up the look and feel of your website and drive the overall user experience. Once that is accomplished, the computer code that will operate the website and turn the design into a reality must be programmed. Both the design and development of a successful website require specialized skills. So if you or the employees in your business don't have experience in this area, it is a good idea to hire a professional website designer and developer (if necessary) to perform these important tasks for you.

As with any form of business, one other option is always just to buy what you need. It may even be possible to purchase a registered domain name, a functioning website, and all of the associated assets as a package. But in most cases, you will want to either start from scratch or use a template and tailor your website to your particular business.

We will now walk you through the process and issues involved in establishing a website that will attract and retain customers and add significant value to your business.

Domain Names

Your domain name will be one of the primary marketing tools of your business, and should be chosen with the same care that you use in choosing the trademarks attached to your products and services. Factors to consider include:

- How effective the domain name will be in driving Internet searches by your target audience to your website

- How memorable the domain name will be for your customers.

- Whether it will be possible to register the domain name as a trademark

- Whether it may infringe the trademarks of another person in places where you intend to do business

Unlike trademarks, domain names are not technically owned by the user. Domain names must be registered in the domain name system ("**DNS**") database, upon which the registrant is granted the "right to use" the name. Therefore, once you've chosen the domain name (or names) that you want to register, first go to any well-known registrar's database and see if the name is available. This may take some time, because hundreds of millions of domain names have already been registered.

You should then do a trademark search against the domain name(s) you intend to register, as well as a general Internet search against the name. If the domain name has been registered or is being used as a trademark or trade name and there is the possibility of a conflict, you should think seriously about selecting a different domain name. You don't want to attract unnecessary litigation, or be forced to change your domain name after your website is up and running.

After finding the available domain name you want to register, the next step is to choose a registrar. Keep in mind that registrars are for-profit businesses, and all are not the same. They offer different prices for different periods of registration, as well as provide different levels of customer service, account security, ease of use, and stability. The last thing you want is for your domain name to be hijacked due to lax security by your registrar, or to have difficulties contacting the registrar in case of a problem with your domain name. So do some research before choosing a registrar.

Once the registrar has entered your domain name into the DNS, you have the right to use that name for the term of your registration, and afterwards for as long as you continue paying the renewal fees. To protect your intellectual property rights, it's also a good idea to register domain names for each of the trademarks and brands that you use in your business. In addition, you should register these domain names under all of the most common top level domains, or TLDs, which is the last part of a domain name, i.e. the .com, .info, .biz, etc..

Buying and Selling a Domain Name

Because there are hundreds of millions of domain names that have already been registered, you may have difficulty finding one that you are satisfied with for your business. And even if you do find an acceptable domain name, you may see a better one that has been registered and is for sale. In these situations, you may want to buy a domain name rather than registering a new name yourself.

Domain names can be offered for sale (i) directly by the current registrant, (ii) through a domain name broker, or (iii) both of the above at the same time. If you wish to buy a specific domain name that is already registered, you can perform both an Internet search and a "Whois" search under the desired name. Most often, you will either be led to a site that is actively using that domain name, or to a site—either individual or brokerage—that says the domain name is for sale. If the name is for sale, the asking price will often be listed as well.

For example, if you search "mrmechanic.com," you will find an active .com site with no indication that the domain name is for sale, and if you perform a Whois search for that domain name, you will locate the registrant and his contact information. However, if you type in "carmechanic.com" you will find a link to a brokerage site that tells you the domain name is currently for sale and the asking price. In addition, a Whois search will take you to a site listing the domain name registrant, its contact information, and statement that the name is for sale.

The method of completing the purchase and sale of a domain name will depend on the circumstances. If a brokerage service is used, it may be able to handle all of the details, including the payment method and arranging for the domain name transfer by the registrant. If an individual is selling the domain name, then the terms and payment method will have to be worked out in a domain name transfer agreement that is either signed or agreed to through email exchanges.

It is important for a buyer to get the further assurances of a seller that if future help is required to complete the transaction, switch registrars, etc., then the seller will provide the assistance needed. In addition, the buyer will want the seller to undertake not to use the domain name or any associated trademark after completion of the transfer.

Domain Names and Trademarks

The intersection of domain names and trademarks has become a complicated area of the law that you should have some familiarity with when selecting and registering, or buying, a domain name. The complications arise from the fact that (i) registered domain names are unique and can only be used by one company at a time, (ii) registered domain names are automatically useable on a worldwide basis, and (iii) domain names can be registered and maintained without being actively used.

The same trademark can be registered by two or more different companies if the trademark is being used with respect to different goods or services. But only one company can have a domain name that contains that trademark. This has led to some famous conflicts over domain names, such as the one between Sun

Photo, Sun Oil, and Sun Microsystems. There is only one sun.com, however, which Sun Microsystems registered first and has the right to use to the exclusion of the others.

While domain names have a global reach, trademarks are registered in the country where goods or services are being sold with the use of the mark. As a result, a company that uses a domain name that is the same as a registered trademark, and also sells the same goods in the same country as the trademark holder, may be liable for infringement. In general, the test will be whether the domain name registrant intended to offer products for sale to persons located in the country in question. But the issue is complicated and should be examined thoroughly if a potential conflict exists.

Websites

A website consists of content accessible through the Internet. The website of a local seafood restaurant could be as simple as a single homepage displaying the business name and logo, a photograph of the restaurant's exterior, a few menu items, location, and contact information. The website for a multinational consumer products corporation could include entire catalog for several product lines, interactive graphics, forums, shopping services, databases, and whatever else is required to conduct the entire business online.

Regardless of how big or small, complex or simple a website is, there are certain steps that need to be taken to get it up and running, make it successful, and maintain it going forward. First you need to think through exactly what you want to accomplish with the website and who the target audience will be. For example, will you use the site purely for informational purposes, or do you want to sell products over the site as well?

Then you need to visualize how the website will look and feel, and how you would like visitors to interact with the available content. Are static photographs sufficient, or are interactive graphics and animation required? Do the customers need to perform pricing and other forms of calculation? Every function of the website needs to be identified and analyzed for it to be successful. If this is not done upfront, then your site could turn away as many customers as it attracts.

Once this basic description of the commercial requirements of the site is in place, then the technical work begins. The entire website needs to be designed and developed to realize your commercial vision. This includes an interwoven system of software programs that operate the website, including the user interface and all of the text, graphics, and sounds that will be included on the site. Then content must be developed or otherwise obtained and added to the site.

Finally, the programs and content that make up the website must be hosted on a server. This is where the website will reside and be maintained, and where your visitors will be directed via your domain name to view your website content. Typically, websites are hosted on servers owned by external hosting companies, who have the resources to cost-effectively maintain servers of sufficient bandwidth in a safe and secure environment.

There is one last thing to keep in mind when creating and launching a website. Both in the development of the computer programs operating the website, and with respect to the content that appears on the site, care must be taken to ensure that applicable intellectual property, consumer protection, and other laws are adhered to.

Website Design and Development

Your website is the first impression that many potential customers will have of your business. For that reason, it is crucial that the site be visually appealing, easy to navigate, and function quickly and smoothly. With a well designed and developed website, visitors will linger, browse, and come back often. A poor website will have the opposite effect, sending customers racing out the virtual door, often never to return.

Although often used interchangeably, website "design" and "development" are technically two different terms. Website design refers to how a site looks and operates on the surface—its graphic appearance and usability. It also entails making the website "search engine friendly," i.e. using key words and other techniques that cause your site to appear prominently when customers are searching the Internet for what you sell.

Website development refers to the underlying computer code that allows the website to look and operate the way the designer intended. The software that must be programmed to operate a website is extensive. It must control everything from the ability to enlarge a photograph to links to other websites to accepting credit cards.

As a result, most businesses that are just starting out don't have the technical capability or capacity to program website software, but fortunately they don't have to. For a simple website, downloadable design software is available for which the development work has already been done. For more complex sites, there are many website designers and developers available and willing to perform the service for a fee.

If your business has limited resources and you just want a very basic Internet presence that will simply perform the function of making potential customers aware of the goods and services you offer, as well as provide your location and contact information, then you may want to go online and download a proven website design software package to create your own site.

Be aware, however, that even a website design program that performs all of the functions you desire will require a significant amount of thought, as well as trial and error, if you want your site to be a successful marketing and sales tool for your business. You will need to consider carefully the appearance of the site and how the visitors will interact with the information you provide. To realize the importance of this, just think about some of the websites you have visited that had poor graphics and difficult to read text, or were complicated and counter-intuitive to interface with. This type of website screams out "unprofessional" and reflects poorly on the business involved.

For these reasons, even if you are starting a new business it is probably worth the investment to hire an experienced website designer to help you create an easy to use site that will attract and retain customers, as well as a developer if you intend to write the software code for your own site rather than using a template. Keep in mind when looking at candidates that you need a person or a team who can perform both the design and development functions. A website designer who dabbles in development, or vice versa, is not good enough. You need an expert in both areas.

In searching for a website designer and/or developer, you should consider a range of issues, from their experience and skill level to their responsiveness and ability to listen and communicate. When analyzing whether a candidate is the right fit, take a close look at his or her portfolio of websites, particularly those that are similar to your own specifications. Get your hands dirty with these sites and gauge your own reactions as if you were a potential customer.

For example, ask yourself these questions when reviewing the portfolio sites: Do you find the website design user friendly? Is it easy to find all of the information you desire and return to pages you have previously viewed? Is the site uncluttered and visually appealing? Is the text easy to read? Are the graphics clear and relevant? Do you feel like you can quickly learn about what the company has to offer and the features of its products? With a good designer, the answer to all of these questions will be "yes."

Also pay attention to the functionality and production values of the site. Is it fast and efficient? Do the links operate properly? Are the graphics, animation, sound, etc. of high quality? If you are able to interface with the site quickly and easily without even thinking about how it is functioning, then the developer has done a good job. If there are glitches, delays, and unprofessional functions and appearances that frustrate your enjoyment and use of the site, then you should look for another developer.

In addition to reviewing a candidate's portfolio, get referrals and talk to previous customers about whether the designer/developer readily understood the needs of their business and created a site that added significant value to their operations. In this respect, look for designer/developers who have worked on sites for other companies in your line of business. Hopefully, they will already be familiar with your target audience and how best to attract and retain customers.

Once you've selected a website designer and/or developer, you need to put together a website design and development agreement.

The development of the website provisions should be specified in great detail, either in the body of the website design and development agreement or in attached schedules. Most often, the design and development work will be broken down into phases, with explicit instructions as to the work that will be performed during each phase and what performance levels must be achieved.

Following the completion of each phase, there should be an acceptance test to make sure that the specifications are being met and the project is on track. If the customer feels that the deliverable for a given phase has not met the specifications outlined in the development schedule, then it will provide the designer/developer with its objections and the cure provisions will kick in. If the designer/developer fails to cure the deficiencies, then the customer will either be able to terminate the agreement or reduce the fees, depending on the negotiated terms.

In addition to allowing the periodic testing of the website in progress, the designer/developer should represent and warrant that the final product will be free from defects and will operate according to specifications and up to the required performance levels.

Some of the trickiest issues to negotiate in a website design and development agreement are the rights and liabilities related to intellectual property. A fully developed website will include many different forms of copyrighted software and content, as well as trademarks and possibly even patented material. Some of this software and content will be developed or provided by the designer/developer, some will come from the customer, and some will be sourced from third parties.

The first thing that must be decided, and clearly specified in the website design and development agreement, is who owns what part of the end product and the pieces used to put it together. As the customer, you will want to own everything associated with the website, and intuitively may feel that since you paid for the design and development work, you already own the end result. But this will not be the case unless the agreement says so.

The person who creates the design, software code, text, graphics, music, etc. is the owner of the copyright in that material. So initially at least, the designer/developer will own what he or she creates for your website. This includes everything from the overall website design to the specific code to the content. Therefore, whatever you wish to own must be specifically assigned to you in the website design and development agreement. It cannot be emphasized too strongly that it is in your best interest to obtain this assignment so you have complete control over your website going forward.

However, there may be certain portions of the site for which the designer/ developer will demand ownership. For example, the designer/developer may have previously created some basic design templates, or developed code that performs certain functions, that he or she reuses over and over for different websites. If this is the case, however, then you need to receive a perpetual, non-cancellable, worldwide license to use this material in your website.

In addition, the designer/developer may incorporate software programs and content in your website that is owned by third parties. If so, then you once again need to make sure that you have the proper license to use the material in your website without infringing the third party's copyright, trademark, patent, or other intellectual property rights.

Once the website is developed, the question is who will host, maintain, and have the ability to alter the site going forward. Some designer/developers can be contracted to perform some or all of these services, in which case the appropriate provisions can be included in the website design and development agreement, or in a separate contract for future services. Website owners who have qualified employees may also do some or all of the maintenance and content alteration work themselves, while hiring a separate web hosting service where the site will reside.

If it sounds like creating a website will take a lot of thought, time, effort, and money, it probably will--especially if you want a site that adds value to your business. There are times, however, when it is possible and makes sense to buy an existing website rather than developing one from scratch.

Buying a Website

In some cases, rather than recreate the wheel it may be a good idea to buy an existing website. This would make the most sense if you want to enter the business already being operated on the website, or if you find a site for sale that could easily be altered to suit the needs of your own business.

Website owners offer sites for sale directly or through brokers. In addition, you can search the Internet for sites that appear to be dormant and attempt to contact the owner to make an offer to buy. The other instance where websites are purchased and sold is in connection with the sale of an ongoing business.

Purchasing a website is much the same as purchasing any other asset that includes technology and intellectual property. You should perform your own due diligence to make sure the website and all of its components are owned or licensed by the person selling the site, that the seller has the right to sell or assign licenses to the website and associated assets, and that the site functions the way it purports to.

If you are satisfied with the results of your due diligence and have agreed on a purchase price with the seller, you will want to enter into a website transfer agreement.

The sale, assignment, and transfer provisions should be inclusive enough so that the purchaser receives ownership of, or a license to, everything necessary to operate the website as intended. This will include the website, all of its associated pages and content, all of the associated software used in building and/or maintaining the site, all lists and databases containing user information, all associated trade secrets, all website designs, all trademarks and copyrights associated with the website, any other intellectual property or content related to the website, and the domain name and registration.

The purchase price can be paid up front, or part of it can be paid in stages as part of a negotiated earn-out amount based on the website's future performance. Most often, the purchase price will be paid into an escrow account, and then released when all of the assets have been transferred and assigned.

Due to the nature of a website, which incorporates an interwoven network of technology, computer programs, and content that often involves every form of intellectual property, it is important that the seller represents and warrants in the transfer agreement that it owns or has a valid license to all of the assets being transferred and assigned, and there is no infringement of any third party rights. The seller should also warrant the website operates properly, i.e. there are no underlying defects.

E-commerce

If you decide to use your website as more than just a marketing tool and actually sell your products via the site, then you have entered the exciting but very challenging world of e-commerce. Doing so successfully will require that you not just become familiar with, but actually master, all of the aspects of Internet marketing we touched on in Chapter 12 and website design we discussed in this chapter. In addition, you will need to develop detailed knowledge of every function involved in selling products over the Internet. Therefore, in this section we will simply highlight the areas that you need to research thoroughly and understand completely.

With an e-commerce website, you will be able to promote and sell your products all over the world 24 hours a day/7 days a week while avoiding the high-cost of leasing and staffing a retail store. You will be able deliver large amounts of information to your customers, allow them to compare products and prices almost instantaneously, and make a purchase without leaving their home or office. However, in order to take advantage of these positive aspects of e-commerce, you need to be better than the competition at driving potential customers to your website, convincing them to make a purchase when they arrive, and bringing them back as repeat customers. This is much easier said than done.

In the previous sections we discussed the basics of website design and development that you must know in order to get a site up and running. But an e-commerce website requires all of that and much more. The elements of a successful e-commerce website/business include:

- An Internet marketing strategy that is comprehensive, integrated, and drives a high volume of qualified traffic to your website

- A customer conversion strategy and related techniques that turns a high-percentage of viewers into customers, and then repeat customers

- A user experience that keeps customers on your website and keeps them coming back for more

- A competitive and effective online pricing strategy

- A profitable business model

- A navigation system that is easy to use, consistent, and intuitive

- A hosting solution that is high performance, feature-rich, and reliable 24/7

- An order mechanism/shopping cart system that is fast, easy to use, and functional

- A payment gateway that is fast, efficient, and accurate

- A merchant account that is professional, reliable, and cost-effective

- Security software that protects your customers' payment/transaction details

- A privacy policy that protects your customers personal data

- An order management system that efficiently tracks sales, orders, and inventory

- A fulfillment/shipment system that quickly, cost-effectively, and accurately delivers products to customers and handles returns

- Excellent pre-sale and post-sale customer service and technical support

- An integrated M-commerce (mobile commerce) and F-commerce (Facebook commerce) strategy

- Measurement tools for tracking and analyzing key performance indicators

Each one of these elements demands a section, if not a chapter, of its own. If you are going to rely on online sales to drive your business, you must become an expert in every area listed above. This is true regardless of whether you decide, as you likely will, to use an e-commerce hosting solution to host your website.

While third-party solutions provide many, or even all, of the necessary tools and applications you will need to start an e-commerce business, you will have little chance of success unless you understand the most effective way to utilize those tools and applications. In addition, you need to understand every element of e-commerce in order to select the best hosting solution and applications for your business.

If you don't get it right, customers who are accustomed to shopping with ease on popular e-commerce sites will depart quickly and never return to your site. However, if you do get it right, you will have increased your marketing and sales reach exponentially, and the world will literally become your economic oyster.

Exotic Universe, Inc.

The further she progresses towards starting her new business, the more Cindy McKay realizes that just as her friend/investor Nancy said, Exotic Universe, Inc. is in essence an Internet marketing company, and her efforts in that respect will be just as important as the artwork she sources. Therefore, her website will be one of the key factors for the success of her business because it will constitute the primary vehicle for her marketing and sales efforts. In order to conform to her branding strategy, the site has to be highly professional, both visually and in terms of content. As an artist, creating a website is one of the aspects of starting a business that Cindy is most excited about, and when she sits down with Roger to begin work, she discovers that designing a website actually is tantamount to creating a work of art. Roger tells her that the first thing they need to do is to design a logo. "Why?" Cindy asks. "Let's get the content down and we can do that later." Because, Roger tells her, the logo is like the focal point of a painting, and everything on the website flows from the logo. In a well-designed website, the color schemes, style, and other design elements of the entire website all begin with and are derivative of the logo. And starting with the logo, they must all reflect and enhance the company and brand image you want to create. A black and red logo with sharp angles communicates something very different than a violet and yellow logo with a rounded form. The design and color schemes must then match those of the rest of the home page and linked pages. This is only one element of website design. Many choices have to be made. For example, Roger asks whether Cindy wants to give the site a gallery look and feel, a home décor look and feel, or an exotic travel look and feel. Each would communicate something very different and appeal to a different target audience. Then there are the functional aspects of the website, all of which needed to be woven into the creative environment. The ability to easily browse the artwork, learn about the artists, purchase items, contact customer service, navigate from page to page, etc. have to be efficient and seamless. The fewer clicks the better; the less thought required the better. Another key question is whether to use a website template or to design the website from scratch and find a web developer to program it. The former is by far the cheapest and least complicated option, but it would limit the flexibility of what could be done with the website. On the other hand, having to find someone to write the code for a website would cost a considerable amount of money and take up more of Cindy's time. In addition, it would have to be made compatible with all major browsers, and that compatibility would need to be maintained in the future. The major template companies take care of all that for you. So in the end, Cindy decides to go with Roger's preferred template. She instructs him to design a site that reflects her branding strategy of high quality exotic artwork for the home. As such, in addition to the catalog she wants high quality representations of paintings placed in stylish living room, bedroom, and office settings. In the future, she wants to include a feature where a potential customer could relate interactively with the site, placing a particular painting within an image of their own home to see how it would look if purchased. She also wants to include video interviews with artists to supplement the text. Template or not, Cindy sees that creating her website is going to require, and deserve, a considerable amount of time and effort. This was the center of her business, and would require the center of her attention.

CHAPTER 14:
CLOSING THE DEAL

Chapter

14

CHAPTER 14

CLOSING THE DEAL

Start-up Sales and Distribution

It's a statement of the obvious to say that a company needs sales in order to survive and thrive. But what's not so obvious is the best way to generate and optimize those sales. As the founder of a new company, you may think that you should just go out and hire some experienced sales persons, tell them to do their thing, and wait for the orders to roll in. But in most cases you would be wrong, and you'll probably be surprised to learn that the best person to sell your products at the start-up stage is actually—now look in the mirror—you.

In most cases, the evolution of a company's sales program will take place in three general phases:

- Start-up

- Growth

- Scaling

In the start-up phase, it is important for many reasons that the person running the business is out pitching the products and having personal interactions with customers. Once the product, business model, and marketing strategy have been refined, then it will be time to bring on a salesperson or two to give you the bandwidth for growth. Then, once you're ready to significantly scale the business, you can look to hire a sales manager and create a sales team for him or her to manage.

The 'Me, Myself, and I' Method of Start-up Sales

As the founder of the business, you should be directly involved in selling your products during and after their initial launch. This does not mean you sit behind a desk and manage a team of sales people; it means you are actively out in the field, meeting with customers, and pitching your products. This is true regardless of whether you consider yourself to be "the salesperson type," and it is true for more reasons than just garnering initial sales.

Going out and pitching your product to customers gives you the ability to connect directly with your first buyers and develop long-term relationships. And most importantly, it provides the opportunity to receive direct customer feedback at a crucial time for your company. You may have a business plan and a marketing plan that provide substantial information on your target customers and their needs, but until you sit down with customers in a genuine sales presentation and listen directly to their desires and concerns, your information will still be incomplete.

The reason for this is that despite your best pre-launch efforts, it is almost impossible to develop an exact match between your product and your customers' needs before the product is out there in the marketplace. When you are the one in the sales meetings, personally demonstrating your product, gauging your customers' reactions, asking questions and listening to their answers, you get the most valuable information possible about how to improve both your product and your message—especially when you start hearing the same responses from many customers.

If you've never sold anything before, don't worry. Your intimate knowledge of your own product combined with a passion to solve your customers' problems will overcome initial weaknesses in technique, and the more sales meetings you lead the more you will improve. And regardless, the fact is that as an entrepreneur, you need to learn to pitch your product. To get you started, here are some key factors to keep in mind, each of which will serve you and your business well through every phase of developing a strong start-up sales effort.

Know Your Customer

It is extremely important that before you pitch your products to a potential customer, you know that individual person and business as well as possible. This allows you to ask more individualized questions designed to discover a customer's specific "pain points" and give you the information necessary to craft solutions to the customer's problems. It also allows you to "put yourself in your customer's shoes," a key requirement both for effective sales and good product development. Taking the time to understand your potential customers and asking the right questions gives them assurance that you are in tune with their individual needs, and gives you the best opportunity to glean valuable information from the meeting and learn from every interaction. While it takes time to prepare and learn about an individual customer, and this becomes more difficult to do as your business scales, as things progress you will develop standardized sales processes that allow you to do so more easily.

Ask Questions

This is probably the most important and underappreciated aspect of sales, especially at the start-up stage. In order to understand your customer's problem and how to solve it, you have to ask the right leading questions, listen to your customer's responses, and observe his or her reactions. As such, the term "sales pitch" is misleading, because your goal in a sales meeting should be to collect even more information than you provide. Try to determine which features of your product the customer believes will most benefit his or her business, which features they need that your product lacks, what competing products they are interested in and why, etc. Also find out how the purchasing decision will be made, by whom, and when—information which is critical in order to qualify your lead.

Qualify Leads

In addition to getting important feedback about your own business, the questions you ask potential customers will allow you to determine whether they are a "qualified" lead, meaning they are a customer that has a need that you can solve and is ready to buy. In order to qualify a lead and place them in the category of a buyer that is worth spending substantial immediate time on, determine the following:

- Does their budget allow for the purchase?

- Does the person you are speaking to have the authority to make a purchase decision?

- Do they have a need that your product can fill?

- Will they make a purchase in the near future?

If the answer to any of these questions is no, you have to question how much of your time is worth spending on this potential customer. Remember that you can't push your products on a customer who isn't ready or who is unable to buy. Spend your time on the deals that are real, and with the people who can close those deals.

Educate the Right Persons

In order to truly determine whether you have identified a qualified lead, you need to track down two people within every organization, or family unit for that matter, that you are selling to. The first is the person who sees the need for your product and the second is the person with the authority to buy. Often they will be one and the same person, and once you have identified them, you need to educate them about your products and your business.

Sell Your Strong Points

When speaking to your potential customer, remember two related things: don't oversell, and focus on the most important benefits that your products will provide to your customer. To do so, you must first listen to the answers your customer gives to the questions you ask, making sure you fully understand the specific problem they need solved. A customer may have a long list of needs, but there is usually one key concern that will get the person to buy. Once you have identified what they are really buying, educate them on your value proposition—the benefits your product offers that solves that problem better than the competition. It is more important to sell your prospective customer on the principal benefits your products or services provide them, rather than the many smaller features that adorn your products or services. In doing so, don't oversell—educate. Aggressive sales tactics are almost always counterproductive.

Eliminate Objections

In almost every sales situation, you will have to deal with a potential customer's objections to making a purchase. Some objections will provide valuable information that allows you to make important changes to your product, pricing, and messages. The others are simply hurdles you must leap to close the sale. The best salespersons are those who can identify, understand, and overcome a potential customer's objections to buying their product. They do not accept vague reasons not to buy, but rather probe and zero in on the real reason, and then use that information to offer up a solution, thus eliminating the objection. Ask for specifics and work towards a win-win solution. As you get more experience making sales calls, you'll become familiar with different objections. Keep a log of common objections and ways you have successfully overcome them. This will be useful both at present and in the future, when it comes time to train your sales team.

Price Appropriately

Some of the most common objections that must be overcome involve cost. The best way to overcome those objections is to price your product appropriately and educate your customer on the value they will receive. If potential customers point out that your particular product or service is more expensive than your competitor's product, don't be defensive, walk them through the advantages you offer and the added value you provide. Keep in mind that while a low price may attract some customers who care only about price, it can also dilute the value of your product or service. So before lowering your price to win a deal, calculate the return on investment ("**ROI**") your potential customer will receive by using your product (you can find ROI spreadsheets to do this).

Ask for the Sale and Follow Up

Many founders with no sales experience are afraid to step up and directly ask for the sale out of fear of appearing overly aggressive and losing the customer. Set aside that fear and ask for the business. After all, closing the sale is the reason you are there. Afterwards, follow up as often as necessary. Do so without being obnoxious, but do so until you get a clear answer.

Create a Sales Process

Your goal should be to develop a sales strategy and process that you can teach others as you grow and scale your organization. In order to do so, track as much data as you can. This includes calls and emails, connections to decision makers, qualified leads, closed deals and times to close, the deal value and returns. Systems like Salesforce.com come highly recommended for these purposes. The goal should be to codify all of the knowledge you gain from your start-up sales and use it to establish standard operating procedures and train your sales team going forward.

Building a Sales Force

At some point after launching your business, you will determine that you've had enough customer contact and received enough feedback to properly align your product with the needs of your customers. In addition, you will have had the time to refine your sales strategy and put in place a scalable sales process. That will be the time to hire your initial sales personnel.

If done properly, adding salespeople can free you up to spend time and energy on other tasks, as well as result in increased sales by expanding your pipeline of leads and creating the bandwidth necessary to qualify those leads and close sales. But always remember, your sales team will be responsible for more than just generating revenue—they will be the persons with the most direct and frequent contact with your customers. Therefore, hiring the wrong salespersons, handing them the wrong strategy, or using an ineffective and/or un-scalable process could actually damage both your brand and your sales.

Hiring the Right People

Before hiring your first salesperson, you need to determine exactly what you want them to do, and that will depend on the nature of your business. For example, if you are an enterprise software company, you will want each salesperson to generate qualified leads, meet frequently with potential customers to demonstrate your product and educate them on its benefits, receive feedback and deliver it to your product development team, and close deals—basically everything we spoke about in the previous section. However, if you are strictly in the e-commerce business, you may only need your salespeople to respond to customer inquiries and take orders.

Once you've created a job description, next imagine your ideal salesperson for that position, including his or her personality, experience, energy level, reputation, and abilities. Think of the specific qualities to look for, such as intelligence, creative thinking ability, communication and listening skills, the ability to identify and solve problems, and the willingness to accept responsibility and follow-through. In addition, all customers want sales people who understand their needs, understand the product or service, take the time to listen, and can trust that what they're telling them is being properly communicated to your office. So when hiring salespeople, put yourself in your customer's shoes, and ask whether you would want to work with and buy from this person.

But it's not just your customers' needs that must be served by your sales force. Once you stop selling personally, you will need people you can rely on to perform the tasks that you were previously performing—primarily gathering valuable feedback. This means your sales people must know what kind of questions to ask and in what manner to ask them. Otherwise, you will be in the dark about what your customers' evolving needs may entail.

One other thing to consider is that the type of salesperson you require will change as your business grows—the skills to be successful at a large company are very different than those who would work well at a start-up. At the beginning, you need someone who is able to perform in a less-structured environment and still get qualified leads, close deals, and keep customers happy. In addition, early-stage selling is much more "educational" than process driven. But this means you need somebody comfortable working with a lack of a defined process.

Later, as the business scales, you will want to add more process-oriented people who understand the importance of following your standard operating procedures and can utilize those defined sales systems to great benefit. Ideally, at the outset you will find people who can do both—and they may well become the superstars of your organization.

Compensation

By nature, good salespersons are high-energy, highly motivated people. But the fact is that money is what motivates them the most, and if you want to attract good people and get good results, you will have to incentivize them properly. Commission plans and financial incentives based on sales success are standard parts of sales compensation packages. However, maintain your ability to create metrics that align with your goals and make sense for your company.

Territories

A sales territory is a segment of your market that you've assigned to a salesperson. While a sales territory is usually composed of a geographic area, it should really be thought of as a group of customers and created with an emphasis on customer type. Be careful, few things in business are as potentially problematic as the divvying up of sales territories. You want everyone to feel they've been treated fairly, while at the same time making the most of everyone's individual skills and talents. That means you don't have to divide everything equally.

Measuring Productivity

Once you have a sales force, it is critical that you have the ability to evaluate their performance, and the best measure when it comes to evaluating a sales force is sales productivity. Dividing the volume of sales by the number of salespeople on staff will give you an average sales productivity figure and let you know how the average salesperson in your organization is doing. More useful, though, is to know how each individual salesperson is doing compared to the average. This will tell you whether you have a few productive people who are doing most of the heavy lifting, or whether everybody is pulling their weight.

In addition, keep in mind that sales productivity involves more than simply generating sales revenue. If your sales force creates good volume but does so at the cost of customer retention due to poor relations or service, or if they experience large numbers of returns, then their productivity numbers may be misleading.

Hiring a Sales Manager

Ultimately, you will need to hire a manager to lead your sales team, and this requires an additional skill set that many pure salespeople don't possess. In fact, the best salespersons often do not make good sales managers.

A good sales manager has to be able to:

- Oversee salespeople

- Develop sales strategies and plans

- Set targets for the sales team

- Monitor sales performance

- Personally handle key customers

- Prepare sales reports and other reports

- Implement and manage a scalable sales process

A great sales manager needs to get a team of people to be able to follow a sales process methodically and with enthusiasm. Look for someone with experience both selling and managing—as first time managers normally go through a teething phase that is hard on the organization.

Sales Agents

The best salespersons often demand hefty salaries and bonuses. For this reason, and to expand the reach of the sales force as broad and as deep as possible, many companies contract with outside agents to sell their products. This provides many of the benefits of an in-house sales team, while keeping the costs variable rather than fixed (no guaranteed salaries and benefits). It also minimizes the difficulties of reducing sales staff when necessary, or replacing those who are underperforming, and to some extent the cost of doing so as well.

Sales agents are legally authorized to act on the company's behalf within a set of defined parameters. As a result, the agent can take orders and make agreements regarding price and delivery on behalf of the company in the same way that an internal sales person could. However, the agent is not an employee, and is typically paid only in the form of a commission on products sold.

A key issue with sales agents is whether they will be granted exclusive rights to their territories. If they are, you may want to require them to meet minimum sales targets, or at least use best efforts to do so.

Because an agency arrangement specifically authorizes a sales agent to act in the name of the company (as opposed to a distributor, which acts and contracts in its own name), it is extremely important to select agents as carefully as you hire employees. Even if an agent takes actions that he or she has not been given specific authority by the company to perform, such as giving payment terms to a customer that are more favorable than company policy allows, the agent may have "apparent authority" in the eyes of the customer and the law, and the company may be liable to comply with the terms the agent agreed to.

Although it's possible to build indemnification provisions into the related agency agreement to cover this type of scenario, the right to indemnification and the ability to collect are two entirely different things, especially when it comes to individual sales agents. So choose reliable agents, and prepare your company's sales agency agreements with care.

Distribution

The ultimate goal of all your product development, marketing, and sales efforts will be to get your product into the hands of the end user, because it is the end user who will drive product demand. You can have the best product in the world and thousands of eager buyers, but if you can't get your product to your customers where and when they want to buy, none of it has any meaning. While direct sales are one way to accomplish this goal, it is not the only or necessarily the best way to do so. Your strategy should be to sell to the person or organization in the distribution channel that will best deliver your product to the end user.

A distribution channel is the chain of individuals and organizations involved in getting a product or service from the producer to the consumer. There are many factors to consider when selecting the appropriate distribution channel for a given product. You need to fully understand who it is you are planning to market to and select distribution routes that will make the most sense for those targets.

Depending on the type of product your start-up offers, the best distribution channel may be obvious, or you may have multiple viable routes to choose from. Keep in mind, however, that while increasing the number of ways in which a consumer can find your product has the potential to increase sales, it also creates complexities that can make distribution management difficult and costly. In addition, the longer the distribution channel, the less profit you might get from the sale.

In addition to direct sales, the basic distribution alternatives are:

- Wholesalers

- Distributors

- OEM (Original Equipment Manufacturer)

- Manufacturer's Representatives

- Online Sales

As opposed to a sales agent, a distributor buys products from the manufacturer, stores them, and resells them to retailers, end users, or customers. Most distributors also provide marketing, technical support, and other services that benefit the supplier. The strength of your distribution network can make or break your business, and it is often more effective and efficient to have distribution performed by third parties that are familiar with the local market and close to the customers. This will especially be the case when you are selling products outside of your home state, or the United States for that matter.

It also makes sense to hire businesses that specialize in distribution because they will have the infrastructure and systems in place to most efficiently get your product in the hands of your customers, and will often be responsible for marketing in their assigned region as well. In addition, distributors will be responsible for warehousing and shipping and will take on credit risk for uncollectible accounts receivable.

Distributors need to make a profit as well, however, so in return for shouldering these responsibilities the distributor may request preferable terms for the purchase of your product. In addition, the distributor might demand exclusive rights to the territory they cover, which will add a whole new level of negotiation when it comes to the distribution agreement.

In fact, many of the most important parts of a distribution agreement will be driven by whether or not exclusive rights are granted. These clauses include the efforts the distributor must make to sell your products, the territory covered by the agreement, and the termination provisions. In an exclusive distribution deal, you will want to clearly spell out the marketing and distribution efforts that you require from the distributor, the level of organization it must maintain, and minimum sales targets for the area covered. You do not want to get locked into an exclusive arrangement with a distributor who is either not using its best efforts to promote your product or who is simply not up to the task, so the default, cure, and termination provisions are very important.

In addition, the territory covered by the distribution agreement should be specifically defined, because you don't want to end up in breach of another exclusive distribution agreement if one distributor strays into the territory of another. You also don't want a distributor with insufficient reach attempting to sell your products where it cannot provide the appropriate level of customer service. On the other hand, the distributor will want the ability to "cure" any failure to meet minimum sales targets as long as it is using its best efforts to meet the goals.

It is very important to thoroughly investigate a distributor and the local market before any distribution agreement is signed. In many respects, the distributor will be the face of your company with respect to your customers, and the distributor's reputation will become your reputation. Make sure your distributors have the business skills and resources to represent your company well and deliver on their promises to customers.

Exotic Universe, Inc.

Because Exotic Universe, Inc. will be primarily an online business, it will not require in-person sales pitches to most customers. However, Cindy McKay intends to generate additional revenue through direct sales to two very different types of businesses. The first will be art galleries and dealers. Cindy intends to select the cream of the crop from the artwork she sources overseas and market them to these customers. This will require her to get out there and sell using the techniques outlined in this chapter, but it will also allow her to get a constant stream of feedback about what potential customers are looking for and develop valuable contacts within the art industry. In addition, Cindy intends to develop a B2B source of revenue by targeting larger online retailers who offer diverse product lines that include artwork. In this case, Cindy will not only be looking for current qualified leads, she will be looking to develop a list of contacts and form relationships that may pay bigger dividends in the future, when she branches out into handicraft items such as jewelry and home décor. While she has decided for strategic reasons not to include these items in the launch of her initial business, she will still be developing relationships with artisans. If she can land even one contract with a large retailer, it could provide consistent cash flow that would greatly support her product lines, reduce the amount of additional capital she will need, and allow her to expand much more quickly.

Where Cindy will really have to use her sales skills and efforts, however, is at the other end of the supply chain. Her primary job will be to travel overseas and convince artists to sell their artwork through Exotic Universe, Inc. on an exclusive basis. This will be no easy task. She must sell them on her vision for the company and convince them to list their artwork in her online catalog, forsaking other opportunities. The supply arrangements have to be exclusive, because Cindy cannot have customers order pieces that turn out to have been sold elsewhere. She will also want the artwork to be sold on a commission basis as well, so she does not have to purchase and store inventory. This brings up one of the trickiest aspects of Cindy's business model—distribution. Her main vehicle will be direct to customers, but the challenge will be the logistics of physically getting the artwork from the supplier to the customer as quickly and cheaply as possible. Cindy's instincts tell her to demand that the artists allow her to ship paintings in bulk to the United States and hold them there on consignment. However, this will be a very difficult sell. She will have to convince the artists that creating a worldwide market for their products is worth the risk and give them assurances their artwork is safe in her hands. At minimum, she will need trusted local representatives to maintain good relations with artists in the countries where she sources artwork. Her business depends on working these supply and distribution issues out as efficiently as possible. Once again, Cindy's relationship skills will be a key to her business success.

CHAPTER 15:
INTANGIBLE VALUE

Chapter

15

CHAPTER 15

INTANGIBLE VALUE

Securing and Protecting Intellectual Property Rights

Intellectual property rights allow you to legally protect the inventions, trade names, brands, logos, written material, software, and the like that you create for your business. The legal protections come in the form of patents, trademarks, and copyrights, all of which allow the owner to prevent another person from using the work created and sue for damages if unauthorized use occurs.

These rights can be very valuable, so in operating your business it is important to first understand what intellectual property rights you have, and then take the necessary steps to secure, protect, and enforce them. Conversely, you should become aware of the intellectual property rights held by others in your line of business. If you fail to do so and inadvertently violate the patent, trademark, or copyright of another person, you may find yourself in receipt of a "cease and desist letter" demanding that you to stop using a brand or machine that has become an important part of your business, not to mention facing a claim for significant damages for infringement.

Some intellectual property rights require government registration and approval to be enforceable, while others do not. To receive a patent on an invention, a patent application meeting the appropriate tests and requirements must be filed and approved by the United States Patent and Trademark Office ("**USPTO**"). Otherwise, inventions can only be protected to the extent they remain confidential trade secrets.

Trademarks can in theory be protected without government registration under state unfair competition laws and common law prohibitions against "passing off"—the misleading use of a name, brand, etc. to make the consumer believe that the product being offered originates from someone who has previously developed goodwill in the trademark. However, enforcement of federally registered trademarks is much easier and more effective, and there is significantly more value in a registered trademark.

Copyrights also do not require government registration. In fact, a copyright is automatically created as soon as a copyrightable work such as literature, computer code, art, music, or video is reduced to a tangible form by its author. However, as with trademarks, there are definite benefits to the federal registration of copyrighted material.

In order for a patent to be issued on an invention or for a trademark or copyright to receive federal registration, the created work must meet the appropriate legal test and not fall within one of its exceptions. In these areas of intellectual property law, this is an extremely complicated subject and often requires the advice of legal counsel. Don't assume you can glance at the legal requirements and assume you understand their implications. They are often not as simple as they appear.

In addition, once an intellectual property right is created, it must be maintained and enforced to keep its value. Certain rights such as patents require periodic maintenance fees or they will lapse, and trademarks must be put to use within a certain time frame and not abandoned by continued non-use after registration. Time, money, and effort must also be spent policing potential infringements and following up with letters, negotiations, and possible legal actions. In addition, if you are planning on selling your product outside of the United States, you will have to think about filing patent applications and trademark registrations in other countries as well.

All of this effort and expense is often worthwhile, however, because intellectual property rights may become one of your business's most valuable and easily exploitable assets. The value of intellectual property rights is not only in their usefulness to your business. They can be sold and licensed as well, often for considerable amounts of upfront money or downstream royalties that can supplement your business revenues. As a result, your intellectual property will increase the value of your company, increase the collateral available when seeking bank financing, and provide an asset that can be exploited in joint ventures and other strategic relationships.

Therefore, to identify and maximize the potential value of your intellectual property, when establishing a new business you should analyze all of the intellectual property that your business intends to use and assess whether it is eligible for patent, trademark, or copyright protection. This means you should look at all of the technology and machines, brand names and logos, written materials and software that will be used in your business, and develop a plan of action to ensure your right and ability to protect those assets. Then each time a similar item is added to your business, perform the same analysis. Conversely, you should analyze all of those same items of intellectual property and make sure that they do not violate the rights of another person or business.

Finally, it is important to take adequate steps to protect your trade secrets, know-how, and other confidential information that provide your business with a competitive advantage. For example, there may be reasons not to file a patent application on a process you developed to manufacture your product, but it is still extremely valuable as long as it has not been disclosed to the public. By keeping access to that secret process restricted to persons who have a clear duty to maintain its confidentiality, you can still protect the asset, restrict its use outside your business, and exploit its value by selling or licensing it to third parties. However, if the process is made available to the public, whether intentionally or accidentally, the commercial value in that process could be severely depleted.

We'll now take a closer look at the major forms of intellectual property rights—patents, trademarks, copyrights, and trade secrets—including how to secure, protect, maintain, and enforce those rights, as well as the methods for maximizing their value.

Patents

A patent is a property right granted by the U.S. government to an inventor to exclude others from making, using, offering for sale, or selling the invention throughout the United States, or importing the invention into the United States, for a specified period of time. So if you have invented a machine that harnesses solar power and uses it to convert straw into gold, and you are then issued a patent on the invention, you can prevent anyone else from using the machine in any way. Importantly, this includes someone who arrives at the same invention on their own, completely independent of your work.

Unfortunately, preparing a patent application is an extremely complex process that requires the ability to thoroughly understand the science or technology involved in the invention. In addition, it requires the ability to describe the invention in a manner that is both specific and clear enough to satisfy the patent examiner of its uniqueness and broad enough to adequately protect the invention from use by others. In addition, the patent application will require you to publicly disclose the details of your invention after 18 months, and in the end there is no guarantee that a valid patent will be issued.

However, if a patent is issued, you will be able to prevent any competitor from using your invention for a period of 14-20 years, depending on the type of patent you receive, and in most cases will have an asset that will increase the value of your business and that can be licensed out for royalties.

The first question you need to answer in deciding whether to try and obtain a patent on an invention is whether it is even patentable. So what constitutes a patentable invention? The short answer is that any process, machine, article of manufacture, composition of matter, or improvement of any of the above, is patentable if it is:

- Useful

- New/Novel

- Non-Obvious

To be "useful," an invention must have the potential to be applied in a product or process for making a product—it cannot be simply a theory that has no practical use. The requirement that the invention is "new" means that no one else has created the invention and either publicly written about it or demonstrated it, meaning there is no "prior art" available or "prior use" of the invention. Finally, the mandate that an invention be "non-obvious" means the invention must be different enough from what has been used or described before such that it is not obvious to a person having ordinary skill in the area of technology related to the invention.

On the face of it, this all sounds fairly straightforward. But determining what inventions are useful, new, and non-obvious, and describing an invention in a way that the USPTO will agree that this is the case, is one of the most complicated areas of the law and requires specialized technical and legal expertise. This is why filing a patent application is almost always a time-consuming and expensive process.

Therefore, before you even begin to prepare a patent application, you should conduct a thorough "patent search" in order to determine as definitively as possible that there is no prior use or prior art with respect to your invention. Patent searching is a difficult, learned skill, and so it's a good idea to retain an experienced attorney or patent agent to conduct the search.

If your search does not turn up any results that would preclude the invention from being patented, the next question is whether you will receive priority from the USPTO with respect to any other inventor who may be out there. In the past, U.S. patent law was based on a "first to invent" system, meaning that the person who could prove they invented the article first would receive priority. But that changed dramatically on September 16, 2011, when the United States patent system received a major overhaul in the form of the America Invents Act ("**AIA**").

The AIA was implemented in several phases and ushered in many substantive changes. The most significant change took effect on March 16, 2013, when the United States joined the rest of the developed world in becoming a "first to file" country. This means that the first inventor to file a patent application has priority, rather than the first person to invent. As a result, an inventor who does not take prompt action to protect his or her invention faces a higher risk that a later inventor will end up with the patent.

One relatively cheap and easy way to win this "race to the USPTO" is to file what is called a "provisional" patent application. A provisional application allows the establishment of an early effective filing date without a formal patent claim or many of the other details required to receive a patent. The provisional application is not examined—you cannot obtain a patent through this filing alone—and automatically lapses twelve months after filing. During that period, you must file a non-provisional application, which includes a large amount of information and which will be examined by the USPTO.

Among other things, a non-provisional patent application must include a detailed description of the invention, and the process of making and using the invention, in full, clear, concise, and exact terms. The description must also distinguish the invention from other inventions, and it must be sufficient so that any person of ordinary skill in the pertinent art, science, or area in question could make and use the invention without extensive experimentation.

Most importantly, a non-provisional application must have at least one claim specifying exactly what the inventor or inventor regards as the invention. The claim or claims define the scope of the protection of the patent, and whether a patent will be granted is determined in large measure by the scope of the claims.

The USPTO is the government agency responsible for examining non-provisional patent applications, determining whether a patent should be granted in a particular case, and issuing patents. Patent application fees vary depending on the type of patent application you submit and the way you claim your invention. The basic fees for most patents are:

- The Filing Fee

- The Issue Fee

- The Maintenance Fees (paid $3\frac{1}{2}$, $7\frac{1}{2}$, and $11\frac{1}{2}$ years after a patent is granted)

There are three principal types of patents: utility, design, and plant. A utility patent, by far the most common, is issued for a new and useful process, machine, or manufacture; a design patent is issued for a new design for a manufactured item; and a plant patent protects a distinct and new variety of plant life. Utility and plant patents are granted for a term which begins with the date of the grant and usually ends 20 years after the date you first applied for the patent. Design patents last for 14 years from the date you are granted the patent.

Patent Maintenance and Enforcement

Once a patent has issued on your invention, you will be able to preclude anybody else from using it for the term of the patent. However, you need to maintain the patent by filing the periodic maintenance fees. In addition, you must enforce the patent, as there is no governmental body that will do that for you.

If you identify someone infringing your patent, there are several courses of action available. The first step is often to notify the person or company violating your patent rights and request that they stop immediately. If you wish, you may also attempt to negotiate a license deal with the infringer. If these actions aren't successful, you may be forced to file an infringement suit and ask the court to issue an injunction and an order to destroy infringing products, as well as award your business damages for lost profits.

The most common defenses to a patent infringement claim are that (i) there has been no infringement (because the patent claims do not cover the activity of the third party), and (ii) the patent is invalid (because, for example, there was previously undisclosed prior art). As with the patent application process, patent litigation is often drawn out, complex, and expensive. However, in order to protect the considerable value of a patent, it is often considered a necessary if unpleasant process.

Maximizing Value: How to Sell or License a Patent

After spending a large amount of time and money obtaining, maintaining, and enforcing a patent, it makes sense to get as much value out of that asset as possible. The most obvious way to do this is to exploit the competitive advantage you have obtained by using the patented invention in your business while precluding competitors from doing so in theirs. If you have a patent on a better mousetrap and have the ability to manufacture, market, and sell that mousetrap, then by all means you will want to do so yourself and not give away profits to a middleman.

But in many cases, there may be more value in selling or licensing all or a portion of your patent than in retaining exclusive use for your own business. For example, your business may not have the geographical reach to distribute and sell your patented mousetraps in every foreign market. In this case, you may want to license the patent rights to local companies, or large companies with worldwide manufacturing and distribution capabilities, and receive royalties in return.

In addition, some patents may not add much value to your business but would be very valuable to others. Or you may want to withdraw from your business and sell its assets; or simply sell a specific product line. Under these circumstances, you may want to sell the patent outright so you don't have to worry about maintaining and enforcing it in the future. In addition, the asset buyer may require a patent assignment so that it can control enforcement and licensing in the future.

There may also be times when it makes sense, or be necessary, for your business to buy or license a patent. Your company may be the "local business" that can provide efficient sales and distribution of a foreign company's patented product in the United States. Or if patented complementary technology would improve the efficiency of your manufacturing process, you may want to license that technology. You may also want to buy the assets of a business that include a patent.

Finally, you may find that certain patents give you the opportunity to team up with other companies holding complementary technology or capabilities. Here it may make sense to form a joint venture that creates synergies and increases the value of both companies' intellectual property.

Licensing a Patent

Licensing a patent is much more complicated than a simple assignment. In fact, a patent license agreement could be one of the most complex agreements any company has to negotiate. But a well-planned and executed patent licensing strategy can provide the owner of a patent with the best of all worlds: the ability to receive substantial revenues from a patent without having to build extra manufacturing, distribution, and sales capacity, while at the same time maintaining ownership and control. Licensing also allows the patent owner to select more than one licensee based on their ability to exploit a given territory and/or type of patented product.

What makes a patent license so complex is also what makes it appealing: it begins with a clean slate upon which any conceivable form of deal can be negotiated. Some of the open-ended issues that can be discussed include whether all or only a portion of the claims covered by the patent will be licensed, what territory will be covered, what field of use will be covered, what level of exclusivity will be granted, and how royalties will be determined.

Trademarks

A trademark is a word, phrase, symbol, and/or design that identifies and distinguishes the source of the products of one party from those of others, while a service mark identifies and distinguishes the source of a service. The term "trademark" is often used to refer to both trademarks and service marks.

Trademarks include names, brands, logos, designs, shapes, and sometimes even colors. The goodwill associated with a trademark can be one of the most valuable assets a business possesses, and the use of the same or similar trademark by a competing business can significantly dilute its value. That's why most well-known companies go to extreme lengths to protect their trademarks.

You can develop rights to a trademark in one of two ways:

- By being the first to use the trademark in commerce—conferring limited protection under state common law

- By being the first to register the trademark with the USPTO— conferring broad protection under federal law

"Use of a trademark in commerce" means the actual sale of a product to the public with the trademark attached. Under these circumstances, protection of the trademark is limited to the geographic area in which the product is being sold or could be expected to be sold. If you claim common law rights to use a trademark, you can attach a "TM" or "SM" to notify the public of your claim.

The best way to protect a trademark is to register it with the USPTO. This gives you the right to use the trademark nationwide and prohibit others from doing so. However, to the extent that your trademark is already being used by others within a specific geographic area when it is registered, then the prior user retains the right to use the trademark within that geographic area, and you get the right to use it everywhere else.

In order to receive protection, a trademark must be "distinctive," meaning it must be capable of identifying the source of a particular good. There are four categories used in determining whether a trademark is distinctive:

- Arbitrary or Fanciful

- Suggestive

- Descriptive

- Generic

Arbitrary or Fanciful

An arbitrary or fanciful trademark is one that bears no logical relationship to the underlying product. Arbitrary or fanciful trademarks are inherently capable of identifying an underlying product and are given a high degree of protection. "Apple" for computers is an example of an arbitrary trademark, and "Reebok" for sport shoes is an example of a fanciful trademark.

Suggestive

A suggestive trademark is one that evokes or suggests a characteristic of the underlying product. Like arbitrary or fanciful marks, suggestive marks are inherently distinctive and are given a high degree of protection. "Coppertone" for suntan lotion is an example of a suggestive trademark.

Descriptive

A descriptive trademark is one that directly describes a characteristic or quality of the underlying product. Unlike arbitrary or suggestive marks, descriptive marks are not inherently distinctive and are protected only if they have acquired "secondary meaning." A descriptive mark acquires secondary meaning when the consuming public primarily associates that trademark with a particular producer, rather than the underlying product. "Vision Center" for an optics store is an example of a descriptive trademark.

Generic

A generic term is one that describes the general category to which the underlying product belongs. Generic terms are not protected by trademark law because they are not distinctive, i.e. they are associated with a type of product rather than the source of the product.

How to Register a Trademark

The first step in protecting a trademark used in your business is to identify the names, brands, logos, etc. that you want to register, as well as the goods and/ or services to which the mark will apply. There is more to this than initially meets the eye. Most businesses have numerous protectable trademarks, and new business owners are often unaware of the trademarks they possess which could in fact be registered.

For example, if you look at the label on a bottle of Johnnie Walker Black Label Whisky, you will find several trademarks: the brand name "Johnnie Walker," the striding man logo, the words "Black Label," and the label design as a whole. All of these trademarks have value because if any were found on the label of another bottle of whisky, the consumer would likely assume that a company affiliated with the producer of Johnnie Walker produced that whisky as well. Without proper registration and enforcement of the trademarks, the competing company could benefit from the goodwill that the owner of the trademark "Johnnie Walker" has established in its brand, as well as dilute the value of that brand at the same time.

The next step towards trademark registration is to conduct a trademark search to make sure that nobody else is using your desired trademark. Trademark searches are generally performed by specialized search companies, such as Thomson & Thomson, or by individual trademark attorneys. While you are not required to use a search firm or attorney, doing so may save you from future costly legal problems by ensuring a comprehensive search of federal registrations, state registrations, and "common law" unregistered trademarks. Once the trademark search is completed, you can obtain additional comfort by employing a trademark attorney to give an "availability opinion" based upon the search. The attorney will review the trademark search and, based upon their experience, give a legal opinion as to whether your mark is available for use and for registration.

When it comes time to file your trademark application, you can do so online using the Trademark Electronic Application System. If you have already used your mark in commerce, you may file under the "use in commerce" basis. If you have not yet used your mark, but intend to use it in the future, you must file under the "intent to use" basis. This means you have a bona fide intent to use the trademark in commerce—i.e. although you have not already used the trademark to market your product, you have taken some initial steps towards doing so.

After receiving your application, the USPTO will conduct a search and will refuse to register your trademark if there is another registered or pending mark similar to yours. The total time for an application to be processed may be anywhere from several months to several years, depending on the basis for filing and the legal issues that may arise in the examination of the application.

The most common reasons the USPTO examiners give for refusing to register a trademark are:

- The trademark is likely to cause confusion with another registered trademark or trademark in a prior application

- The trademark is descriptive of the goods/services it is attached to

- The trademark is a geographic term or a surname

Trademark applicants and registrants are expected to monitor the status of their applications or registrations. You should check the status of your application through the Trademark Status and Document Retrieval system every 3-4 months. If the USPTO has taken any action, you may need to respond promptly.

Once your trademark has been registered by the USPTO, to avoid abandonment you have 6 months to file either a Statement of Use with respect to the goods and services named, or an Extension Request (up to five extension requests are allowed). The trademark registration is valid as long as you timely file all post-registration maintenance documents.

However, the rights to a trademark can be lost through abandonment or lapse in other ways as well. For example, a trademark is abandoned when its use is discontinued with intent not to resume its use. Non-use for three consecutive years is considered prima facie evidence of abandonment.

Trademark rights can also be lost if the trademark is licensed without adequate quality control or supervision by the trademark owner. Similarly, where the rights to a trademark are assigned (legally transferred) to another party without the corresponding sale of any assets, the trademark may be canceled. The rationale for these rules is that in these circumstances the trademark no longer serves its purpose of identifying the goods of a particular provider.

Enforcement of Trademarks

Once you have registered your trademark, no one may use the same or a similar trademark in relation to the same class of goods or services without your permission. While the USPTO attempts to ensure that no other party receives a federal registration for an identical or similar trademark for related goods/services, the owner of a registered trademark is responsible for enforcing the trademark rights and bringing any legal action to stop a party from using an infringing trademark.

You may challenge the unauthorized use of your trademark in several ways, depending on the situation. One option is to sue for trademark infringement, with the standard claim being "likelihood of confusion." In deciding whether consumers are likely to be confused, the courts will typically look to a number of factors, including the proximity of the goods, the similarity of the trademarks, and evidence of actual confusion.

Successful plaintiffs are entitled to a wide range of remedies under federal law, including injunctions against further infringing or diluting use of the trademark. In trademark infringement suits, monetary relief may also be available, including the defendant's profits, damages sustained by the plaintiff, and the costs of the legal action. Damages may be trebled upon the showing of bad faith.

Maximizing Value: Sale or License of a Trademark

Both in order to grow your business and realize its potential, you may want to exploit your trademarks by selling or licensing them to others. Licensing the use of a trademark to companies operating outside of your home region allows you to receive royalty income while at the same time establishing brand awareness in the licensed territories. There may also be times when it makes sense to sell a trademark and capitalize on the value of its underlying goodwill.

Trademark Licensing

Creative trademark licensing can greatly increase a company's revenues, as well as expand its brand identification and sales reach into territories that otherwise would fall outside of its manufacturing and distribution capacity.

Licenses can be granted for a particular country or for a particular product. For example, a U.S. company may hold a registered trademark for "Kennedy's Candies" that covers both a line of hard candy products and a line of soft drinks. If the company has also registered the trademark in England, but does not have the capacity to sell its products in that market, it may want to license the trademark, manufacturing, and distribution rights for its hard candies to one company and the soft drink line to another. This would allow it to find the best possible manufacturer and distributor for each particular product.

In addition to determining which products will be covered by a trademark license, the licensor needs to decide whether to grant an exclusive or non-exclusive license. An exclusive license will receive a much higher royalty rate and will typically motivate a licensee to invest more in terms of advertising and sales support for the licensed product. However, it will preclude the licensor from exploiting its own products in the territory, and if the licensee does not perform up to expectations, the company will lose potential revenue and the damage to its brand may be irreparable.

It is therefore very important when licensing a trademark to choose a licensee that will enhance the value of the brand and give it adequate support, because the ripple effect of the licensee's efforts may extend beyond the territory and the term of the license. As a result, many of the terms included in a trademark license agreement are intended to ensure that the licensee performs up to expectations and maximizes the value of the trademark in the licensed territory.

The "licensed products" in a trademark license agreement are those that can be manufactured and sold using the licensed trademarks. The use of the trademarks to sell any other product, or for any other commercial purpose, will fall outside of the scope of the license and constitute infringement.

Royalties can be calculated in many ways, but the two most common are a percentage of net sales or a set amount per unit sold. In the case of an exclusive license, it is common to have a minimum royalty amount payable on a monthly or quarterly basis in order to make sure that the licensee is using its best efforts to exploit the trademark. The licensor may also specify minimum sales targets, minimum amounts to be spent on promoting the products within the territory, and other mandatory marketing and distribution activities of the licensee.

The provisions that cover protection and use of the trademark, as well as quality control of the underlying products, are vital for several reasons. The most obvious is that the improper use of the trademark and/or failure to meet the trademark owner's quality control standards will diminish the value of the brand and thereby decrease the goodwill underlying the trademark. In addition, if the trademark owner does not closely monitor the manner in which the trademark is used and the quality of the products and materials to which it is applied, the trademark registration may actually be revoked on the grounds that it is likely to mislead the public by not representing a product of consistent quality.

This means that the licensor must include provisions in the trademark license agreement that specify how the trademark will be used with respect to all licensed products, packaging, and marketing material, and give the licensor the right to closely inspect such use and remedy any misuse. One method of setting the appropriate standard for a licensee's use of a trademark is to attach detailed requirements in the form of an appendix to the trademark license agreement.

Copyrights

A copyright provides legal protection for the creator of "original works of authorship," including literary, dramatic, musical, and artistic works. It protects the way an idea is expressed in tangible form, rather than the idea itself. The categories of protected works are viewed broadly under the law. For example, computer programs are considered "literary works."

Persons Who Can Claim a Copyright

Copyright protection exists as soon as a covered work of authorship is created in fixed form. No publication, registration, or additional action is required. At that time, the copyright immediately becomes the property of the author who created the work. Only the author or a person receiving rights from the author can claim a copyright. However, in the case of a "work made for hire," the employer and not the employee is considered to be the author. Under the copyright law, a work prepared by an employee within the scope of his or her employment is considered a work made for hire.

Works Protected by a Copyright/Exclusive Rights under a Copyright

Copyright protection is available to both published and unpublished works. It is important to understand, especially when assigning or licensing a copyright, that a copyright is actually a bundle of rights, with the owner of a copyright having the exclusive right to do and to authorize others to do the following:

- Reproduce the work

- Prepare derivative works

- Distribute copies of the work

- Sell or transfer ownership of the work

- Rent, lease, or lend the work

- Perform or display the work publicly

Material that is not eligible for federal copyright protection includes:

- Titles, names, and slogans

- Works that have not been fixed in a tangible form of expression

- Listings of ingredients or contents

- Ideas, procedures, methods, systems, processes, concepts, principles, discoveries, or devices, as distinguished from a description, explanation, or illustration

- Works consisting entirely of information that is common property and containing no original authorship

Notice of Copyright

The use of a copyright notice is not required under U.S. law. However, a copyrighted work that is published can contain a notice of copyright that includes the copyright symbol © or the word "Copyright," the year of publication, the name of the copyright owner, and the language "All rights reserved." It is a good idea to include this notice on all copyrighted works, because it informs the public that the work is protected by copyright. As a result of such notice, if the work is infringed then the defendant in a lawsuit cannot claim innocent infringement and therefore may be liable for greater damages. The use of the copyright notice does not require advance permission from, or registration with, the U.S. Copyright Office.

Duration of Copyright Protection

A copyrighted work is protected from the moment of its creation until 70 years after the author's death. In the case of "a joint work prepared by two or more authors who did not work for hire," the duration of the copyright is 70 years after the last surviving author's death. For works made for hire, the copyright lasts until 95 years from publication or 120 years from creation, whichever is shorter.

Copyright Registration

Although registration of a copyrighted work is not required, it is definitely a good idea because registration is necessary in order to file a lawsuit for copyright infringement. Registration may be made at any time within the life of the copyright, but registration within specified time periods also provides a presumption of originality and ownership, and allows for the owner to receive remedies such as statutory damages and attorney fees in such a lawsuit. In addition, registration allows U.S. Customs to stop the importation of infringing works.

An application for copyright registration consists of a completed application form, a non-refundable filing fee, and a non-returnable deposit of the work being registered, and you can apply either online or by mail with the U.S. Copyright Office. If the application is accepted, you will receive a certificate of registration.

Transfer of a Copyright

The owner of a copyright may transfer all or a subset of the exclusive rights under the copyright. However, the transfer of exclusive rights is not valid unless it is in writing and signed by the copyright owner. Transfer of a right on a non-exclusive basis does not require a written agreement. A copyright may also be bequeathed by will or pass by intestate succession. The law does not require that a transfer of copyright be recorded in the U.S. Copyright Office, but recordation does provide certain legal advantages and may be required to validate the transfer as against third parties.

Trade Secrets

Because they are not registered with the government, trade secrets are probably the most overlooked aspect of a company's intellectual property portfolio, despite the fact that often they can be the most valuable.

Trade secrets are protected by an assortment of federal and state laws, and the law governing trade secrets varies from state to state. However, a majority of states have adopted a version of the Uniform Trade Secrets Act ("**UTSA**").

There are four important parts to the definition of a trade secret under the UTSA, each of which must be present to invoke "trade secret" protection:

- A "trade secret" must consist of information, which can include technical information or business information (including a formula, pattern, compilation, program, device, method, technique, or process)

- The information must derive economic value (actual or potential) from the fact that it is secret

- The information cannot be generally known to the public, industry competitors, or others who could realize economic value from its disclosure or use

- The information must be treated as a secret by its owner, who must exercise reasonable efforts to maintain its secrecy

Technical information trade secrets may include plans, designs, patterns, processes, formulas, methods and techniques for manufacturing, and computer software programs or code. They also may include "negative information," e.g. designs that didn't work. Business information trade secrets may include financial information, cost and pricing information, internal market analyses, customer lists, and business and marketing plans.

Trade secrets exist as long as they remain secret. However, once previously secret business information is released or otherwise becomes generally known, it loses any trade secret protection that it might have enjoyed.

What constitutes "reasonable efforts to maintain its secrecy" depends on the circumstances, but normally would include such efforts as advising employees of the existence of a trade secret, limiting access to trade secret information on a "need to know basis," using security passwords for computer files and programs containing trade secrets, requiring employees to sign confidentiality agreements, including a strong trade secret policy statement in employee handbooks, and marking trade secret documents "confidential" and keeping them under lock.

In addition, requiring outside contractors, visitors, and other people who may come into contact with trade secret information to sign non-disclosure agreements, which put the parties on notice that certain information is considered confidential and provide a contractual duty to keep the covered information secret, can help to ensure that the information retains its trade secret status.

It is generally illegal to "misappropriate" trade secrets owned by someone else. Under the UTSA, the definition of misappropriation can be broken down into three types of prohibited conduct:

- wrongful acquisition

- wrongful use

- wrongful disclosure

Information that is "readily ascertainable" by proper means, such as availability in trade journals, reference books, or published materials, is normally not protectable as a trade secret. In addition, independently developed information and reverse engineering, which means starting with the known product and working backward to find the method by which it was developed, are not considered to have been misappropriated under trade secret law.

Under the UTSA, remedies for trade secret misappropriation come in the form of both monetary damages and injunctive relief. For example, trade secret owners may:

- Obtain an injunction prohibiting actual or threatened misappropriation

- Recover compensatory damages for actual loss caused by the misappropriation

- Recover compensatory damages for the defendant's unjust enrichment

- Obtain payment of a reasonable royalty

- Recover punitive damages if the misappropriation is "willful and malicious"

- Recover attorneys' fees for willful and malicious misappropriation

In addition, state laws governing unfair business practices may also impose liability for improper use of confidential information. And finally, a slew of state and federal criminal statutes directly or indirectly prohibit trade secret misappropriation.

Assignment of Intellectual Property to the Business

One of the most common and biggest mistakes that many entrepreneurs forming a new company make is not making sure the relevant intellectual property is assigned to the business, both at the start-up phase and going forward.

Among other problems, this can result in the nightmare "lost founder" scenario, where after a company becomes successful, someone who worked on the business but left early on in the process returns to claim an interest in the company's intellectual property assets—and demands huge payments as a result. It could also result in the company not even owning the intellectual property the company's business is based on.

If intellectual property is being created prior to the incorporation of the business, and everyone involved does not sign a contract assigning their intellectual property rights to the corporation when it is formed, then this is exactly what could happen. In addition, if you plan on raising money from angel or venture investors, be aware that they will require that you trace and prove ownership in your key intellectual property assets. Therefore, it is critical that when starting your new business you take the following steps:

First, at the time of incorporation have all of the founders sign an agreement assigning all of their intellectual property rights associated with the business to the corporation. This includes both intellectual property that he or she created in the past, and that he or she may create in the future. In many cases, the founders will make this assignment in connection with the stock purchase agreement under which they are issued their founders' shares. In addition, check to see if government filings are required to perfect the assigned rights in the corporation.

Second, make sure that any independent contractors doing work for the business— including friends giving a helping hand getting the business started—also contractually assign any intellectual property created in the course of that work to the corporation. Make sure that every such person is paid something for their efforts, so that the consideration necessary for a binding contract of assignment is present.

Third, have every employee sign an intellectual property assignment agreement before starting their new job. This agreement should state that any intellectual property they create in the course of their work for the company or using any company resources is assigned to the company.

Do not take these issues lightly—your entire business may depend on it. If your company is at all reliant on intellectual property, then it is highly recommended that you retain an experienced intellectual property attorney who can advise you on setting up a program to protect these assets.

Exotic Universe, Inc.

If Cindy McKay runs her business properly and executes her branding strategy the way she has mapped it out in her marketing plan, one of her company's most valuable assets will be her trademark/trade name. As mentioned briefly in Chapter 6, however, choosing a name for her business turns into a very frustrating experience. Cindy thinks she has it nailed with ExoticArt.com, but her attorneys quickly rain on that parade. "Exotic Art," they explain, is a descriptive term that stands almost no chance of being registered as a federal trademark, and will not even be protectable under state law. Adding ".com" to the mark does not help, as the courts ruled during the dot.com boom that this was also descriptive and did not turn a generic or descriptive phrase into a protectable one. So Cindy sets about finding a new name that she knows she can protect, register, and turn into an identifiable brand. Surely that will not be difficult? But it is. Cindy goes through dozens of name combinations related to global art, but every name she comes up with is already in use in some manner. In addition, names related specifically to art are too limiting, and would not be appropriate when she expands into other product lines. The best way to do find a clearly protectable trademark is to come up with a fanciful name, but doing so will require even more branding effort to establish name recognition with customers. Finally, Cindy decides on the name "Exotic Springs." This name, she feels, connotes that the source of her art is exotic foreign countries, which she wants from her trademark. In addition, the name is original and unique enough to build a brand around, and it is flexible enough to encompass future expansion into different product lines. However, when she tests "Exotic Springs" out on some friends, many associate the word "exotic" with "erotic," and say they would expect the website to sell racy paintings. This could potentially turn off some of the customers Cindy was trying to attract, but she feels she is willing to take that risk. But others say that "springs" made it sound like a mattress company, which would be amusing to Cindy if this weren't such a serious issue for her business. Together, these concerns sour Cindy on the name, and she decides to keep looking. This time, she settles on Exotic Universe, which her attorney David tells her is suggestive rather than descriptive, and which is cleared by the trademark search process. Having decided on a name, Cindy instructs David to file an intention to use application with the USPTO at the same time he reserves the corporation name with Delaware. She also instructs him to purchase the domain name exoticuniverse.com on her behalf. During their discussions, David also advises Cindy that if she intends to sell her products overseas, she should think about protecting her trademark in targeted foreign countries as well. This is an additional expense, but Cindy decides to make sure her trademark and logo are secure in Europe and Japan in addition to the United States. After all, she intends to build her brand into something instantly recognizable to everyone around the world.

CHAPTER 16:
BY THE NUMBERS

Chapter

16

CHAPTER 16

BY THE NUMBERS

Accounting and Financial Planning

Every company, no matter how small, needs an organized accounting
system. What that consists of—now take a deep breath—is a set of methods,
procedures, and controls designed to gather, record, classify, summarize,
analyze, and present accurate and timely data that allows management to
prepare financial statements, understand the company's financial position and
results, properly forecast and budget for future operations, make good strategic
and tactical decisions, and file accurate tax returns.

Got all of that? If it sounds like a mouthful of information, it is. But every
word and clause is an important component of your accounting system and
your overall business operations. Let's break that opening paragraph down, and
it will be easy to see how all the pieces fit together.

An Accounting System consists of:

- Methods

- Procedures

- Controls

Designed to:

- Gather

- Record

- Classify

- Summarize

- Analyze

- Present

Accurate and timely data allowing:

- Preparation of Financial Statements

- Understanding of Financial Position and Results

- Proper Forecasting and Budgeting

- Good Management Decision Making

- Accurate Tax Reporting

Fortunately, good accounting software is available that can perform many of the basic bookkeeping and accounting functions. But don't make the mistake of thinking you can buy accounting software without knowing anything at all about financial accounting because the software will do everything for you. First, you need enough knowledge to choose the right software for your business, and then you need enough knowledge to use the software in the proper way—if you don't understand what you're putting into the software and how it works, you won't get good results from using the software. In order to properly utilize even the best accounting software, or to manage accounting staff that are using the software on your behalf, you need to understand the basics of how an accounting system works. And in order to take advantage of the information generated and make good strategic and financial decisions, at minimum you need to understand how to read financial statements and how to create a budget.

We'll start with some accounting nuts and bolts, and then progress to more high-level strategic matters.

Bookkeeping and Accounting

Contrary to the belief of many new entrepreneurs, bookkeeping and accounting are not the same thing. Bookkeeping is the recording and classifying of all financial transactions pertaining to a business. This includes all sales, expenses, and bank transactions. Accounting, on the other hand, is the process of taking the recorded information and summarizing, analyzing, reviewing, reporting, and interpreting it for the company's management team.

In most businesses, the bookkeepers operate under the chief accountant, who is responsible for setting up and maintaining the company's accounting system and performing the accounting functions. As a start-up, your chief accountant may be a controller, or you may even want to outsource this function. When your business gets larger, however, it will be time to hire a full-blown chief financial officer.

The bookkeeping/basic accounting process consists of the following levels, each of which is a necessary component of the system described in the introduction to this chapter:

- Chart of Accounts

- Source Statements, i.e. receipts

- Journal Entries

- General Ledger Entries

- Trial Balances

- Financial Statements and Reports

Before diving into a description of each component, it's important to understand the foundation of every accounting system, which is called the "Accounting Equation." Everybody has heard the phrase "I've got to balance my books." Well in business, the Accounting Equation is the formula for making sure your books always balance, and that formula is: Assets = Liabilities + Equity.

Assets are what your company owns, such as its inventory and accounts receivables. Liabilities are what your company owes, such as accounts payable and bank loans. What your company owns minus what it owes is the equity that you and your investors have in the business.

Now we'll take a look at the steps that must be taken in order to, in fact, balance your books.

Chart of Accounts

Creating a chart of accounts is the first step in establishing your company's accounting system. There are five general categories on every chart of accounts, and these constitute the five categories of data that an accounting system is designed to keep track of:

- Assets

- Liabilities

- Owner's Equity

- Revenue

- Expenses

Within these categories, there will be many specific "accounts," which collectively will constitute a record of increases and decreases in the amount of specific assets, liabilities, equities, revenues, and expenses. The types of accounts included will depend on the nature of your business—you only need those that will be relevant to recording your particular company's financial transactions. For example, if you sell computer hardware, you will need an inventory account. But if you are in the cleaning business, you may not.

Source Documents

Every time you make a sale or incur an expense, the transaction must be supported by some form of written or computerized record, such as a receipt or cash register record containing the amount, the date, and other relevant information. The source documents are what you use to record your journal entries (discussed below), but they are also your back-up documentation for tax returns. Therefore, any original paper documents should be kept and backed up by scanning them into a computer file for safekeeping.

Journal Entries

The information contained in the source documents is recorded in an accounting journal, which is simply a chronological record of all a company's transactions. Most companies have a general journal and a range of special journals such as a sales journal, cash receipts journal, and cash disbursements journal to take care of recurring transactions. Collectively, they form a detailed record of every financial transaction of your business.

The most common and practical form of making journal entries is called the "double-entry" method of bookkeeping, and this is where the Accounting Equation first comes into play. With a double-entry bookkeeping system, at least two entries are made for each transaction. A debit is made to one account and a credit is made to another account. Debits increase assets and decrease liabilities and equity—they go in the left column of the journal. Credits increase liabilities and equity and decrease assets—they go in the right column.

For example, if you own a supermarket and use $100 cash to purchase twenty gallons of milk to sell, then your cash journal would be credited $100 and your inventory journal would be debited $100. The most important thing to remember is that debits must always equal credits.

This can get confusing, but fortunately many accounting software programs are designed so that you enter each transaction once, and the software program makes the corresponding second entry for you. The program will also perform the next step, posting the journal entries to the general ledger.

General Ledger Entries

After financial transaction entries are made in the appropriate journals, they are posted in the general ledger. The general ledger is the main accounting record for your business. The accounts in the general ledger are based on your chart of accounts and include the main accounts that will be shown in your financial statements such as current assets, fixed assets, current liabilities, long-term liabilities, sales revenue, and each specific expense account. While a journal records transactions as they happen, the general ledger groups transactions according to their type, based on the accounts they affect. Double-entry accounting is also used in the general ledger, with a debit and a credit recorded for each transaction.

Trial Balance

Probably the most useful aspect of double-entry accounting is the requirement that accounting records will always be "in balance." As a result, most accounting errors are automatically exposed by the lack of balance in the debits and credits. Therefore, after posting all financial transactions to the accounting journals and summarizing them in the general ledger, a trial balance is prepared to verify that the debits equal the credits on the chart of accounts. The trial balance is the first step in the "end of the accounting period" process. The trial balance is prepared by adding up all the account balances in your general ledger. The sum of the debit balances should equal the sum of the credit balances. If total debits don't equal total credits, you must track down the errors and correct them.

Cash versus Accrual Accounting

There is no official "right" way to organize your books. As long as your records accurately reflect your business's income and expenses, you will be able to use that information in strategic and financial planning, and the IRS will find them acceptable. Most businesses, however, typically use one of two basic accounting methods in their bookkeeping systems: cash basis and accrual basis.

The cash method is the most simple in that the books are kept based on the actual flow of cash in and out of the business. Income is recorded when it is received, and expenses are reported when they are actually paid. The cash method is used by many sole proprietors and businesses with no inventory. It may be appropriate for a small, cash-based business or a small service company. From a tax standpoint, the cash method is sometimes advantageous for a new business, because earned income which has not yet been received can be put off until the next tax year while expenses are counted right away.

That being said, most businesses use the accrual method of accounting. With the accrual method, income and expenses are recorded as they occur regardless of whether or not cash has actually changed hands. This means that for accounting purposes:

- Revenue earned does not necessarily correspond to the receipt of cash

- Expenses incurred are not necessarily related to the expenditures of cash

- Accounting income for a given period is determined by matching the expenses incurred in that period with the revenues earned in that period

- Income is not the same as cash flow

An example is a sale on credit. The sale is entered into the books when the invoice is generated rather than when the cash is collected. Likewise, an expense occurs when materials are ordered, not when they are actually paid for.

While most businesses use the accrual basis, the most appropriate method for your company depends on your sales volume, whether or not you sell on credit, and your business structure. The accrual method is required if your annual sales exceed $5 million and your venture is structured as a corporation. In addition, businesses with inventory must also use this method. It also is highly recommended for any business that sells on credit, as it more accurately matches income and expenses during a given time period.

Financial Management System

While a good bookkeeping system is important, even more critical is what you do with the numbers in order to establish your methods for financial management and control. Financial Management is the process you use to put your numbers to work to make your business more successful. With a good financial management system, you will know not only how your business is doing financially, but why you have achieved the results you have. And you will be able to use the information generated to make decisions to improve the operation of your business.

Financial Statements and Reports

Financial statements collectively summarize all of the information recorded in the general ledger and present the results of operations and the financial position of the company. At minimum, the financial statements you produce should include the big three: a balance sheet, income statement, and cash flow statement. To manage your company's finances proactively, you should plan to generate financial statements and reports on a monthly basis.

Balance Sheet

The balance sheet provides a snapshot of your company's financial position at a point in time, and does so in a format reflecting the Accounting Equation. It therefore has three major sections: assets, liabilities, and equity. Assets list the total resources of the business, liabilities list claims against the business, and equity lists the amount left over after the claims are deducted from the resources.

The key components of the balance sheet are:

- Current Assets
  These are the assets that can be converted into cash in one year or less. They include cash, accounts receivable, and inventory.

- Fixed Assets
  These are the tangible assets of a business that will not be converted to cash within one year during the normal course of operations. They include land, buildings, equipment, and vehicles.

- Intangible Assets
  These are assets that have no physical properties but still have value. They include intellectual property (such as patents) and goodwill.

- Other Assets
  Some companies include this category of assets in their balance sheet in order to break certain assets, such as life insurance and long-term investments, out from their other asset categories.

- <u>Current Liabilities</u>
  These are the obligations of the business that are due within one year. They include accounts payable, accrued expenses (such as payroll), amounts due on lines of credit, and current amounts due on long-term debt.

- <u>Long-Term Liabilities</u>
  These are the obligations of the business that will not come due for at least one year. The most common long-term liability is bank debt.

- <u>Owner's Equity</u>
  This figure represents the total amount invested by the stockholders plus the accumulated profit of the business.

Note that the excess of current assets over current liabilities is called "net working capital." For most companies, current assets should be twice as much as current liabilities. This is to protect against unexpected bad debts, declines in inventory value, unanticipated liabilities, etc. that could cause the company to become insolvent.

Income Statement

The income statement shows the financial performance and profitability of your company over a specific period of time—it presents the flow of revenues, costs, and expenses through your business during that given period. If you created a balance sheet at the beginning of the specified period and at the end of the period, the income statement would show how you got from the financial position depicted on the first balance sheet to the next.

The income statement is prepared by summarizing the information on revenue and expenses contained in the general ledger. The bottom line of the income statement is net income, meaning the actual profit your business earned during the period reported.

The key components of the income statement are:

- Sales

  This number constitutes the gross revenue generated from the sale of your product, net of any returns and discounts allowed.

- Cost of Goods Sold

  This is the direct cost associated with producing your product. These costs include materials costs, direct factory labor, and factory overhead costs.

- Gross Profit

  Your Gross Profit equals Sales minus Cost of Goods Sold. Here you can see the amount of direct profit generated by the production of your product, before other indirect income and expense items are included.

- Operating Expenses

  These are the selling, general, and administrative expenses incurred in running your business, such as marketing programs, rent, and salaries.

- Operating Profit

  Your Operating Profit equals Gross Profit less Operating Expenses. This tells you the amount of profit you have earned from normal business operations.

- Depreciation

  Depreciation results when a company purchases a fixed asset and expenses it over the entire period of its planned use. Depending on the type of asset, depreciation expense is included either in operating expenses or cost of goods sold.

- Other Income and Expenses

  Other income and expenses report transactions that did not take place occur during the normal course of business. Capital gains income and interest expense on debt are included in this category.

- Net Profit Before Taxes

  This is the earnings of your business before you pay taxes. The amount is calculated by adding/subtracting the amount of Other Income and Expenses to/from Operating Profit.

- Net Profit After Taxes
  This is the "bottom line" earnings of your business—your net income for the period being measured.

Cash Flow Statement

The cash flow statement is one of the most useful and important tools in running your business. This statement shows all of the sources and uses of cash and cash equivalents during the period measured. It also details the overall change in the total of cash and cash equivalents during that period.

Normally, the cash flow statement measures cash flow from three major sources: operating activities, investing activities, and financing activities. In order to do so, the statement is prepared by converting the accrual basis of accounting used for the income statement and balance sheet back to a cash basis.

Once again, two time periods of comparative balance sheets are examined in order to prepare a statement of cash flows, and the statement is divided into four categories:

- Net Cash Flow from Operating Activities
  Operating activities are the daily internal activities of a business that either generate cash or use it. Items contributing to this category include cash collected from customers and cash paid for operating expenses, interest, and taxes.

- Net Cash Flow from Investing Activities
  Investing activities are discretionary investments made by management. These primarily consist of the purchase (or sale) of plant and equipment.

- Net Cash Flow from Financing Activities
  Financing activities are those external sources and uses of cash that affect cash flow. These include sales of common stock, changes in short or long-term loans, and dividends paid.

- <u>Net Change in Cash and Marketable Securities</u>
  The results of the first three categories are then used to determine the total change in cash and marketable securities during the period being measured.

While understanding historical sources and uses of cash is important, even more important is to understand future cash flows so you can plan your operations to grow in an optimum manner without ever running short on cash. Good financial management, therefore, requires the preparation of a budget.

Preparing a Budget

A budget is a detailed financial plan that shows estimated revenues and expenses for a specific period. Properly constructed, it spells out the specific course of action for your business and then compares the intended results with the actual results. It is therefore a method for maintaining control over your finances and making necessary adjustments as the business progresses.

Some business persons question the need for a budget, arguing that the time and effort spent in creating the document does not justify an outcome that can quickly change based on many variables. But budget creation does not have to be as inefficient as many people experience, and budgets do not need to be 100 percent accurate to be beneficial. The bottom line is that every successful business needs a budget in order to plan, manage, and control its finances. The budget allows you to understand both the amounts your business has to spend and the amounts it needs to spend to reach its goals.

You can also use the budget to make strategic adjustments. If your business is either not generating the targeted revenues or spending more than the budgeted expenses, the budget will give you visibility into out how you can reduce expenses or lower profit expectations and adjust accordingly.

A budget should include your revenues, your costs, and your profits and cash flow. Start with sales and/or profits, because this information will drive the rest of your estimates for costs, expenses, and capital expenditures.

Keep in mind that budgeting actually begins with the business planning process. The budget is created to chart a path to accomplishing your strategic goals. Any budget created in a vacuum without being grounded in strategy will be less than useless, it will be detrimental.

The basic components of a budget include:

- Revenues
  Revenue forecasts are the cornerstone of the budgeting process. The main component of forecasted revenues will be from sales, but the forecast should include all sources of revenue for your business. Forecasting revenue is also the most difficult aspect of budgeting, especially for a business in the start-up phase. Clearly identify all assumptions you are making and don't be overly aggressive in your estimations.

- Expenses
  Here you must identify all the costs and expenses that you will have to incur to earn the forecasted revenues. Budgeted expenses can be divided into fixed, variable, and semi-variable costs.

  - Fixed Costs are those expenses that remain the same regardless of the level of sales you achieve. They include rent, salaries, and insurance.

  - Variable Costs are directly related to sales volumes. These include the cost of raw materials and shipping costs.

  - Semi-Variable Costs are fixed costs that can be variable when influenced by volume of business. These can include some salaries and advertising.

- Gross Profit Margin
  This requires an estimate of your cost of your goods sold, which is then subtracted from your forecasted sales revenue.

- Net Profits
  You can either end with the bottom line or begin with it. Many believe it makes sense to begin with the net profit percentage you wish to

achieve and believe is possible, then do a sales forecast, and then create your expense budget to achieve the desired bottom line results. The budgeting process will then flesh out whether this is possible.

Accounting Software

Accounting software is a requirement for almost any sized business these days. Even the cheapest and easiest to use can help you run your business more efficiently, reduce costly errors, and collect and present valuable information about how your business is performing.

The first step in choosing accounting software for your new business is to determine exactly what you need, both from a financial accounting and management perspective. It is critical that you think this through in as much detail as possible. Otherwise, you might find yourself having paid for, and more importantly taken the time to implement and learn, a software package that you soon have to change. This can be an expensive and very disruptive prospect for your business.

There is now a wide range of accounting software products available for small businesses. The options range from basic small business payroll and accounting applications to more full-service business management programs, and both desktop and Web-hosted packages are available.

Factors to consider in choosing accounting software include:

- Required Features

- Size and Nature of Your Business

- Industry-specific Requirements

- Ease of Use

- Training Required

- Customer Support

- Scalability as Your Business Grows

- Ease of Upgrade

- Compatibility with Associated Software (e.g. your accountant and bank's software)

- System Requirements

First, make a list of the features you absolutely need to run your business. Any accounting software that you purchase should give you the ability to input to the general ledger and develop financial statements such as the income statement, balance sheet, and cash flow statement for your business, as well as any additional reports you need to give to your accountant on a monthly, quarterly, and annual basis. In addition, most businesses will require their software to provide applications for:

- Payroll Functions

- Accounts Receivable Tracking

- Accounts Payable Tracking

- Business Tax Reporting

- Budget Preparation

Depending on the nature of your business and industry, you may also want applications that provide:

- Inventory Management

- Sales Tracking

- Customer Relations Management

- Credit Card Payment Support

- Online Banking Support

- Multiple Currency Support

- Time Billing and Tracking

- Customizable Financial Reports

- Job Costing

- E-commerce Support

- Industry-specific Applications

You can begin educating yourself on accounting software options by investigating popular providers such as Intuit (QuickBooks), Sage, and Peachtree, each of which has tiered offerings for different levels of business requirements. Before making your decision on what accounting software to purchase, consult with your accountant, employees who will use the software, and any entity such as your bank whose software needs to be compatible. Also consult with others in the industry about the software needs of their business and the software package they use.

Take your time and be thorough in your approach. You will be relying on your accounting software package to produce all of the financial information you need to properly run and manage your business. It is worth the time and effort to get this right.

Exotic Universe, Inc.

When Cindy McKay first asks Bill whether he feels there would be any difficult accounting issues in setting up her company, he just rolls his eyes. "I'm not even sure where to start," he replies. Then he walks her through some of the issues her accountants will face. With respect to the basic bookkeeping function, they will be required to put in place the proper systems and controls to keep track of expenses being incurred in the same exotic locations that her artwork is created. Somebody will have to accept delivery of the artwork and the payment will have to be made in the local currency. It's possible that foreign bank accounts and even subsidiaries will have to be set up. There will likely be other local expenses incurred, and Cindy and other members of her team will also be incurring overseas travel expenses on a regular basis. At the sales level, a failsafe system for online

274 | ENTREPRENEUR'S GUIDE TO STARTING A BUSINESS

purchases and payments will have to be set up. The bottom line, Bill says, is that from the very beginning Cindy needs to invest in the appropriate accounting software and a good controller who understands international and online operations—otherwise the accounting systems and controls could spin out of control very quickly. At the next level, the company will face significant accounting issues as well. Particularly, the question of when to book revenue could be a tricky problem. The answer will be driven in large part on whether the company purchases the artwork and holds it in inventory, or sells it on consignment on behalf of the artists. How to reserve for returns will also be a difficult issue until a history can be established. Given the nature of the product—artwork purchased before live viewing—and in order to compete with other online sellers, Cindy will have to allow customers to return pieces that they are unsatisfied with. Given the fickle nature of art buyer's in general, it should be expected that returns will be substantial and will have to be adequately reserved for. These issues will also play a large part in budgeting and preparing financial projections, particularly in order to manage cash flow. Forecasting sales for the first year will be very difficult, with many factors to be taken into account. To start with, Cindy has yet to actually source her products. She will have to spend the first few months lining up artists, gathering information and images, and creating the website and methods of payment and distribution. When she does launch, sales will be highly dependent on the marketing effort and how much traffic it drives to the website. Knowing what he now knows about the business, Bill recommends that Cindy revise her forecasts to anticipate delays in generating significant amounts of revenues. This means another unpleasant conversation with Nancy, and places increased importance on Cindy being able to find secondary sources of revenue until her Internet sales are running full throttle.

CHAPTER 17:
TAXING SITUATIONS

Chapter

17

CHAPTER 17

TAXING SITUATIONS

Paying Federal and State Taxes

It's time to deal with the inevitable. Filing tax returns and paying taxes are a necessary evil for any business, so you need to have a good understanding of the process. In this chapter, we'll look at the two main federal tax issues you will immediately need to confront when starting a new business: income tax and payroll taxes/withholding. In addition, if you're in the retail business you'll need to collect and pay sales taxes, so we'll look at that and other state tax issues as well.

As a preliminary matter, if you have employees and/or operate your business as a corporation or partnership, you will need an Employer Identification Number ("**EIN**"), which is issued by the IRS for tax administration purposes. You can obtain an EIN online or by phone. To apply online, go to www.irs.gov. To apply by phone, call toll-free at (800) 829-4933. If you choose to call, before doing so complete Form SS-4, Application for Employer Identification Number, so you have all relevant information available. The person making the call to the IRS must be authorized to sign the form.

Federal Income Taxes

All businesses must file either an annual federal income tax return or information statement. Who exactly will incur the tax, file the form, and make the payments, as well as what the tax rate will be and what form will be required, depends on what type of legal entity your business is operating under.

Sole Proprietorship

If you operate your business as a sole proprietorship, from the IRS's perspective you and your business are identical—i.e. the business is not a taxable entity. Therefore, all of the assets, liabilities, income, and losses of the business are owned by you personally—and all of the taxes are incurred and paid by you personally. Sole proprietors pay income tax and self-employment tax on their net income, i.e. profits. They must file a Form 1040 Individual Income Tax Return, a Schedule C (Profit and Loss from Business), and a Schedule SE (Self-Employment Tax).

General Partnership

A partnership is also not a taxable entity under federal law and therefore it does not pay taxes. Instead, it "passes through" any profits or losses to its partners. But a partnership must still file Form 1065, Return of Partnership Income, which is an information statement used to report the income, deductions, gains, and losses from its operations. Each partner then includes his or her share of the partnership's income or loss on Schedule E (Supplemental Income and Loss), which is filed along with his or her Form 1040 Individual Income Tax Return. The partners will also have to pay self-employment tax and file Schedule SE along with their Form 1040.

Limited Liability Company

An LLC is a business structure allowed by state statute. Owners of an LLC are called members, and most states permit "single-member" LLCs. Depending on the number of members and the elections made by the LLC, the IRS will treat an LLC as a corporation, partnership, or what is termed a "disregarded entity." Specifically, an LLC with at least two members is classified as a partnership for federal income tax purposes unless it files Form 8832 and affirmatively elects to be treated as a corporation. An LLC with only one member is treated as an entity disregarded as separate from its owner for income tax purposes, but as a separate entity for employment tax purposes (unless it files Form 8832 and elects to be treated as a corporation).

As such, LLCs that have not elected to be treated as a corporation have pass-through taxation, so no tax on the LLC's income is paid at the business level.

Income/loss is instead reported on the personal tax returns of the members, and any tax due is paid at the individual level using the same forms as general partners or sole proprietors, as the case may be. In both cases, shares of profit are subject to self-employment tax and Schedule SE must be filed along with the members' Form 1040s.

C Corporation

For federal income tax purposes, a standard C corporation is recognized as a separate taxpaying entity. A corporation conducts business, realizes net income or loss, pays taxes, and then may distribute profits to stockholders. The profit of a corporation is taxed to the corporation when earned, and then is taxed to the stockholders when distributed as dividends. This creates a double tax. The corporation does not get a tax deduction when it distributes dividends to stockholders, and stockholders cannot deduct any loss of the corporation. C corporations must file a Form 1120, Corporation Income Tax Return. Any distribution of dividends to stockholders will be reported on the individual's Form 1040 and taxed as part of their total income.

S Corporation

S corporations are corporations that elect to pass corporate income, losses, deductions, and credits through to their stockholders for federal tax purposes. Stockholders of S corporations report the flow-through of income and losses on their personal tax returns and are assessed tax at their individual income tax rates. This allows S corporations to avoid double taxation on the corporate income.

In order to become an S corporation, the corporation must submit Form 2553, Election by a Small Business Corporation, signed by all the stockholders. The S corporation must file Form 1120-S, Income Tax Return for an S corporation, which is an information statement used to report the income, gains, losses, deductions, credits, etc. Its stockholders file Form 1040, Individual Income Tax Return, and Schedule E (Supplemental Income and Loss). One of the benefits to S corporations, as opposed to other pass-through entities such as LLC's or partnerships, is that S corporation stockholders normally do not have to pay self-employment tax on income.

Paying Estimated Taxes

Under the federal income tax system, taxes must be paid as income is earned during the tax year. Employees normally have income tax withheld, so they don't have to worry about making payments themselves. But for corporations and individuals whose taxes are not withheld, estimated payments must be made on a quarterly basis. Individuals do so using Form 1040-ES, and corporations use Form 1120-W.

Federal Employment Taxes

When you have employees, you as the employer have certain federal employment taxes that you must pay and forms you must file. Employment taxes include the following:

- Federal income tax withholding

- Social security and Medicare taxes

- Federal unemployment tax

When you hire an employee, you must have your new hire complete Form W-4, Employee's Withholding Allowance Certificate, which indicates the employee's filing status and withholding allowances. These allowances are used to determine how much federal income tax to withhold from an employee's wages.

Federal Income Tax

Employers generally must withhold federal income tax from their employees' wages. To figure out how much tax to withhold and understand your tax responsibilities as an employer, review the information in and use the withholding tables described in IRS Publication 15, Employer's Tax Guide (available at www. irs.gov), together with the information contained on your employees' Form W-4s.

Social Security and Medicare Taxes

Employers must also withhold social security and Medicare taxes, which are known as Federal Insurance Contributions Act ("**FICA**") taxes. To calculate the tax you need to withhold for each employee, multiply an employee's gross wages by the applicable tax rates. In addition, employers are required to pay a matching amount of FICA taxes on each of their employees.

Additional Medicare Tax

Beginning January 1, 2013, employers are responsible for withholding a 0.9 percent additional Medicare tax on an employee's wages and compensation that exceeds a threshold amount. They are required to begin withholding the additional Medicare tax in the pay period in which it pays wages and compensation in excess of the threshold amount to an employee. There is no employer match for the additional Medicare tax.

Deposit of Income and FICA Taxes

In general, employers must deposit federal income tax withheld and both the employer and employee social security and Medicare taxes. There are two deposit schedules, monthly and semi-weekly, and before the beginning of each calendar year you must determine which of the two deposit schedules you are required to use based on IRS rules. You must use electronic funds transfer ("**EFTPS**") to make all federal tax deposits (to enroll, go to eftps.gov). EFTPS allows you to go online or use the phone to make payments, and funds are moved from your account to the Treasury Department's on the date you indicate.

Reporting of Income and FICA Taxes

In addition to making monthly payroll deposits, employers are required to file a quarterly Form 941, Employer's Quarterly Federal Tax Return. This is a form that provides the government with information on the federal income taxes you withheld from your employees' pay as well as the FICA taxes you withheld and paid. It also tells the government when the taxes were withheld so the IRS can determine if the federal tax deposit was made on time.

At the end of the tax year, employers must prepare and furnish copies of Form W-2 (Wage and Tax Statement) to each employee who worked for you during the year. Form W-2 provides information on how much money each employee earned and the amount of federal, state, and FICA taxes you withheld. You must also send copies of the W-2s to the Social Security Administration using Form W-3, Transmittal of Wage and Tax Statements.

Federal Unemployment Tax

Employers report and pay federal unemployment tax ("**FUTA**") separately from Federal income tax and social security and Medicare taxes. Your business pays the FUTA tax—which is used to compensate workers who lose their jobs—only from its own funds. Employees do not pay this tax or have it withheld from their pay. Your business generally deposits FUTA taxes quarterly. In addition, it must file an annual return for its FUTA taxes using Form 940, Employer's Annual Federal Unemployment Tax Return, which must be filed by January 31 of the following year.

Self-Employment Tax

Self-employment tax is a social security and Medicare tax primarily for individuals who work for themselves, which includes sole proprietors, partners in general partnerships, and members of LLCs. It is similar to the social security and Medicare taxes withheld from the pay of most employees. Generally, you must pay self-employment tax and file Schedule SE to Form 1040 if your net earnings from self-employment are $400 or more.

State Taxes

In addition to the taxes required by the federal government, you and/or your business will have to pay state and local taxes. The most common types of state tax requirements for small business are income taxes, employment taxes, and sales taxes.

Income Taxes

Forty-two states have a personal income tax and, as with federal income tax, your business's income tax requirement will depend on the legal structure of your business. In most states, corporations are subject to a corporate income tax while income from "pass-through entities" is subject to a state's tax on personal income. Every state has different rules and rates for both corporate and personal income taxes, so you'll need to check with your state and local governments to be sure you understand them.

Employment Taxes

Similar to federal employment taxes, business owners with employees are also responsible for paying certain taxes required by the state. In addition, all states require payment of state workers' compensation insurance and unemployment insurance taxes. A few states also require a business to pay for temporary disability insurance. Check with your state's department of revenue to find out about the forms and requirements for withholding, depositing, and reporting state employment taxes.

Sales Taxes

Sales taxes vary by state and are imposed at the retail level. If you engage in retail sales, you probably need to register for or get a sales tax license or seller's permit. This lets you collect sales taxes from your customers, which you'll pay to the state. A license or permit is important because in some states it is a criminal offense to undertake sales without one. In addition, if you fail to collect sales tax, you can be held liable for the uncollected amount.

Not every state and locality has a sales tax, and those that do have an exemption on certain items such as food and clothing. If you are charging sales tax, you need be familiar with the applicable rules and rates.

In addition, keep in mind that service revenues are generally not taxed. So if your business generates revenue from both products and services, you should keep your revenues from services separate from your revenues from the sales of goods. Some states have changed their laws, however, and are now requiring sales tax on some services. If you operate a service business, contact your state revenue and local revenue offices for information on the sales tax laws where you do business.

One of the trickiest questions in the sales tax arena involves whether an out-of-state seller, such as an online retailer, must pay sales tax on sales to persons within the state. Generally, if the seller has a physical presence in a state, such as a store, office, or warehouse, it must collect applicable state and local sales tax from its customers. If the seller does not have a presence in a particular state, it may not be required to collect sales taxes, but it should not automatically assume this is the case.

Some states have enacted legislation that requires large online sellers to collect sales tax even with no physical presence in the state. In addition, there is a pending federal bill called the Marketplace Fairness Act of 2013 which would require online retailers to collect state and local sales taxes from all customers in the United States.

Note about Tax Deductions

Federal and state income taxes are paid on net income. In order to arrive at net income, the taxpayer is allowed to deduct certain business expenses from gross income. Understanding the rules about what expenses are deductible is an important component of any business's financial and tax planning, because the more you can deduct, the less taxes you have to pay.

Under Section 162 of the Internal Revenue Code, all the "ordinary and necessary" expenses paid or incurred during the taxable year in carrying on any trade or business are deductible. This includes:

- A reasonable allowance for salaries or other compensation for personal services actually rendered;

- Travel expenses (including amounts expended for meals and lodging other than amounts which are lavish or extravagant under the circumstances) while away from home in the pursuit of a trade or business; and

- Rentals or other payments required to be made as a condition to the continued use or possession, for purposes of the trade or business, of property to which the taxpayer has not taken or is not taking title or in which he has no equity.

Section 162 also describes specific items that can't be deducted, and in some cases, the IRS provides specific instructions for determining whether or not an expense is "ordinary and necessary" either through IRS regulations or publications.

Exotic Universe, Inc.

At the time of incorporation, Cindy McKay told her attorney David that she intended to file an "S" corporation election. Fortunately, she had not yet instructed him to proceed with the election before Nancy committed to fund her business as an angel investor. S corporations can have only one class of stock, and like most outside investors, Nancy will require that she be given preferred stock with rights that are separate from the common stock held by Cindy. So now that Nancy is coming on board in the near future, Exotic Universe, Inc. will remain a standard "C" corporation. This means that for federal and state income tax purposes, the company will have to file its own income tax return and pay its own federal and state income taxes. Payroll taxes are an issue that Cindy is not prepared to handle, so until she can recruit a financial controller who can set up a system for payroll and payroll tax withholding and deposits, she will have to outsource the operation to her accounting firm, incurring yet another unanticipated expense. As an online retailer, she is also going to have to determine whether she has to pay state sales taxes in the many states where her customers will reside. At first glance, it appears that she will not be required to do so unless a particular state has passed a law that encompassed her form of online sales. But when she tells Bill that she may have sales agents selling to galleries in certain states, or enter into agreements with galleries to exhibit her paintings, he informs her that they will have to take a close look to determine whether a nexus has been created in some states that will require the payment of state sales tax. Finally, her accountants are going to have to research whether any of the company's overseas activities will require the payment of income or other taxes in foreign countries. At minimum, Cindy is sure to have to pay certain export fees and duties. As Bill said back at the initial planning session: "This isn't a local pizza parlor you're opening, this is an international business." Time and again, this had been reinforced to Cindy. But she is learning every day and has surrounded herself with a good team of experienced people, keeping her confidence level high despite the huge task ahead. In fact, she's actually starting to enjoy the details of running a business—even learning about taxes.

CHAPTER 18:
LEGAL MATTERS

Chapter

18

CHAPTER 18

LEGAL MATTERS

Keeping in Compliance with the Law

Nearly every aspect of running a business is affected by some combination of federal, state, and local law. As an entrepreneur focused on producing and selling products, you may feel that devoting the time and energy necessary to stay in compliance with those laws is a waste of valuable resources. But failure to do so puts at risk everything else you have worked so hard to build. This may not be the most exciting part of your start-up experience, but it is a necessary one.

Although it is not possible to cover every legal detail you will need to familiarize yourself with, in this chapter we will highlight the areas of law that you need to research and understand in order to start and run a business. You can use the framework below to get you started, but you will need to dig into the details as well. Remember the old adage: ignorance of the law is no excuse.

Business Licenses and Permits

Virtually every business needs a variety of federal, state, and/or local licenses and permits to operate. Which ones you will need depends on the type of business you intend to engage in and where it is located. Inevitably, you will need to contact many sources to determine what licenses and permits are required, but one of the best ways to get started is to utilize the "Permit Me" search tool on the Small Business Association's website, www.sba.gov. But don't rely solely on that site. Also contact your state government, local government, and any relevant industry or trade association to enquire about what licenses and permits are required for your business and location.

Here is an overview of what to look for in your search:

Federal Licenses and Permits

Federal laws and regulations touch many aspects of running a small business, most notably employment and taxes. But unless your business is regulated by a federal agency, it is unlikely you will need a special federal license or permit to operate. Businesses that are regulated by government agencies include those involved in providing or selling investment advice, pharmaceutical products, public transportation, broadcasting, alcohol, and firearms. There are others as well, so check with any relevant trade associations, ask others in your line of business, and search online to make sure you are not in an industry where a federal license or permit is required.

State Licenses and Permits

State licensing requirements are more pervasive than federal. For example, you may need a state license to produce or sell food, liquor, gasoline, or firearms. Most states also have licensing requirements for professionals such as lawyers, doctors, accountants, teachers, architects, insurance agents, and engineers, and for tradespersons such as auto mechanics and massage therapists. Depending on the state and the product being sold, the individual, business, or both may be required to obtain a license. In addition, if you're engaged in retail sales, you will most likely need a sales tax license allowing you to collect taxes from your customers.

Local Licenses and Permits

As you drill down to the local level, you really need to do some research and make some phone calls to determine what is required, because the more you zero in on your exact location, the more licenses and permits you will find are necessary to run your business. To begin with, almost every business needs a local business license, sometimes called a tax registration certificate, which is normally issued either at the city or county level. Beyond that, contact the following local departments to determine what other licenses and permits are required:

- City Clerk and County Clerk

- Planning or Zoning Department

- Health Department

- Assessor or Treasurer

- Fire Department

- Police Department

- Public Works Department

- Building and Safety Department

After you have determined what federal, state, and local laws and regulations your business must follow, you need to set up internal systems and controls to make sure you stay in compliance on an ongoing basis. Maintain a copy of all licensing and permit forms and keep track of renewal dates. In addition, most states and localities require businesses to prominently display their business licenses and permits so customers can see them. Keep in mind that if your business changes, you may be required to obtain additional licenses and permits as well.

Employment and Labor Law

Probably the most comprehensive set of laws and regulations that your new business will need to comply with kick in once you hire your first employee. This is an area where federal law is pervasive, and most federal employment and labor laws fall under the jurisdiction of the U.S. Department of Labor ("**DOL**"), the EEOC, or the IRS.

The DOL issues regulations under and enforces the following laws (among others):

- Fair Labor Standards Act: prescribes minimum wage and overtime pay requirements

- Employee Retirement Income Security Act: regulates pension and welfare benefit plans for employees

- Occupational Safety and Health Act: regulates workplace safety and health conditions

- Family and Medical Leave Act: covers minimum leave requirements

- Labor-Management Reporting and Disclosure Act: deals with the relationship between a union and its members

- Uniformed Services Employment and Reemployment Rights Act: governs reemployment obligations regarding armed services personnel

The statutes and regulations enforced by the DOL often require recordkeeping and reporting by the employer. In addition, some require that notices be provided to employees and/or posted in the workplace, informing employees of their rights and employer responsibilities under labor laws.

The EEOC is responsible for enforcing federal laws that make it illegal to discriminate against a job applicant or an employee because of the person's race, color, religion, sex, national origin, age, disability, or genetic information. It is also illegal to discriminate against a person because the person complained about discrimination, filed a charge of discrimination, or participated in an employment discrimination investigation or lawsuit.

Federal laws enforced by the EEOC include:

- Title VII of the Civil Rights Act of 1964: makes it illegal to discriminate against someone on the basis of race, color, religion, national origin, or sex

- The Equal Pay Act of 1963: makes it illegal to pay different wages to men and women if they perform equal work in the same workplace

- The Age Discrimination in Employment Act of 1967: protects people who are 40 or older from discrimination because of age

- Title I of the Americans with Disabilities Act of 1990: makes it illegal to discriminate against a qualified person with a disability

- The Genetic Information Nondiscrimination Act of 2008: makes it illegal to discriminate against employees or applicants because of genetic information

As we detailed in Chapter 17, there are numerous federal employment-related requirements with respect to withholding and payment of taxes, which are administered and enforced by the IRS. As an employer, you will be required to obtain an EIN from the IRS, withhold federal income tax and FICA tax from your employees' paychecks and deposit those amounts with the federal government, and file Form W-2 federal wage and tax statements.

In addition, all businesses with employees are required to carry workers' compensation insurance coverage through a commercial carrier, on a self-insured basis, or through their state's Workers' Compensation Insurance program.

Finally, federal law requires employers to verify their employees' eligibility to work in the United States. Within three days of hiring a new employee, you must complete an Employment Eligibility Verification Form, commonly referred to as an I-9 form. This requires examining acceptable forms of the employee's documentation to confirm his or her citizenship or eligibility to work in the United States. Be aware, you can only request documentation specified on the I-9 form. Employers who ask for other types of documentation not listed on the I-9 form may be subject to discrimination lawsuits.

You do not file the I-9 with the federal government. Rather, you are required to keep the form on file for three years after the date of hire or one year after the date the employee's employment ends, whichever is later. The U.S. Immigration and Customs Enforcement agency conducts routine workplace audits to ensure that employers are properly completing and retaining I-9 forms, and that employee information on I-9 forms matches government records.

The Immigration Reform and Control Act which introduced the I-9 form also included anti-discrimination provisions. Under the Act, most U.S. citizens, permanent residents, temporary residents or refugees who are legally allowed to work in the United States cannot be discriminated against on the basis of national origin or citizenship status.

Workplace Safety and Health Law

Under the federal Occupational Safety and Health Act ("**OSHA**"), employers must provide a workplace free from recognized hazards that cause, or are likely to cause, death or serious physical harm to their employees.

The following are selected OSHA standards that apply to many employers:

- Hazard Communication Standard
  This standard is designed to ensure that employers and employees know about hazardous chemicals in the workplace and how to protect themselves.

- Emergency Action Plan Standard
  An Emergency Action Plan describing the actions employees should take to ensure their safety in a fire or other emergency situation is mandatory when required by an OSHA standard.

- Walking/Working Surfaces Standard
  The OSHA standards for walking and working surfaces apply to all permanent places of employment, except where only domestic, mining, or agricultural work is performed.

- Medical and First Aid Standard
  OSHA requires employers to provide medical and first-aid personnel and supplies commensurate with the hazards of the workplace.

In addition to these general standards that apply to most businesses, a number of other OSHA standards may apply to your particular workplace. For example, if you have employees who operate machinery, you may be subject to OSHA's Machine Guarding requirements, and if your employees service or maintain equipment that could start up unexpectedly or release hazardous energy, you may be subject to OSHA's Lockout/Tagout requirements. In addition, OSHA's Electrical Standards include design requirements for electrical systems and safety-related work practices. And employers whose employees are exposed to excessive noise (e.g., conditions that make normal conversation difficult) may be required to implement a hearing conservation program.

Advertising and Marketing Law

All businesses have a legal responsibility to ensure that any advertising claims are truthful and not deceptive. The **FTC** oversees and regulates federal advertising and marketing law in the United States, and every state has consumer protection laws that govern advertisements running in their jurisdiction.

The main consumer protection statute enforced by the FTC is the Federal Trade Commission Act ("**FTC Act**"). Section 5(a) of the FTC Act provides that "unfair or deceptive acts or practices in or affecting commerce" are unlawful. According to the FTC Act and the FTC, an advertisement or business practice is unfair if:

- It causes or is likely to cause substantial consumer injury which a consumer could not reasonably avoid; and

- It is not outweighed by the benefit to consumers.

In order to determine if an ad is deceptive, the FTC looks at the advertisement from the point of view of the "reasonable consumer," i.e. the typical person looking at the advertisement. In doing so, the FTC looks at both "express" and "implied" claims. An express claim is literal, while an implied claim is one made indirectly or by inference. The FTC also looks at what the advertisement does not say, and whether the failure to include information leaves consumers with a misimpression about the product. Finally, the FTC looks at whether the business has sufficient evidence to support the claims in the advertisement. Before a company runs an advertisement, it has to have a "reasonable basis" for the claims, meaning objective evidence that supports the claim.

Keep in mind that the FTC pays closest attention to advertisements that make claims about health or safety, advertisements that make claims that consumers would have trouble evaluating for themselves, and advertisements directed at children.

In addition, you should be aware that the FTC regulates the following other matters with respect to marketing and advertising:

- Specific Industries: the FTC has some rules and compliance guides for specific industries including franchises, real estate, and clothing manufacturers

- Telemarketing: if you will be telemarketing, pay specific attention to the National Do Not Call Registry and other laws governing the practice

- Email spam: the law is very specific on what email you can send and to whom

- Bait and Switch Advertising: it's illegal to advertise a product when the company has no intention of selling that item, but instead plans to sell a consumer something else

- Children's Advertising: the FTC pays particular attention to advertisements aimed at children because children may be more vulnerable to certain kinds of deception—advertising directed to children is evaluated from a child's point of view, not an adult's

- Disclosures and Disclaimers: some laws and regulations enforced by the FTC, such as the Truth in Lending Act, have specific requirements that certain information must be "clearly and conspicuously" disclosed when the disclosure of qualifying information is necessary to prevent an advertisement from being deceptive

- Food: as a general rule, advertising for foods, over-the-counter drugs, dietary supplements, medical devices, and cosmetics is regulated by the FTC, while labeling for these products is regulated by the U.S. Food and Drug Administration

- Contests and Sweepstakes: sweepstakes-type promotions that require a purchase by participants are illegal in the United States. Other agencies, including the U.S. Postal Service and the Federal Communications Commission, also enforce federal laws governing contests and prize promotions. And each state has laws that may require promoters to make disclosures, seek licensing, or post a bond

- "Free" Claims and Rebate Offers: when a "free" offer is tied to the purchase of another product, the price of the purchased product should not be increased from its regular price—other laws govern "sales," "rain checks," "new products," etc.

- Guarantees: if an ad mentions that a product comes with a guarantee or warranty, the ad should clearly disclose how consumers can get the details

- Made in the U.S.A.: a product has to be "all or virtually all made in the United States" for it to be advertised or labeled as "Made in the U.S.A."

Consumer and Employee Privacy

The FTC also regulates and oversees business privacy laws and policies that impact consumers. In general, your online and offline privacy policy is your company's pledge to your customers about how you will collect, use, share, and protect the consumer data you collect from them. As with advertisements, the FTC prohibits deceptive practices in this area. In addition, if in your business you collect sensitive consumer and employee information, it is your legal responsibility to take steps to properly secure or dispose of this information. Financial data, personal information from children, and material derived from credit reports may raise additional compliance considerations.

Advertisers should also be aware of the privacy issues raised by Internet marketing. Basically, the FTC strongly encourages companies to implement four fair information practices: giving consumers notice of a website's information practices; offering consumers choice as to how their personally identifying information is used; providing consumers with access to the information collected about them; and ensuring the security of the information collected.

In addition, if you are marketing online then become familiar with The Children's Online Privacy Protection Act, a federal law that requires websites to obtain verifiable parental consent before collecting, using, or disclosing personal information from children, including their names, home addresses, email addresses, or hobbies. The FTC has issued a rule outlining the procedures for commercial websites to use in obtaining parental consent.

Environmental Regulations

The U.S. Environmental Protection Agency and state environmental agencies enforce environmental laws, and violation of these laws could result in enormous costs to your business. If you produce products that could potentially harm the environment, release pollutants into the air, land, water, or sewers, or store, transmit or dispose of hazardous or non-hazardous waste, make sure you know the federal and state environmental laws and comply with them. Many small businesses which do so are required to obtain some form of environmental permit from state or local authorities to operate legally.

Antitrust Law

Antitrust laws promote vigorous competition and protect consumers from anticompetitive business practices. Their basic objective is to protect the process of competition for the benefit of consumers, making sure there are strong incentives for businesses to operate efficiently, keep prices down, and keep quality up.

Here is an overview of the three core federal antitrust laws:

- The Sherman Act
  This law outlaws "every contract, combination, or conspiracy in restraint of trade," and any "monopolization, attempted monopolization, or conspiracy or combination to monopolize." The U.S. Supreme Court has decided that the Sherman Act only prohibits the "unreasonable" restraint of trade. However, certain actions are considered to be so harmful to competition that they are almost always illegal. These include plain arrangements among competing individuals or businesses to fix prices, divide markets, or rig bids.

- The Federal Trade Commission Act
  This law bans "unfair methods of competition" and "unfair or deceptive acts or practices." Because the U.S. Supreme Court has said that all violations of the Sherman Act also violate the FTC Act, the FTC can bring cases under the FTC Act against the same kinds of

activities that violate the Sherman Act. The FTC Act also reaches other practices that harm competition.

- <u>The Clayton Act</u>
  This law addresses specific practices that the Sherman Act does not clearly prohibit, such as mergers and interlocking directorates. Section 7 of the Clayton Act prohibits mergers and acquisitions where the effect "may be substantially to lessen competition, or to tend to create a monopoly." The Clayton Act also bans certain discriminatory prices, services, and allowances in dealings between merchants.

In addition to these federal statutes, most states have antitrust laws that are enforced by state attorneys general or private plaintiffs.

Exotic Universe, Inc.

Having learned numerous lessons already about not letting details slip through the cracks, Cindy McKay takes legal compliance seriously and uses this chapter to create an initial checklist to help keep her business on the "straight and narrow." First, she will need a local business permit to begin operations. She will also need a Colorado state employer tax ID number and a state sales tax ID number and seller's permit. In addition, she will need to file a "Doing Business as Trade Name" registration with her local county. While her operations will be simple and she will be leasing an office in a building where the landlord is present, she doesn't take anything for granted and makes the requisite calls to the health, police, and other departments to make sure permits aren't required, even enquiring if a permit is required to serve wine at her launch party. She also does some research to make sure that art dealers are not required to have a special license in Colorado. Next, Cindy turns to federal and state employment law. Since she will begin recruiting employees almost immediately, she learns as much as she can about the legal anti-discrimination requirements she must follow and documentation she should produce and keep. She also collects the information necessary to make sure her small office, which is in an old building, is up to health and safety standards. Of course one of the key areas she will also have to keep in mind is her online marketing material. Browsing the websites of other online art dealers, she has seen many questionable claims about the pieces they have for sale. Cindy wants to develop a site that is beyond reproach, but that means she will have to verify claims as to originality, materials used, etc. from the artists themselves. Also, she previously had in mind some potential "grand opening" promotions that may not conform to the FTC's rules and regulations, so now may have to rethink some of her ideas. Another thing she had not given much thought to was her company's privacy policy, but that will be front and center for many of her customers. She will have to develop a policy and make sure she has systems and controls in place to make sure their private information stays private. Previously, she never thought that things like antitrust and securities laws would apply to a small fish like her. But now she realizes that discussion among art dealers regarding pricing could run afoul of the law, and any time she issues shares of stock in her company, she needs to make sure she has an exemption and supplies her investors the appropriate information. Her attorneys also advise her that now is the time to start keeping good track of her contracts and obligations, to make sure her document retention and compliance system doesn't fall behind as her company grows as quickly as everyone hopes.

All of these details keep Cindy busy every evening and weekend from her winter break business planning sessions until school lets out for the summer. And when the bell rings on the last day of school, Cindy weaves her way through the crowd of celebrating teenagers and heads directly to her favorite coffee shop, where Nancy is waiting in the back room. Nancy asks how she feels, and Cindy replies, "Excited and terrified!" Nancy smiles and says "Good, you can channel both those emotions for what you're about to do." A few minutes later Cindy's good friend Rita, an Internet marketing guru who works for a large retailer with a substantial online presence, joins them holding a double latte. After some initial small talk, the first substantive meeting of the Exotic Universe, Inc. board of directors commences. Cindy begins by giving her fellow directors a status report so all three women are up to date at the same level. Over the last three months, Cindy has formed a corporation in Delaware, funded it with $25,000 of her own money, and had the corporation issue shares to her as the sole stockholder. She has also registered Exotic Universe as a trademark with the USPTO, and purchased the domain name exoticuniverse.com. On the personnel side, she has made one hire, a young man named Steve who graduated seven years ago from the University of Colorado with a degree in business administration with a minor in international relations. He has traveled extensively and spent three years working for an NGO in Thailand, where his task was to work with local village groups on forming small businesses funded by the NGO. Steve is the new director of international operations for Exotic Universe, Inc. He is young, but he is smart and highly motivated, and willing to work for a reduced salary as long as he is granted a good number of stock options. In addition, while Rita likes her current job and is not ready to take the risk of jumping onboard a start-up, she has extensive contacts in the Internet marketing field and has put Cindy in touch with a very good candidate for the director of marketing position. And finally, Bill has continued to be extremely helpful and has passed along resumes for several good controller candidates. But Cindy and Nancy have already spoken offline, and before Nancy funds the company, Cindy must provide some proof of her commitment and ability to pull this thing off. What they have agreed is that Cindy will use a good portion of the money she has invested in the company for her and Steve to take a 10-week trip, where they will visit Mexico, Argentina, South Africa, India, and Thailand. Nancy has told Cindy that if she can secure 30 artists who will commit to selling their works through Exotic Universe, Inc., then Nancy will commit to investing $400,000 in the company in September, a number based on a revised business plan and business model that Nancy and Cindy have worked on over the last month. The other thing Cindy has been doing is reaching out to all of her contacts in the countries she has visited, informing them of her new business venture, setting up appointments for her trip, and asking them to provide her with as many other contacts as possible. So she is confident, but experienced enough to realize that in many of the countries she will be doing business in, people don't like to say "no" to a friend even if the answer will ultimately be just that. This means that nothing is guaranteed until Cindy gets their firm commitment and has their artwork in hand. But in August, Cindy and Steve return from their trip with over fifty artists in hand. "Congratulations," Nancy says. "You've got yourself an investor." The next day, Cindy hands in her resignation at the high school. She is no longer a teacher, she is now an entrepreneur.

RESOURCES

This section provides some additional useful resources for entrepreneurs wishing to start their own business.

Small Business Association	http://www.sba.gov/
Business Guides by Industry	http://www.sba.gov/category/ navigation-structure/starting-managing-business/managing-business/business-guides-industry
IRS Small Business start-Up Checklist	http://www.irs.gov/Businesses/ Small-Businesses-&-Self-Employed/ Checklist-for-Starting-a-Business
Business USA	http://business.usa.gov/
Small Business Notes	http://www.smallbusinessnotes.com/
Entrepreneur.com	www.entrepreneur.com

 Additional Resources

Enodare's resources area includes free information and forms to help you get your business up and running. To access the online repository, simply use the unlock code below.

Web: http://www.enodare.com/downloadarea/

Unlock Code: EB786573

enodare

Business Name

Your business name is key and web presence is key to most start-up businesses. Before deciding on a business name, check if your business name is available. A quick search on www.godaddy.com will enable you to identify if your chosen web domain name is available.

Next, check if another company has already trademarked your desired name. To check existing trademarks registered in the US, you can use the Trademark Electronic Search System to conduct a free online search of the USPTO database at www.uspto.gov. This will give you a good understanding whether you can proceed with your chosen business name in the US.

If your name is available, begin by registering the domain name, and then register your business name. While it is not necessary to register your trademark just yet, it can be advisable.

Company Incorporation

Now that you have verified that your company name is available. Various companies are available online to help you register your business. Your first step is to decide which state to register in, each state has different requirements and costs. Once you have decided on your state and name, you are ready to begin the process of company incorporation. Incorporation can start from as little as $99 from websites such as www.bizfilings.com. Their single focus is to help entrepreneurs and business owners start, run and grow their companies. You'll find lots of useful resources on this website.

Business Planning

The next step in your business journey, may just be your business plan. Business planning is often one of the most crucial aspects of your business and one, which causes most companies to fail. Enodare's book on business modelling has brought together serial entrepreneurs with vast experience in planning and raising funds. Enodare's book entitled "Developing an Effective Business Plan" is a must read. You'll learn to develop the business model in conjunction with your business plan. Develop your business plan in conjunction with this book and you will be on the right path to creating a successful business. See page 338 of this book for more details.

Research

When starting your own business, researching is a critical element to identify competitors and verify the existence of a market. Tools such as those contained on www.Alexa.com, www.Similarweb.com and www.Hoovers.com will provide much needed insights to markets, competitors etc. Don't simply dive into planning or getting work completed, spend time researching first. The more you research, the more solid your business will become.

Staffing – Once you have completed the planning stages, your next step is to identify and secure people who can help get your business started can be difficult. Several websites offer the ability to hire staff on a temporary or permanent contract. Work can range from legal to writing to software development. Websites include UpWork.com, Hired.com and Guru.com offer you access to key personnel. Simply sign up for an account, post your requirements and contractors will bid on your work. Ensure you brief is very detailed; this is to avoid any ambiguities at later stages. Before engaging with any contract for hire, review the contractor's background in detail, speak to previous customers and rate each contractor against the other. A bad choice could cause further issues down the line.

Data Analytics

Most entrepreneurs aspire to find financial investors to back their business. Learn about some of the key metrics required by investors when making a decision to invest. Alistair Crolls's book entitled "Lean Analytics" (ISBN -978-1449335670) is a must read for start-ups. Together with analytics, some of the key elements investors require are traction and revenue over 4-6 months to validate your business.

Given that most businesses start with a small website, it is therefore useful to install Google Analytics on your website at an early stage to help monitor tragic growth and visitor behaviour.

E-commerce

Historically E-commerce solutions have commanded a high price for start-up businesses. This prevented many companies getting up and running. Luckily this situation has changed and a variety of options exist for new businesses. Websites such as www.shopify.com can prove an excellent way to get your website selling online without the need for programmers of cash outlay. Some other recommended options include solutions offered by companies such as 3Dcart, X-cart and BigCommerce.

Distribution

Once you have completed your product, identifying distribution channels can be difficult. Some distribution channels can be simple to identify such as Amazon, Ebay etc, others may require that you identify wholesale companies or buyers within specific business. They key here is research once again, most websites will have information about submitting products or you may find retail buyers through a linkedin.com search.

Accounting & Invoicing Software

Accounting and invoicing software can help you appear professional and drive your business forward. Some of the most frequently talked about software includes Quickbooks, available at www.quickbooks.intuit.com/ or Freshbooks at www.freshbooks.com/ or Zoho Invoice at www.zoho.com are all excellent tools in a young entrepreneurs tool bag.

INDEX

I

T

X-Y-Z

Other Great Books from Enodare's Estate Planning Series

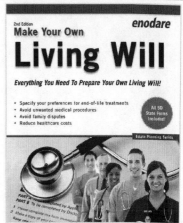

How to Probate an Estate - A Step-By-Step Guide for Executors

This book is essential reading for anyone contemplating acting as an executor of someone's estate!

Learn about the various stages of probate and what an executor needs to do at each stage to successfully navigate his way through to closing the estate and distributing the deceased's assets.

You will learn how an executor initiates probate, locates and manages assets, deals with debt and taxes, distributes assets, and much more. This is a fantastic step-by-step guide through the entire process!

Make Your Own Living Trust & Avoid Probate

Living trusts are used to distribute a person's assets after they die in a manner that avoids the costs, delays and publicity of probate. They also cater for the management of property during periods of incapacity.

This book will guide you step-by-step through the process of creating your very own living trust, transferring assets to your living trust and subsequently managing those assets.

All relevant forms are included.

Make Your Own Living Will

Do you want a say in what life sustaining medical treatments you receive during periods in which you are incapacitated and either in a permanent state of unconsciousness or suffering from a terminal illness? Well if so, you must have a living will!

This book will introduce you to living wills, the types of medical procedures that they cover, the matters that you need to consider when making them and, of course, provide you with all the relevant forms you need to make your own living will!

Other Great Books from Enodare's Estate Planning Series

Make Your Own Medical & Financial Powers of Attorney

Estate Planning Essentials

Funeral Planning Basics - A Step-By-Step Guide to Funeral Planning

The importance of having powers of attorney is often underappreciated. They allow people you trust to manage your property and financial affairs during periods in which you are incapacitated; as well as make medical decisions on your behalf based on the instructions in your power of attorney document. This ensures that your affairs don't go unmanaged and you don't receive any unwanted medical treatments.

This book provides all the necessary documents and step-by-step instructions to make a power of attorney to cover virtually any situation!

This book is a must read for anyone who doesn't already have a comprehensive estate plan.

It will show you the importance of having wills, trusts, powers of attorney and living wills in your estate plan. You will learn about the probate process, why people are so keen to avoid it and lots of simple methods you can actually use to do so. You will learn about reducing estate taxes and how best to provide for young beneficiaries and children.

This book is a great way to get you started on the way to making your own estate plan.

Through proper funeral planning, you can ensure that your loved ones are not confronted with the unnecessary burden of having to plan a funeral at a time which is already very traumatic for them.

This book will introduce you to issues such as organ donations, purchasing caskets, cremation, burial, purchasing grave plots, organization of funeral services, legal and financial issues, costs of pre-arranging a funeral, how to save money on funerals, how to finance funerals and much more.

Personal Budget Kit

Budgeting Made Easy

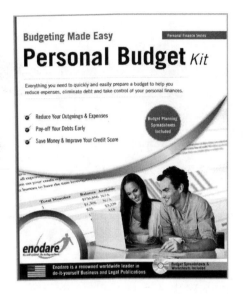

In this kit, we'll guide you step-by-step through the process of creating and living with a personal budget. We'll show you how analyze how you receive and spend your money and to set goals, both short and long-term.

You'll learn how to gain control of your personal cash flow. You'll discover when you need to make adjustments to your budget and how to do it wisely. Most of all, this kit will show you that budgeting isn't simply about adding limitations to your living but rather the foundation for living better by maximizing the resources you have.

This Personal Budget Kit provides you with step-by-step instructions, detailed information and all the budget worksheets and spreadsheets necessary to identify and understand your spending habits, reduce your expenses, set goals, prepare personal budgets, monitor your progress and take control over your finances.

- Reduce your spending painlessly and effortlessly

- Pay off your debts early

- Improve your credit rating

- Save & invest money

- Set & achieve financial goals

- Eliminate financial worries

Budget Planning Spreadsheets Included

enodare

Developing an Effective Business Plan
A Business Modle Path to Success

To develop and write a successful business plan, you need to begin by creating and validating an effective business model. The business model is the core of your business plan, it's your unique recipe for making sustainable profits. The business plan is your strategy for developing and running each major aspect of your business in a way that successfully executes your business model. You will be show step-by-step how to use one of the most highly regarded business modeling techniques, the Business Model Canvas, to identify, test and validate the optimal business model for your enterprise. Next, you will learn how to develop and write a business plan that will most effectively implement your validated business model.

A detailed case study is used throughout the book to illustrate and help you understand how the process of creating a business model and writing a business plan plays out in the real world. By reading, studying and applying the techniques we discuss in this book, you will be able to lay a solid foundation for launching a successful and profitable business.

Business Planning and Development

- Identify the correct business model
- Write and implement an effective business plan
- Develop a successful marketing plan
- Learn from real-world case studies

Includes
Real-Life
Case Study!

enodare

NEW TITLE